PAT CHAPMAN'S
Vegetable Curry Bible

Also by Pat Chapman

In the same series as this volume:

Pat Chapman's Curry Bible

Pat Chapman's Balti Bible

Other Pat Chapman books:

Curry Club Indian Restaurant Cookbook

Curry Club Quick After-Work Curries

Pat Chapman's Thai Restaurant Cookbook

Pat Chapman's Taste of the Raj

Pat Chapman's Noodle Book

The Good Curry Guide

PAT CHAPMAN'S
Vegetable Curry Bible

Hodder & Stoughton

Edited by Grapevine Publishing Services
Designed by Lovelock & Co.
Photography by Colin Poole
Jacket Photograph by Gerrit Buntrock
Food cooked and styled for photographs by Dominique and Pat Chapman
Props by Dominique

First published in Great Britain in 1999 by Hodder and Stoughton
A division of Hodder Headline PLC

A CIP catalogue record for this book is available
from the British Library

ISBN 0 340 75158 4

Printed and bound in Great Britain by
The Bath Press

Hodder and Stoughton
A division of Hodder Headline PLC
338 Euston Road
London NW1 3BH

Photography by Colin Poole

I would like to thank various individuals, restaurants
and organisations in Britain and in India for their
enthusiastic co-operation.

Thanks to: Sira, Dokal and Bhai Bhai stores, and Abdul Pazzaq
at the Tandoori Express on Jalebi Junction (all on the Broadway, Southall); the High
Commission of India, the Spices Board, and Kerela Tourist Board for their help with
photographs, ingredients and information used in this book, and their kind invitation
to attend their 1999 Malabar Pepper Fest in Calicut, India, sponsored by Silk & Spice
Travel and Communication Company (Wyanad Road, Calicut, Kerela, India).

Thanks also to Sherin Alexander, Director and Mernosh Modi, Executive Chef at Porte
des Indes, 32 Bryanston Street, London, and their sister establishment, the Blue
Elephant Thai Restaurant, Fulham Broadway, London, for specially air-freighting in
some of the tropical fruit and vegetables depicted in the Vegetable Ingredients File in
this book; and to Richard Bishop and David Burrows for their assistance, Raji Balan,
and Helena and and Eric Bennet for loaning props.

And my special thanks to Mr Haridas, owner of the Sree Krishna Restaurant (Upper
Tooting Road, London SW17) and Ragam (Cleveland St, London W1), Malabar
Junction Restaurant (107 Great Russell Street, London WC1) and Chef Sujatha from
Hyderabad, who allowed me to help her in her kitchens.

Vegetable Curry Bible Menu

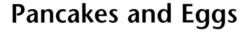

Introduction

Whatever you do, please don't be put off by this book's title. Until recently many of us in the developed world had an inbred dislike of vegetables. Indeed, in Victorian and Edwardian times, such items were regarded with innate suspicion. But in our new enlightened age we are told that a vegetarian diet is perfectly adequate nutritionally. Add curry spices, however, and the food is not just adequate – it is stunning, and with this book, I hope to prove it to you. But this is by no means a book just for vegetarians; it is written to satisfy all curry lovers with the possible exception of the most confirmed carnivores. So welcome to my *Vegetable Curry Bible*.

In spite of various sensationalised meat scares, the vast majority of the population continues to eat meat, poultry and fish. (I myself am not a vegetarian, nor am I likely ever to become one.) However, no one can deny the relationship between excess consumption of meat, particularly fatty meat, and heart disease. And there are many other factors which contribute to long-term ill health, including over-eating, chemicals in processed foods and one's general state of fitness. Today's consumers are resigned to the pitfalls of the modern Western diet, and are looking for solutions. Cutting down on or eliminating meat, and/or poultry and/or fish might offer a partial solution, but the benefits of doing this can be wasted if one replaces such items with an excess of cholesterol-laden dairy products and sugary processed foods.

In fact, health is not the only reason for people choosing to stop eating meat. Often there are financial, sentimental, religious, or ethical considerations, or simply having been brought up as a vegetarian. And for the true vegetarian, nowhere is there a better choice or a greater range of tastes than in India and the subcontinent when it comes to non-meat based food.

But already I find I am stumbling about with definitions. 'Non-meat', 'non-vegetarian' and 'vegetarian' all are labels which do not describe this particular book's concept very accurately, and can, indeed, be off-putting to the great majority of the population. My first vegetarian book, *The Vegetarian Cookbook* was retitled by my American publisher as *Non-meat Curries* for the US readership. Obviously there are no meat recipes in that book but, to the Americans, it was a code that told them there are no poultry or fish recipes in it either. It probably wouldn't work elsewhere as a title.

The choice of a title is never easy. I explained in my book *The Curry Bible* that the word 'Bible' had been chosen to convey the idea of 'an authoritative work'. The book and its title proved popular, so we followed it up with a second book, the equally successful *Balti Bible*. Both books examine their respective subjects comprehensively and are self-contained works, the one not needing the other for the reader to achieve total success in all departments. This book does the same: its 200 recipes enable the reader to cook anything from a snack to a six-course banquet using, as its title suggests, no meat, poultry, fish or shellfish.

Malabar Junction's chef Sujatha cleans the hotplate with water in preparation for dosa making.

She ladles the batter onto the hotplate . . .

and quickly spreads it in a widening circular motion.

Note the steam coming off as the batter firms up.

When the steam stops, oil is brushed onto the dosa.

When cooked, it is eased off the hotplate.

I have studiously avoided the word 'Vegetarian' in the book's title, since while it is a must for vegetarians, it is by no means written exclusively for them. So by calling it *The Vegetable Curry Bible*, it is hoped that the message will be carried to both vegetarians and non-vegetarians alike.

Of course, the title does not do the book's contents full justice. Flip through the pages and you will see straight away that, though vegetables are indeed a major feature, they are not the only feature. As well as the numerous vegetable curries, there are starters and snacks, soups and salads, pancakes and egg dishes, rice dishes, breads, chutneys and pickles. There are whole chapters devoted to the Indian restaurant top sixteen curries, to restaurant vegetable favourites, and to authentic specialities and vegetable curries from outside India. There is also a complete chapter on vegetable and dhal curries, and desserts too have a chapter to themselves.

As did its predecessors, this 'bible' includes a thorough examination of ingredients in the **Vegetable Ingredients File**, along with studies of other important ingredients, such as dairy items, eggs and nuts. There is also

a **Fruit Ingredients File**. These sections help readers to find their way through the ever-increasing choice of exotic vegetables and fruit available today. All of these help to enhance the range of tastes and textures for our non-meat recipes.

But it has taken us in the West a long time to 'discover' many of these wonderful foods, and no one could claim that the subcontinent of India can be bettered for spicy food. Archaeological evidence proves that cooking with spices has taken place there for at least 7,000 years. While Britain was still covered in ice and populated with individuals in bearskins whose main activities included hunting berries, India was already cooking refined spicy food. Today's distinctly different northern Indian style, using whole aromatic mild spices and the south's use of pungent, hot spices wet-ground with garlic and onion, have changed remarkably little over the millennia.

Among the earliest inhabitants of India were the dairy-farming Ayrans in the north, and, in the south, the rice-cultivating Dravidians. The Ayrans were meat-eaters but, in the course of time, the numbers of cattle they bred for

meat and milk came to be revered, not slaughtered. By 1000 BC this dogma had become a key characteristic of the Hindu religion.

Meat-eating gave way to vegetarianism, with a large dependence on dairy produce. The Dravidians, meanwhile, had evolved away from meat-eating very early on, relying instead on their rice, coconut and prolific vegetable crops for subsistence. Apart from those people living by the coast or near rivers who ate fish, India remained almost totally vegetarian for the next 2,000 years.

The ancient Egyptians had developed poultry incubators and hatcheries long before the birth of Christ, while their neighbours, the Arabs, bred sheep and goats for eating. Following the birth of Mohammed in AD 570, the population of the Middle East became largely Moslem. Soon they ruled a vast empire including northern India to which they brought their meat-eating culture. The greatest empire India ever saw was that of the Moghuls, themselves Moslems. From 1500 until 1857 when they were finally replaced by the British, the Moghuls ruled the subcontinent of India in a style of extraordinary power and wealth.

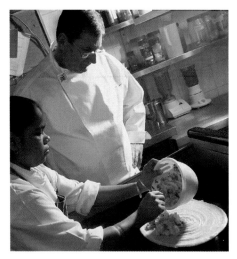

The masala filling is spread onto the centre.

The dosa is folded over the filling . . .

. . . and it is ready to serve.

Most Moslems today are meat-eaters and most Hindus are vegetarian. Seventy-five per cent of India's population are mainly vegetarian. No other place on earth has such a large concentration of vegetarians, and nowhere has more delicious vegetarian food. The result is that one quarter of today's world population are curry eaters and many of these are vegetarian.

Although I have an enormous collection of unpublished vegetable recipes at my disposal, I knew that a special visit to India was called for before I started to write this book. Dominique and I went as guests of the Pepper Fest, held in Calicut on the Malabar coast in south India. South Indian food is particularly strong on vegetables, and I collected many new recipes, some of which appear in this book. Other parts of India are equally strong on vegetable recipes, and they too are well represented here. Indeed, we generally eat vegetarian food on our visits to India. It goes with the territory, so to speak.

A story comes to mind of my thirty-first visit to India since 1982. We often fly Air India, much to the consternation of our Indian friends who prefer BA.

Well I can tell you that BA is certainly not better than Air India, especially in this particular instance which involved 'technical' problems. Whatever anyone tells you, passenger flying is a chore, no matter what airline you use or what class you travel in. It is exhausting and boring, usually running late, with poor (or no) excuses, and with unpleasant passenger handling on the part of the staff. It has, to me at any rate, less charm than travelling by train or coach. In simple terms it is frankly just public transport, often at its worst, and that's when things run normally. When they go wrong, one's tolerance levels are stretched to the limits.

It is then that I reflect that when my ancestors went to India in the 1760s, they travelled on an East India ship on a desperately uncomfortable journey around Africa's Cape of Good Hope which took up to six months, with no guarantee that you would not be shipwrecked somewhere en route. Even when my family left India in the 1930s, by which time the Suez Canal had opened, saving 5,000 miles, the journey still took nearly three weeks to complete. The notion of doing the same journey in just over eight hours

non-stop would be regarded by them as a miracle. A few hours of inconvenience is, I suppose, a small price to pay. And even when things go wrong, there is often a funny side to the story.

Take the journey we took the day after Dominique and I got married some years ago. We got into our economy seats on time. The aircraft was absolutely full, and when I say full, that means there were passengers on the crew jump seats, and older children sitting on their parents' laps. Even in first class, passengers were packed in sardine-like. All that aside, however, Air India pilots are the best in the world; no one lands a jumbo jet as softly. Just this week in fact, the landing was so gentle, that Dominique didn't realise we were on the runway.

To get back to my story: we pushed back on time, and taxied around Heathrow's perimeter, arriving at the back of the queue for take-off. Then a strange thing happened. Firstly we taxied out of the queue, and did a careful U-turn. Going against the traffic, we started slowly threading our way around Heathrow, almost brushing the wing tips of other jets facing the correct way in the queue. After what seemed like an age we finally reached open space, and the pilot speeded up. No announcement had been made, and probably few passengers realised we were no longer in the queue. Finally, we arrived back at Terminal 3 at the same stand we had left 45 minutes earlier and the engines were switched off. Silence. Thirty minutes later, and still no announcement from the pilot or cabin staff. Then I noticed, from my vantage point in a window behind the wing, a small van. An Air India engineer unfolded a step ladder under the starboard inner engine. He climbed to its topmost rung and attempted to hold on to the engine cowling, at fingertip reach. He then clearly burnt his fingers from the still hot jet, and shaking his hand, retreated into his van, and drove off hurriedly. Another hour went by, and a larger truck with hydraulic lift and two engineers turned up. The engine cowling was removed for engine inspection. This took a further hour. By now there were some fifteen personnel standing around on the ground, including one with four gold stripes on his epaulettes, presumably the captain. Clearly animated discussion was taking place,

although, we, the passengers had still not received even a single word about the problem. Finally, it seemed that the meeting came to a decision. The cowling was replaced, the hydraulic lift came down, the personnel dispersed. We're going to go now, I thought.

Thirty minutes later, and exactly four hours after we had first pushed back, the captain came on the public address system. 'Ladies and Gentlemen,' he said, 'I am very sorry, but we have a small technical problem! We are trying to resolve it, but meanwhile, I have instructed the cabin crew to serve your lunch.' And so they began. One thing which no other airline does better than Air India is food. And, unlike other airlines, no passenger ever has to pre-book for vegetarian meals. Dom and I were in the penultimate row of seats at the back of our section, and we were by then very hungry. The service began at the front of our section, and slowly approached us, as the crew served the passengers row by row. When it was our turn we asked for, and were given, Indian vegetarian meals. The crew then moved to the last row behind us. 'Sir,' I heard the stewardess say, 'I'm sorry, we have run out of vegetarian meals.' Sir, a

well-heeled Indian from Bombay exploded in fury. 'How can you possibly run out of vegetarian food on an Indian flight? I do not eat anything else,' he choked. He was apoplectic with rage, and who could blame him? Then the stewardess came up with a possible solution. 'Sir, I'll go to first class and bring you vegetarian food from there if I can.' He was still not happy, and continued muttering at varying volume levels, while we kept a low profile, tucking our meal away as if it were the last supper, in case it was snatched from us. It took ten minutes for the stewardess to return, fortunately with the vegetarian option.

We all enjoyed our meal and while it was cleared away we awaited developments. Finally, with absolutely nothing happening on the ground as far as I could see from my vantage point, the PA system cracked into life again. It was by now seven hours since push back and the captain announced that the aircraft was not going anywhere that day, and we would have to disembark. Another hour went by, and Sir announced theatrically that we should have just been landing in Bombay. Finally we disembarked and, amid considerable chaos and confusion, we arrived at the Heathrow Hotel for the night, with our wash kits and change of clothes safely locked away in the jumbo jet's hold.

I thought about taking a taxi to Southall for a new shirt and some toothpaste, but we were told to be on immediate standby in case the aircraft became ready to fly. At midnight they told us to go to sleep but to be ready to leave at 6 a.m.

You'll not find a better example of dosa than at London's Great Russell Street Malabar Junction restaurant.

To start making jalebi, the batter is squeezed . . .

through a tiny hole pierced in its bag, into hot oil . . .

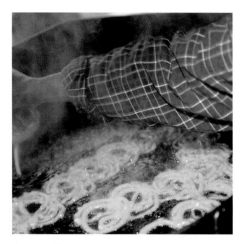

in a continuous process . . .

Next morning we all found ourselves back on the same aircraft, sitting in the same seats, with the same crew at the same stations. Exactly twenty-four hours after the time we should have taken off, we finally did so. Then it was lunch time with, we noticed, a menu identical to that of the previous day. As before, the service began at the front of our section, and again slowly approached us. Again, when it was our turn we asked for and were given Indian vegetarian meals. Again the crew moved to the last row behind us. And guess what? Again they had run out of vegetarian meals! I hardly need to tell

you Sir's reaction. After a scene very much like that of the day before, only somewhat worse, Sir once again got his vegetarian option, and this time the flight arrived in Bombay on time but a day late.

The punch line is that this delay cost us our honeymoon, which we had planned as a long weekend in the entrancingly beautiful Maldive Islands before starting work in India (and a day on the tarmac at Heathrow hardly makes up for it). On arrival in India we couldn't get seats on subsequent Bombay to Maldive flights and so had to put up with Bombay and a visit to a

brewery in Bangalore instead, plus the dubious delights of taking a group around India. Dom and I did get back to the Maldives for three nights a few years later, and I have promised that one day that we will take a fortnight's honeymoon there. But as the one who is always to blame for everything, I have never lived this down.

I said earlier that British Airways are no better. We had a similar experience out of Bombay the following year. The flight took off on time and seemed to be flying smoothly for nearly two hours. Then I noticed the whining noise which accompanies an electrical generator

to create the traditional squiggles.

As soon as they firm up, they are removed from the oil . . .

and are immersed in syrup.

Southall's Abdul Pazzaq makes thousands of jalebi every day . . .

on the pavement outside Tandoori Express on Jalebi Junction, 93 Broadway, to the enjoyment of his customers, of whom Pat is one.

failing and a standby cutting in. It happened again a few minutes later and I then noticed that we had commenced a slow 180° turn. It was around 4 a.m. and most passengers seemed to be asleep. The captain made a quiet announcement concerning a 'minor technical problem' and said that rather than cross into Afghan airspace, he was returning to Bombay.

Two hours later we touched down there at dawn, with the entire complement of the airport's fire brigade, ambulance and police forces racing alongside us. Some minor problem! I suspect it was an engine failure, but of course the passengers never got to know. For a while, many of the sleepy passengers thought we had landed in Heathrow. When the awful truth dawned, we were left for several hours, amid chaos and confusion, with no further information, until we were eventually dispatched to the local

hotels. It was twenty-four hours before we were back in our seats. The similarities between this and our experience just one year earlier were astonishing, although sadly there was no vegetarian food cabaret this time. Indeed there wasn't any Indian vegetarian food.

Following our return from the 'Pepper Fest' on our most recent Air India flight (incident-free, except that the captain went sick before take-off, and we had to wait for three hours on the ground until his replacement could be summoned), I visited one of London's best south Indian restaurants, Malabar Junction, to brush up my dosa-making skills. This rice and lentil flour pancake, filled with spicy potato curry and accompanied by sambar and rasam and coconut chutney is one of our absolute favourite dishes, and recipes for it can be found in this book (see **Index**). Pictured here are the fruits of

my dosa-making labour, or rather those of my tutor, Sujatha, a delightful chef from Hyderabad. Colin Poole (my photographer) and I also visited London's top La Porte des Indes restaurant, whose vegetable displays are legion, and who flew in out-of-season exotic fruit and vegetables from Thailand which we photographed for the **Ingredients File**. From there we went on to Southall, to photograph Abdul Pazzaq's daily pavement performance making jalebis – those scrumptious crispy wiggles dipped in syrup that I talk about in more detail on page 198 – outside the Tandoori Express Restaurant in Southall. It's a remarkable success story, and well worth a visit if you can get there.

Meanwhile, even if you cannot get to such a haven, I hope this book will make a suitable substitute as it takes you on its spicy journey around the curry world.

The Workshop

Traditionally, I call the opening chapter of my books the 'Workshop'. In it we look at the many and varied things which contribute to successful curry cooking. First, we examine the all-important whole and ground spices, in alphabetical order. Next between pages 26 and 29 follows an A to Z of vital flavouring items and staples, such as coconut, garlic, ginger, grain and flour, oils, onion, rice, rose water, salt, silver leaf, and tamarind and vinegar to name a few. Following this comes advice on which utensils, equipment and tools to use, sizzling, keeping curry, portions, serving, as well as nutritional information. By request, the Workshop section ends with a couple of pages on how to avert or correct disasters.

The **Vegetable Ingredients File** is found in among the recipes between pages 55 and 127. This covers, in alphabetical order, many of the major vegetables, familiar and exotic, needed for cooking curry without meat, poultry or fish. We also examine herbs, lentils, nuts, salad leaves and garnishes in this file. The **Fruit Ingredients File**, again in alphabetical order, is among the recipes from pages 131 to 195 and looks mainly at the amazing and tasty selection of exotic tropical fruit now so readily available for our enjoyment.

An appendix on page 205 lists the ingredients you will need in your store cupboard and without which it is impossible to proceed. Before you begin to cook the recipes in this book, I strongly recommend that you read this Workshop chapter and the Store Cupboard page.

To locate a particular ingredient or spice, please refer to the index at the back of the book.

Basic Ingredients

Alkanet Root
Ratin Jot

Alkanet (*ratin jot*), is a wild, deep-rooting plant, with yellow flowers, related to borage. Its root stem is a remarkable beetroot purple-red in colour, and once dried, it forms a wafer-thin bark. In medieval Europe, and until recently, it was used to make a deep red dye to colour make-up, pharmaceuticals and clothing, among other items. It is still is used today for this purpose in India. Alkanet got its name from the Arabic *al-henne*, the deep red-brown dye from the mignonette tree, still used to dye hair, hands and feet in India and Arabia.

In Kashmir, alkanet is used as a food colouring. Alhough it has no flavour, it is important in achieving a deep reddish-brown colour in certain dishes. Another plant, a type of amaranth, called *maaval* in Kashmiri (meaning 'cockscomb', so called because it resembles that part of a chicken's anatomy in both shape and colour), also gives off a gorgeous red colour when soaked in water. The deep red Kashmiri chilli is also used for this purpose (see page 18).

The unique feature of alkanet is that it is impervious to water. However, fried briefly in hot oil, the result is spectacular: at once the oil's colour changes to a deep red. The Roghan Josh with peanuts, tomato and karela gourd, depicted on page 88, is cooked in alkanet.

Allspice
Seenl or Kababchini

Allspice is a spherical, dark purple berry, from a tree related to myrtle, native to the West Indies. Once dried, it becomes a dark brown, slightly abrasive, spherical seed, about 5 mm (¼ inch) in diameter, a little larger and smoother than a black peppercorn. Indeed, allspice got its alternative name, pimento, thanks to the errant Christopher Columbus, whose quest for pepper led to his 'discovery' of the Americas in 1492. Though the native seed was clearly not pepper, Columbus named it *pimienta* (Spanish for pepper), thus creating confusion ever since. In the seventeenth century, owing to its popularity in English cookery, an attempt was made to avoid this confusion and it became known as the 'English spice'. The name 'allspice' was adopted later because, being related to the clove family, its aroma, deriving from the eugenol in its oils, seems to combine that of clove, cinnamon, and nutmeg. Despite these properties, and despite being planted in the East Indies by the British, allspice never became as important in economic terms as other more traditional spices. To this day, the best allspice comes from Jamaica, and, although it is grown in India, mainly for export, it is little used in Indian cookery, although it can be used to give a wonderful aroma to such dishes as Dhansak and Biriani.

Aniseed
Saunf or soonf

This tiny oval, striped, grey-brown seed, about 2 mm (less than ⅛ inch) long, with a little tail, grows on an annual plant with a yellow-white flower. Aniseed is a very ancient spice, native to the Middle East, where its use was recorded by the ancient Egyptians, Greeks and Romans. It was used in English cooking in the Middle Ages, though it is not so commonly used in India as its near relative, the larger, but slightly less aromatic fennel seed (see page 20), with which it is frequently confused. It is a member of the same (*Umbelliferae*) family as fennel. It even shares the same Hindi name, *saunf*. The similarity in taste, though not appearance, comes about because aniseed also shares with fennel, and with star anise, the very distinctive essential oil, anethole, which comprises a huge 90 per cent of aniseed. It is this which gives aniseed its sweet and aromatic flavour, best known as the principal flavouring in such alcoholic drinks as ouzo and pastis. Aniseed is an occasional, but important, spice in dishes requiring an aromatic conclusion. It is also a major ingredient in supari mix, the digestive mixture of spices eaten after a curry meal, sometimes given a highly colourful sugar coating. It is definitely worth having in stock.

Asafoetida
Hing

This spice is extracted from the carrot-shaped rhizome of a giant perennial plant of the fennel family, native to Kashmir. When the rhizome is mature enough, cuts are made in it to yield a milky-white sap which slowly oozes out, and solidifies into a brown

resin-like substance. This is factory-ground into a grey-brown or bright greenish-lemon powder (depending on the species).

The Persian words *aza*, 'resin', and Latin *foetidus*, 'stinking', indicate that asafoetida has an obnoxious, disagreeable odour, hence its other names – 'devil's dung' and 'stinking gum'. The odour itself is due to the sulphur in the rhizome's composition. Because of its smell, it is a good precaution to store it in its factory packaging, and within an airtight container. It is generally used only in fish and lentil dishes, and fortunately, its unpleasant odour disappears once it is cooked, giving way to a distinctive and pleasant fragrance and sweetish taste.

Bay Leaf
Tej Patta Laurel

Bay, or laurel leaf is pointed and oval in shape, and grows to an average 7cm (3 inches) in length. It can be used fresh or dried. Fresh, it is glossy, smooth, quite fleshy, and dark green in colour, and has a more powerful flavour than dried, with a slightly more bitter undertone. Dried, it is paler, and quite brittle. The leaf grows on an evergreen tree or bush, found worldwide, and is a familiar spice to most people in the West. Bay is used whole in aromatic curries and rice, such as Korma and in Birianis. Ground bay is an ingredient in masalas.

Caraway seed

Caraway may well be the world's most ancient spice, with evidence of its use going back over 5,000 years. Seeds have been discovered amongst pottery remains in a number of archaeological sites in the Levant – the area where both agriculture and literacy, as well as caraway, originated.

The Romans added it to their bread, as do contemporary Germans and Austrians.

It grows as a biennial plant, yielding small seeds about 3 mm (⅛ inch) in length, coloured dark grey-brown, with five lighter-coloured ridges. It is a member of the same (*Umbelliferae*) family, and similar in appearance to black cummin (see page 26), though it is paler in colour and a fraction larger, and has no similarity in flavour. Caraway has an aromatic, agreeably warm aroma, with a hint of astrigency due to the presence of caravone in its essential oil. In England, it is best known as a cake-making spice. It grows in cooler climates, such as northern Europe, Russia and the northern subcontinent, especially the Himalayas. In India, it is used more for medicinal purposes than in traditional Indian cookery. As in Europe, it is enjoyed in bread and cakes, cheese and distilling. As far as curry cookery goes, it is a minor spice, but it gives an interesting flavouring option to bread or rice dishes. A tiny pinch adds depth to aromatic curries.

Cardamom
Elaichi

Cardamom is native to south India, Sri Lanka, Thailand and Guatemala. It grows on a herbaceous perennial plant, related to the ginger family, whose pod contains slightly sticky black seeds, their familiar flavour coming from the cineol in its oils. Cardamom is one of the most elegant, aromatic and expensive spices. It is also one of India's most exported spices, earning the country considerable revenue, and the spice itself, the title, the 'Queen of Spice'. There are three main cardamom types, all of which can be used whole or ground.

Natural white cardamoms are much in demand for their flavour and are of the same species as the green, having a similar flavour, which is rather more delicate than that of the brown (but beware bleached cardamoms, which are old specimens 'livened-up'). Green cardamoms, *chota elaichi*, have a smooth, ribbed, pale green outer casing, about 1 cm (½ inch) long. The greener the cardamom, the fresher it is, though, here again, the use of food dyes is not unheard of to 'freshen-up' older specimens. They are used whole or ground, with or without casing, in many savoury and sweet recipes. Brown (also called black) cardamoms, *bara elaichi*, have a rather hairy, husky, dark brown casing about 2 cm (⅞ inch) long. Used in garam masala, kormas and pullaos, they are strong and astringent, and aromatic, though less so than the other species.

Cassia

Jangli Dalchini

This is the corky, outer bark of a tree, with a sweet fragrance, related to cinnamon (see page 19), and indeed there is considerable confusion between the two, to the extent that many spice manufacturers insist on labelling 'cassia bark' as 'cinnamon'. Cassia originated in Burma. It is now widely grown in Indonesia and south China, giving rise to its alternative name, Chinese cinnamon.

Cassia is an ancient spice, known to the ancient Egyptians. It grows as a large, evergreen, tropical-forest tree, the leaves of which are used in the way that the West uses bay leaves. Branches are cut down, their bark is scraped off, and formed into reddish-brown quills about 1 metre (3 feet) long. These are fragile, and by the time it is packed, cassia bark is usually in chips, averaging 5 cm (2 inches) in length. Cassia's essential oil contains cinnamic aldehyde, giving it a sweet, clove-like, musky flavour. Cassia bark is usually much less fragrant, coarser, thicker and tougher than cinnamon, and it stands up to more robust cooking. It is also cheaper. It is used as an aromatic flavouring in subtle meat and poultry dishes, and as a major flavouring in pullao rice and garam masala. Although widely used in cooking, the bark cannot be eaten.

Chilli

Hari Mirch (Green)
Lal Mirch (Red)

Chilli is a relative newcomer to Indian cooking. It is the fleshy pod of shrub-like bushes of the Capsicum family. There are five species, and thousands of varieties of chilli, all of which start life green and ripen through white, yellow or orange to red or purple. Dried, chilli is nearly always red, and is available whole, crushed, or ground to a fine powder. Though this is simply called 'chilli powder', and is available in different 'heat' grades, there is some confusion about cayenne pepper. This originally came from French Guiana, but is now blended from many types of chilli, and is indistinguishable from 'chilli powder', though it is often dearer. Paprika is simply a Capsicum variety.

Often, when people think of curry, it is 'heat' that immediately springs to mind, chilli being the heat giver. 'Heat' in this context is ambiguous, having nothing to do with temperature. 'Piquancy' is better, referring to the burning sensation in the mouth, caused by the alkaloid 'capsaicin', present to a greater or lesser degree in the flesh and seeds of all members of the Capsicum family, irrespective of their colour (with the exception of bell peppers which contain no capsaicin). Capsaicin is related to caffeine, nicotine and morphine, which explains why chilli is the world's most popular spice.

Larger chillies are generally milder, while the familiar long thin cayenne used in Indian cooking is hotter, and at the

incendiary level are Naga, Scotch Bonnet or Habañero chillies. The chilli level can be varied (up or down) in cooking without being detrimental to a dish's overall flavour, but chilli must not be omitted altogether from basic masala mixes – it acts as a catalyst to the other spices. Rich in Vitamin C, fresh chilli, like onion and garlic, actively helps to reduce blood pressure and cholesterol.

Celery seed

Ajmud or Shalari

This is an ancient spice, native to Europe, Asia, and Africa. In recent centuries it has been taken to America. It is a herbal plant of the parsley family, which grows up to 1.5metres (5 feet) in height, and yields tiny (1mm) oval olive-greenish-brown seeds, with five paler-coloured ribs. From the *same (Umbelliferae)* family, come aniseed, caraway, coriander, cummin, dill, lovage, fennel and parsley. Celery seed, used as a spice, is only distantly related to domestic celery, which is a 'recent' (mid-sixteenth-century) development from Italy and France. Wild celery, also called smallage, was used as a herb and a spice by both Greeks and Romans, who were convinced that it had aphrodisiac qualities. Be that as it may, celery seed has a savoury, aromatic, slightly bitter taste, which when fried or 'roasted', intensifies its 'celery' taste. It is little used in Indian cookery, though it can make an interesting substitute for one of the Bengali five spices (see Panch Phoran, page 39). Celery seed has a further use in medication, for the treatment of asthma, liver disorders, and rheumatism.

Cinnamon
Dalchini

Cinnamon has been used to flavour food for thousands of years, its sweetish aromatic flavour adding a haunting quality to food. In Roman times, Arabs were the middlemen between the Chinese and the Romans. To protect their trade routes, and their monopolies, the Arabs used to invent tall stories. They claimed, for example, that cinnamon bark came from the nest of a great, man-eating, horned eagle, the size of a horse, located on top of a single, high mountain peak. Believing such stories, the Romans would pay outlandish prices, squandering their gold reserves, and ultimately bankrupting their empire, in order to buy such 'luxuries' as spices.

Cinnamom is native to Sri Lanka, and though it now also grows in the Seychelles, Brazil, the West Indies and Indonesia, the Sri Lankan variety is still regarded as the best. Like cassia bark, with which it is often confused, cinnamon is the inner bark of a tropical tree. It is prepared in the same way as cassia, yielding more delicate, parchment-thin, tightly rolled, pale brown quills of around 1 cm (½ inch) in diameter and 10–12 cm (4–6 inches) long. These quills are more aromatic than cassia bark's, though unlike that spice, cinnamon can break up in robust cooking. Little pieces of cinnamon are inedible with an unpleasant mouth-feel, so quills are best confined to infusing drinks and flavouring pullao rice. Cinnamon is also used in its ground form in some dishes.

Clove
Lavang

Clove is Britain's most familiar spice, having been used continuously since the Romans brought it here. We still use it for its flavour in dishes like apple pie, and also to ease toothache because of its pain-killing essential oil, eugenol. Originally native only to two neighbouring tiny Indonesian Moluccan 'spice islands', Ternate and Tidore (now called Soasiu), in the East Indies, wars were fought over the clove. Today it is found in India, Sri Lanka, Zanzibar, Madagascar, Brazil and Grenada.

Clove grows on a smallish tropical evergreen tree, related to the myrtle family, which thrives near the sea. The unopened bud of the tree's flower is bright green at first, and must be picked just as it turns pink. The flower, if allowed to bloom, is dark pink about 1 cm (½ inch) in diameter.

Dried clove is dark reddish-brown, bulbous at one end (this is the bud, and is where the flavour is, so watch out for 'headless' cloves), with tapering stalks, about 1 cm (½ inch) in length. The Romans thought that they resembled nails, *clavus* being the Latin for 'clout' or 'nail'. Clove is the world's second most important spice, earning India alone some £20 million a year. It takes some 8–10,000 cloves to make up just 1 kg (2.2 lb).

Coriander Seeds
Dhania

Coriander is a member of the ubiquitous *Umbelliferae* family. It was native to India but now grows worldwide, as a herbaceous annual plant. Its seed and leaf are widely used, while its rather bitter root is also used in India and Thailand. Coriander leaves are mid-green and flat with jagged edges, and are important, some say indispensable, in Indian cookery (see page 36). However, the musky flavour of the leaves is quite unlike that of the seed, which imparts a sweetish flavour, with a hint of orange.

In terms of volume, but not value, coriander is the most important spice in Indian cookery, and 80,000 tons are exported per year.

There are many coriander species, giving minor variations to the appearance of coriander seed. A Middle Eastern variety has small, buff-coloured spheres (about 3–4 mm/ ⅛ inch in diameter). The most common Indian variety has slightly larger, paler, more aromatic oval-shaped seeds. The seeds are used whole or ground, forming the largest single ingredient in most masalas. They are delicious roasted – try them as a garnish.

Cummin
Jeera

Cummin (always spelt this way by the Raj, but 'cumin' by others, after its Latin name *cuminum*), is an ancient spice, native to Syria and Egypt. It has been found, intact, whole, and apparently still edible, in the tombs of the Pharaohs, having been placed there some 4,000 years ago. Cummin was mentioned in the Old Testament, and was so important to the Romans that it was substituted for salt as a seasoning, causing it to be very expensive. It also became synonymous with excess and greed, to the extent that the gluttonous Emperor Marcus Aurelius was nicknamed Cuminus. It still predominates in Middle Eastern cooking, and has found a new role in the USA in Tex-Mex chilli con carne. Cummin has always played a major role in Indian cooking, its use in volume being second only to coriander. Ground, it is a major component in curry powder.

It grows on a smallish annual herb of the coriander (*Umbelliferae*) family. Its thin seeds are about 5 mm (¼ inch) long. They are grey-brown to yellowish-green in colour, and have nine stripy longitudinal ridges and small stalks. Its oil, cuminaldehyde gives it a distinctive, savoury taste with a slightly bitter overtone. Cummin is important in masalas and curries, and is one of the five spices of panch phoran. Whole cummin seeds benefit greatly in taste from being 'roasted'.

Curry Leaves
Kari Phulia or Kurri Patta

Native to South-west Asia, the neem tree grows to about 6 metres (25 feet) in height, and 1 metre (3 feet) across. It is especially prevalent in the foothills of the Himalayas, and south India. The tree is greatly adored as a garden ornamental, when its size is much smaller. The young curry leaf is a small pale green, delicate thing, which grows up to 4 cm (1½ inches) in length. Leaves are widely used whole in southern Indian cooking, and impart a delicious flavour to dishes such as rasam, sambar, masala dosa and lemon rice. Despite its name, the leaf has a lemony fragrance, and no hint of 'curry'. This is because it is related to the lemon family. Ground curry leaf is used in many commercial curry powder blends. In addition, it is used as a tonic for stomach and kidney disorders. Fresh curry leaves are imported into the UK by air-freight from Kenya, but are hard to locate outside of Asian green grocers. Dry ones are readily available from Asian stores and make passable substitutes. If you enjoy south Indian food, they are a 'must-have' spice.

Dill seed
Sowa or Sova

Dill, a member of the parsley family, grows as a hardy annual to about 1 metre (3 feet) high, and its feathery leaves are used as a (non-Indian) herb. Its seed is an oval, rowing-boat shape, about 3.5 mm (⅛ inch) in length, with a narrow pale buff rim surrounding a grey-brown mass. It has three ridges on its convex inner side. It is sweetly aromatic with a slightly lemony taste, which is bitter in excess. Its volatile oils contain carvone and limonenes, as does caraway, to

whose family it belongs. It originated in Europe and the Mediterranean, and was well known to the ancient Egyptians, Greeks and Romans. Dill got its name from the old Norse word *dilla*, to lull. Medievals held it in high enough regard to use it as a 'magic' brew, strong enough to counter witchcraft.

Today, dill is especially popular in Scandinavia, Germany and Russia. The Indian version of dill seed is slightly longer and narrower than the European, but is similar enough in flavour to make the two interchangeable. There, it is sometimes called soya, but it has nothing to do with soya beans.

It is much more widely used in Indian medication than in cooking, though it is great in naan bread, or rice dishes. In fact, it can be substituted for caraway or fennel, in any dish which calls for either of those.

Fennel
Saunf, Sunf or Soonf

Fennel, a European native, is a hardy perennial which grows to about 2 metres (6 feet) in height. Its leaf and its bulb were used by the Romans, both as a vegetable and medicinally, particularly to assist with eyesight problems. The great fifteenth-century spice explorers, the Portuguese, when probing the uncharted Atlantic, literally followed their noses to the island of Madeira. The strong fragrance of fennel on the prevailing westerlies led them there, and they named the port Funchal, from their word *funcho*, meaning fennel.

Today, fennel bulb and leaf are still relished in Europe, though not in India. What is important there is the small, pale, greenish-yellow stripy seed, slightly plump and greener than cummin, which grows to around 5 cm (¼ inch) in length. It is quite sweet and aromatic. Frequently confused in India with its near relative, the smaller aniseed, whose name and (umbelliferous) family it shares, fennel seed is much more prevalent. Its slightly milder, though similar, flavour comes from the essential oil anethole, which both aniseed and star anise contain too. Fennel is 70 per cent anethole (compared with aniseed's 90 per cent), with a smaller amount of fenchone. This combination gives it a sweet and aromatic flavour, making it ideal for subtle dishes, garam masala, and paan mixtures. It is unique, in that it is the only spice common to the five-spice mixtures of both India (panch phoran) and China. Grown all over north India, fennel from Lucknow is the best quality. It is used medicinally as gripe water, and for eyesight, obesity and chest problems.

Fenugreek Leaf and Seed
Methi

There are two forms of fenugreek used in Indian cookery, the seed and the leaf. The latter grows grey-green in colour on a clover-like annual herb, which produces pale triangular-shaped yellow flowers, hence its botanical name, *Trigonella*. Pronounced *may-tee* in Hindi, fenugreek leaf derives from the Latin *foenum graecum*, dried grass or hay ('Greek hay'), indeed the leaf is still used as cattle fodder. The leaf is popular in north Indian and Punjabi cookery, where it is used fresh or dried in the same way as spinach, although it gives a strong bitter taste, disagreeable perhaps at first. But once acquired, it lends an interesting depth to Indian food, and is least bitter when added late in the cooking. Fresh fenugreek is

available at Asian greengrocers, but in its dried form it keeps like any other spice. It is worth noting that after cropping the leaves are dried in the sun on flat roofs. Consequently, it is necessary to pick through them to remove grit and small stones. Unfortunately, you will always find a lot of tough stalks. These should be discarded. The spice has a very strong smell, so it is a good idea to double pack it, in an airtight container, within another airtight container, and use sparingly. Fenugreek leaf is rich in carotene, vitamin A, ascorbic acid, calcium and iron.

The fenugreek plant also yields bean-like pods, 10–15 cm (4–6 inches) long, containing between ten and twenty tiny, hard, yellow-ochre-brown, nugget-like, grooved seeds about 3 mm (⅛ inch) long. Fenugreek seeds have been found in Egyptian tombs. To this day the spice remains very popular in the Middle East, where fenugreek is a key ingredient in a spicy dip called *hilbeh*. It also appears in Arab bread (*khoubiz*), and the Greeks enjoy it with honey.

India produces over 20,000 tons of fenugreek seed a year. It is an important ingredient in masalas, curry powder, and one of the panch phoran five spices. Though seeming to smell of curry, the seed is quite bitter, its main oil being coumarin. Light roasting gives the seed an interesting depth, and another way of using it is to soak it overnight (see Green Masala Paste, page 45). Fenugreek seed can also be sprouted, like mung beans, for beansprouts with a light curry flavour. It is also said to be a good contraceptive and a hair tonic, and in Java it is used to counter baldness.

Lemon Grass
Takrai

Lemon grass is native to India and South-east Asia, and grows as a perennial grass plant to around 1 metre (3 feet) tall. It is depicted fresh, in the photograph on page 37. Its actual grass blades are quite hard, and are discarded, as is the rhizome, or root base. It is this bulbous, lower end of the grass, measuring between 10 and 15 cm (4–6 inches) in length, which contains its oil, citral aldehyde. This gives it its distinctive fragrance, so familiar in the world of cosmetics, and the unique flowery, slightly zesty, lemony, sweet and aromatic taste to Thai, Indonesian, Malaysian and Vietnamese cooking. Generally, the stalk is not actually soft enough to eat. You'll get more flavour if you cut the fresh stalk into tassels (witch's broom-style), which will enlarge its surface area during cooking. Only if the stalk is particularly fresh and soft, and it is 'cross-cut' into tiny half-moons, can it be eaten.

Lemon grass is not widely used in Indian cooking, though it grows extensively there. It is used to flavour tea, and Parsee and Gujarati soups. The Raj also used it in hybrid curries, such as their coconut-based Malaya curry. Fresh lemon grass is widely available, but if you like its flavour, it is worth keeping it powdered. Lemon peel or zest cannot substitute for the real thing.

Lovage
Ajwain or Ajowan

Lovage is an annual, herbaceous plant, which grows up to 60 cm (2 feet) high, with feathery leaves and pretty vermillion flowers. It is a member of the prolific *Umbelliferae* family, which also includes aniseed, caraway, celery, coriander, cummin, dill and fennel. They share a characteristic taste, which of course comes from the thymol in all of them in varying quantities. But once again, this is a spice with a confusing nomenclature. *Ajwain* is indigenous to Egypt, Afghanistan and north India, and its seed is smaller than its European counterpart, lovage. Its seed is a tiny greyish sphere about 1½–2 mm in diameter, with characteristic stripes. Its taste is a little bitter, with a slightly musky, but quite distinctively intense flavour of thyme, which is an acquired taste. Once acquired, however, you'll enjoy this minor spice in Bombay mix, snacks, and fish dishes.

Mace and Nutmeg
Javitri and Jaifal

Mace and nutmeg grow together on a tall, tropical evergreen tree, which originally grew only on the tiny Moluccan Indonesian island of Ambon. The Chinese knew of its location centuries before Christ, and their dhows took mace, nutmeg and clove back to China, from where it travelled the length of the spice route to the Middle East, and onward to Europe. The Romans introduced such spices into Britain, and although many mark-ups made spices very expensive, by Tudor times they were so much in demand, that no effort was spared in finding their elusive sources. Ambon was eventually discovered by the Portuguese, in 1512, and later taken by the Dutch, and fought over, but never occupied for long by the British,

although they broke the monopoly by deviously obtaining nutmeg/mace, and planting it in Sri Lanka, south India and Grenada, in the West Indies.

Mace is enclosed inside a pithy, inedible, bright green case (resembling a smooth horse-chestnut casing). Mace is a delightful bright crimson or amber and forms a type of blade which surrounds the shiny red-brown inner seed case, the nutmeg, in a tendril-like net. Mace is pliable and easily separated from its nutmeg, and is generally flattened, before being dried in the sun. As it dries, mace often loses its red colour. It is very aromatic and oily, its volatile oil being eugenol, though it has less of this than nutmeg. Its use in Indian cooking is minimal, its subtle flavour tending to go well with lighter fish, vegetables and sweet dishes.

Nutmeg is mace's other half, so to speak. After it is cropped and removed from its casing, nutmeg too is spread out and dried in the sun, after which it turns rather grey in colour. The shell is not wasted and is used like bark chippings, as an attractive flowerbed covering. Nutmeg, with its very aromatic eugenol flavour, has always been popular in Britain, the little hard, egg-shaped nuts working their magic when grated into puddings and cake mixes, and over hot chocolate drinks and mashed potato. Indian cooking does not call for nutmeg often as an individual spice, but it is excellent grated over desserts, and is also an ingredient of garam masala.

Mango powder
Am Chur or Kachcha Am

The mango (am) is India's most revered fruit. It has been cultivated there for over 6,000 years, and has earned itself the title 'Queen of Fruit', as well as substantial revenue for India as an export crop. Mango is also used as a vegetable, particularly for pickling. Mangoes grow seasonally on a pretty tree, whose dark leaves spread out like a huge parasol. In Britain and the West, we are fortunate enough to have mangoes available virtually all year round as they are imported from many countries. In India, this is not the case, and the mango season is a greatly anticipated, yet rather short highlight of the year. One way of prolonging its availability is to dry the fruit, then grind it into a fine grey powder. Only sour, unripened, pitted mangoes are used for this and the resultant spice is exceedingly sour, but very distinctive. It is mostly used in chaats and some vegetable dishes.

Marathi Mokku

This is a very unusual and special spice used in Tamil Nadu and southern Indian cooking. It is not readily available yet in the UK because many of the Asian grocers are not from the south and are not familiar with it themselves. But keep asking your Asian store to order it. If you do manage to get hold of one you should grind the hard casing and the small black seeds inside it, which resemble wild onion seeds in appearance, but not taste. Marathi Mokku adds a distinctive fragrance when used but if you cannot obtain it, don't worry, simply omit it.

Mustard Seed

Rai or Kalee Sarson

Mustard could be the world's oldest cultivated spice. Its branched annual plant is a member of the cabbage family. There are three varieties of mustard seed: brown (*juncea*) from India, with spherical seeds around 1 mm diameter; white (*alba*), which is yellow ochre in colour; and black (*nigra*). The latter two are around 2 mm in diameter and both native to the Mediterranean. White and black seeds are used to manufacture mustard and cress, and the familiar bright yellow powder or paste, although black is cropped less these days. The seeds are de-husked then milled, and flour, and turmeric (for colour) are also added. If you taste mustard powder, you will find that it is not hot at first. Its heat develops when cold water is added. This causes a chemical reaction when its components, including its volatile oil, isothiocyanate, react and develop a pungent heat. Indeed, mustard gets its name from the Latin, *mustum ardens*, meaning 'a burning must'. The brown Indian mustard seed is not as pungent as the others, in fact, tasted raw, it is unappealing and bitter. When cooked, however, it becomes sweet and appetising, and is not as hot as you might expect. It is immensely popular in Bengal, where it is one of the five spices in panch phoran, and in southern India where it appears in many recipes roasted, fried or as a garnish.

Paprika

Paprika is the Hungarian name for pepper. Chillies were first introduced to Hungary by Ottoman Turks in the sixteenth century. At first paprika was deep red in colour and very pungent. Over the years much of the pungency has been bred out of Hungarian paprika, so that what we now expect is a tasty deep-red powder used for flavouring and colouring purposes, but not for heat. However, what we actually get may be wide of the mark: paprika may be mild or it may be hot, it can range in colour from rust to crimson, and it may have unspecified additives. The worst paprika will even be bitter. The reason is that, being a major crop, numerous other countries have become producers. Spain's paprika, called *pimieñto para pimeñton*, is made from a different pepper from Hungary's, but ranks as second only to its Hungarian counterpart in flavour and quality. As with everything else, expect to pay the most for the best, but be sure that it is the best you're paying for. Once you've found your favourite brand the best thing is to stick with it.

Peppercorns

Kala Mirch

Pepper, India's major spice revenue earner for thousands of years, is justifiably called the 'King of Spice'. The Romans brought it to England, where it was used as money: in the thirteenth century you could buy a sheep for a handful of pepper! Foreign ships entering London paid a levy of pepper, and it was also used to paid debts, such as (peppercorn) rent. Until chilli was discovered in the sixteenth century, pepper was the main heat-giving agent in cooking, its heat coming from the alkaloid, piperine.

Peppercorn often grows as a climbing vine on the betel nut tree, which thrives in monsoon forests, and whose heart-shaped leaf (paan) is used in digestives (see page 189). The vine flowers, then it produces berries, called spikes, in long clusters. Green peppercorns are immature when picked, and fresh spikes are occasionally available in the UK. Alternatively, they are immediately bottled, air-dried or freeze-dried. To obtain black peppercorns, the spikes are picked when they start changing colour to yellow. They are then sun-dried, and quickly become black and shrivelled. To harvest white pepper, the spikes are left on the vine until they turn red. The outer red skin is removed by soaking it off, revealing an inner white berry which is then dried. Pink pepper is obtained in the same way, from a specific variety of vine, and it is immediately air-dried, to prevent it turning white. The red peppercorn, is not true pepper. It grows on a south American shrub, whose reddish-brown berry is aromatic, and a little bitter, but not hot.

Pomegranate seed
Anardana

Pomegranate grows on a deciduous tree, up to 7 metres (23 feet) high, native to the Himalayas, Afghanistan and Persia. The tree has deep green leaves and vermillion flowers and its fruit is about the size, colour and shape of the average apple. Indeed its name derives from the Latin *poma granata*, the apple of Carthage. This, however, is where the resemblance ends. Cut the pomegranate open and its remarkable secret is revealed, in the form of a neat package of translucent, bright crimson flesh, encasing numerous seeds. Once dried, the seeds turn a very attractive deep, reddish-brown colour. They are sticky, with a unique taste combination of astringent, sour, bitter and sweet. Pomegranate is an ancient fruit, and was certainly used in pre-biblical times. More intriguingly, it is widely believed to be none other than Adam's forbidden 'apple' in the Old Testament. Owning pomegranate was also considered to be a symbol of prosperity in ancient times.

Today, pomegranate also grows in Africa, the Mediterranean and the USA. It is an ingredient in the syrup grenadine. It is highly prized in its native country, Iran, where it is eaten raw and is used in cooking, especially in the Iranian national dish Faisanjan, an exotic duck concoction. And, of course, it is used in specialist north Indian dishes, contributing both colour and taste to salads and raitas, Moghul curries, and Punjabi chanas and chaats.

Poppy seed
Cuscus

The familiar red poppy is a pretty wild flower, native to Europe and north Asia. Unfamiliar in the West is the Asian poppy, with its white, pink or purple flowers. Both produce seeds which have culinary use, but the Asian poppy has a further by-product: opium.

Poppy is the world's most minuscule spice seed: it is a minute 0.6 mm at the longest part of its kidney shape, and it takes 1 million of them to make up a pound in weight. The European poppy has a further unique attribute. Its seed is blue, which makes the spice truly lovely to look at, and popular as a contrasting colour in baking. This variety, called nigrum, also grows in India, but the blue spice is not used there. What is used from the Asian poppy is the creamy-white (*alba*) seed which is the same size, shape, and has the same neutral, nutty, slightly sweet taste as the blue seed.

Poppy seed is a minor spice, used to thicken curries, and to decorate breads and sweets. As to opium, it is made by extracting a sticky, white sap from the unripe seed capsule of the Asian poppy. Once dried, it is ground to a powder. Opium contains morphine, heroin and codeine, essential in medication as a pain killer, reflected in its Latin name, *somniferum*. Unfortunately, because poppy seed, which incidentally contains no narcotic traces, is so easy to grow, it is equally easy, and far more profitable for the grower, to produce illegal opium, which is difficult for respective governments to detect, let alone prevent.

Saffron
Zafron or Kesar

Saffron imparts unique colour, flavour and fragrance, to savoury and sweet dishes alike. Native to Greece, the saffron crocus is a different species from the springtime, purple-leaved, flowering garden plant. Once it was cropped in and around Saffron Walden in Essex; today the main European saffron-producing area is in the La Mancha district of Spain. Asian producers are in China (where it is called *safalan*), Kashmir (*kesar*) and Iran (*zafran*). It flowers there in October.

Saffron is the world's most expensive spice, its cost reflecting not just its scarcity, but the extraordinary intensity of labour required to harvest it. The edible part of the crocus is the golden stigma (a kind of stamen) and only three of these grow in each flower, which must be picked on the very day the stigma is ready. The stigma are then carefully hand-plucked and dried – in La Mancha, by toasting them over very low heat and in Kashmir by sun-drying. Once dried, a remarkable 200,000 stigma are needed to make up a pound in weight of saffron worth over £1,000, which explains why it is known as 'liquid gold'. There is absolutely no substitute for saffron, and because of its price, many attempts are made to pass off imitation saffron. Always buy a reputable brand and beware the cheap, similar-coloured, but feathery safflower (bastard saffron). And do not use turmeric, even when it is called Indian saffron.

Too much saffron can be poisonous, although fortunately, we need well under danger level, with no more than four to six stigma per person (weighing less than 50 mg) imparting amazing colour, flavour and fragrance, from saffron's volatile oil, photo-rocrocin, to savoury and sweet dishes alike. Throughout history, saffron has been used in medicine, dyeing, cosmetics and food.

Sesame
Till

Sesame is a tropical, herbaceous, annual plant growing up to 2 metres (6 feet) in height. It is native to India and China, Asia and America, and is also found in Africa, where it is known as *benne*. Its capsules contain a large amount of tiny, buff, disc-shaped seeds, which grow to around 3 mm (⅛ inch) in diameter. After polishing, they become creamy-white in colour. Another species grow black seeds.

Sesame was used to make a flour by the ancient Egyptians. It was also a main source of oil. To this day, it is still more popular in the Middle East, than elsewhere. There, it is made into a basic paste called *tahini*, fundamental to the chick pea purée *humous*, both of which were popular with the Romans. The manufacture of sesame cooking oil remains a major industry, and is a role which suits the seed well, since it is already very oily, with 60 per cent of its content made up of oleic and linoeic volatile oils. Though sesame is a minor spice in Indian cooking, it is an important export crop there. It has a somewhat neutral, nutty taste and it is used to texture delicate cooking, and in Indian bread and confectionery. It is also used as a garnish. As with many spices, sesame improves greatly with a little 'roasting'. As a cooking oil, the nutty flavour of sesame oil is delightful, but wasted in anything other than subtle dishes.

Star anise
Anasphal

Star anise grows on a small, evergreen tree of the magnolia family, native to China, the Philippines and Indo-China. It flowers with single, yellow-green petals, followed by the seed, which develops into a green star, the average size of which is around 2.5 cm (1 inch) in diameter. It has eight regularly spaced arms (star points) radiating from the centre. When cropped, the still-closed star is dried, after which it becomes reddish-brown in colour. At this stage, some of the arms may open slightly, revealing a gleaming, pale brown seed. A whole specimen of star anise is arguably the prettiest spice on earth, but it is fragile, and the arms can easily break off in the packaging.

It is not related to aniseed, but is so named because it smells and tastes of aniseed because it contains the same volatile oil, anethole.

Star anise has been used since ancient times in Japanese cooking, and as one of the spices in Chinese five spices. Yet despite the fact that clove, nutmeg and mace were voluminously traded from China via the spice route in Roman times, there is no evidence that star anise was sold to Rome, Arabia or India, so there is no traditional Indian use of the spice, even in Moghul times. Equally, there is no record of star anise being used in Europe until the seventeenth century, when the Dutch used it to flavour tea. Modern Indian master chefs have discovered the attributes of star anise – it is astounding, for example, used in pullao rice as much for its shape as its colour.

Turmeric
Huldi

There are several varieties of turmeric, which like ginger is a rhizome that grows underground. It can be used fresh in certain curries, and for pickles and when halved, its gorgeous vivid orange-yellow is a clue to the role that turmeric plays in giving curry its distinctive golden colour. To achieve the familiar powder, fresh turmeric is sun-dried until it is rock hard and then ground.

Wild Onion Seed or Nigella
Kalonji

In the world of spices there is often confusion between one spice and another, and wild onion seeds are certainly a case in point. Open almost any spice reference book, and you will find this spice mis-named as black cummin. It bears absolutely no resemblance to it, nor is it even a member of the family (*Umbelliferae*) to which black and white cummin belong. Neither is it a member of the onion (*Liliaceae*) family, wild or cultivated, although the seeds of some Indian onions are somewhat similar, which may have been the cause of the misnomer, 'wild onion seeds'. An unambiguous name is nigella, the Hindi for which is *kalonji*. It is a member of the *Ranunculus* family, to which a number of aquatic plants belong, as does the buttercup. Nigella, also known as love-in-a-mist, is a native of Asia and north India, and grows as a herbaceous annual up to 60 cm (2 feet) tall, with pale blue flowers. Its seed, a matt coal-black, irregular, pentagonal nugget, is about 1.5–3 mm in size. Nigella has a distinctive, slightly bitter, intensely aromatic, vaguely peppery taste. It is used whole, in certain curry recipes, especially in the Bengal area, and is one of the five spices in panch phoran. Pressed into naan bread dough, it looks good and it tastes great.

Zeera or Black Cummin

Jeera or Kala Zeera or Shahi Jeera

Zeera's more widely used name is *kala* (black) *zeera* or *kala jeera* (cummin).

Black cummin is a herbaceous plant of the *Umbelliferae* family, which grows up to 45 cm (18 inches) in height. It yields dark brown seeds with stripy, longitudinal, charcoal-coloured ribs, ending in a short, curved tail. The seeds closely resemble caraway (see page 17), at about the same length of 3 mm (⅛ inch), though they are darker and narrower. White cummin, on the other hand, is much paler, fatter and longer and, in taste, less subtle and more savoury, than black cummin, which has an aromatic, astringent flavour, with a hint of liquorice. Its flavour comes from its oils which contain limone and cyonene. Its use is limited, but it is worth having in stock, for its great effect in such dishes as pullao rice and certain vegetable dishes.

Other essential basic ingredients

Coconut
Narial

Coconuts grow high up on palm trees in tropical climates. After harvesting, each huge nut is divested of its green case, revealing a pallid item, which when sun-dried, becomes the familiar brown hairy coconut. Once dried, it is opened to create an array of coconut products.

First, there is the liquid which should be present in all coconuts, and can be used in cooking (this is not coconut milk). The coconut flesh is scraped out as chippings, which can be dried and desiccated. Desiccated coconut is a substitute for fresh coconut, and can be used by adding it dry to your cooking, or by simmering it in water and straining it to create coconut milk. Fresh grated coconut can be mixed with water and strained to create coconut cream or milk, readily available canned. Coconut cream is the result of a first straining (or pressing) and is thick, creamy and rich. Coconut milk is the result of a second and third pressing, using new water each time, but the same

flesh. After a second pressing the liquid resembles milk; after the third, it is more like cloudy water. The best canned brands are those taken from first pressings.

Fresh grated flesh can also be freeze-dried and finely ground to create coconut milk powder, which, when reconstituted with water, creates rich coconut milk. It is convenient in this form, because it can be stored in a jar like a spice, and used gradually, unlike its canned counterpart which needs to be used at once.

Coconut oil is extracted by a distillation process, and used for cooking. It is white when solid, and transparent when hot. The oil is also mixed with freshly ground flesh to make blocks of creamed coconut. These must be kept under refrigeration and to use it simply cut off the amount required and melt it in boiling water. If you try to fry it without water, it will burn.

Nothing from the coconut goes to waste. The empty husks are used as containers, or for fuel. The hairs become coir, or coconut matting, well-known for its use in door mats and other floor coverings.

Garlic

Lasan

Garlic has a fascinating history: it probably originated in Turkistan and Siberia, and was highly valued by the ancient Egyptians who believed that a bulb of garlic represented the cosmos, each clove being a part of the solar system. It was fundamental to their diets.

Garlic was also used for bartering: 7 kg (15 lb) of garlic could buy one slave. An inscription on the great pyramid of Cheops states that the slaves were given a daily ration of garlic and radishes for their health. Indeed, history's first recorded industrial dispute took place 3,000 years before Christ, when these slaves mustered up the courage to go on strike because their garlic ration was cut. Garlic was found in Tutankhamen's tomb and it was also thought to play a significant role in warding off the evil eye.

The Babylonians of 3000 BC considered garlic to have miraculous medicinal properties, as did the Greeks. In 460 BC Hippocrates extolled its virtues, and Aristotle did the same eighty years later. Aristophanes believed it enhanced virility and the Phoenicians carried garlic in their Mediterranean trading ships. Mohammed recommended the use of garlic to counteract the stings and bites of venomous snakes. Yet he warned that it could have powerful aphrodisiac qualities, and had a vision of Satan in the Garden of Eden with onion on the ground at his foot and garlic on his right.

We know how the Europeans have revered garlic for centuries, but strange though it may seem, it was not until the 1980s that fresh garlic became widely available in Britain.

Garlic is indispensable to curry cooking. It is best to buy one or more bulbs on which are clustered a number of individual cloves. The skin is discarded leaving you with the creamy, plump, firm cloves. To use, I prefer to chop the cloves finely, but you can use a garlic crusher. You can also simply crush them under the flat side of a knife blade. To purée garlic, use an electric food processor or a mortar and pestle.

Indian restaurants often use large quantities of garlic power in place of real garlic, which saves a lot of time. It also helps to capture that distinctive restaurant flavour, assisted no doubt by the sulphur dioxide and chemical stabilisers it contains. It also seems to cause dehydration – how often have you woken during the night with a raging thirst after eating an Indian restaurant curry? Fresh garlic does not seem to have that effect. If you do use garlic powder, use 2 teaspoons for every clove specified in the recipe. I sometimes use powder and sometimes fresh, and a combination of the two can be interesting.

An expensive (but good) product is garlic purée in tubes. I have also used (as do many restaurants) dehydrated garlic flakes. To use these, soak them in water for three minutes then mulch down in a food processor or blender. They taste nearly as good as fresh garlic and the texture is indistinguishable.

If you and your friends like garlic, add more (a lot more if you like) to the recipes. If you are worried about what it will do to your career, your social or love life, you can cut down on the quantities if you must, but don't omit it altogether.

Ginger

Adrak

Ginger originated in India, and the best and juiciest ginger still grows in south India. Other ginger grows in Thailand, Malaysia, Indo-China and China itself. Ginger is a rhizome which grows underground, to a considerable size. It imparts an important flavour in Indian cooking, though it is not used in every dish. Externally, its beige-pink skin should have a bright sheen or lustre. When cut in half, the flesh should be moist and a creamy-lemon colour, with no trace of blue (a sign of age). Ginger is also available dried and powdered, though, with fresh ginger now so readily available, it is not used in these forms here in this book.

GRAIN
Wheat
Ata or aata or atta

Wheat is a grass plant, which grows in temperate areas. Its grain seeds grow in clusters, or 'ears'. When ripe, the ears are harvested, and the grain is separated from the chaff by threshing. The all-important wheat grain, or kernel, is composed of starch and proteins, called gluten. The harder the grain, the more gluten it contains. Wheat is milled to make flour of varying grades and fineness. The addition of a raising agent results in self-raising flour. Strong white flour is milled from one of the hard varieties of wheat grain, which has more gluten, and this creates a more elastic dough, good for Indian bread. Bran is separated from the grain, ground separately, and is blended into white flour, producing coarser, browner wholemeal flour. The Indian version of this, *ata,* is similar to British wholemeal flour, but is finer ground, from a harder, more glutinous grain.

Oils

Butter is rarely used in Indian cooking because of its low burning temperature. Instead, clarified butter or butter ghee is commonly used in the cooking of the northern subcontinent. It is valued for its flavour and for its high burning temperature, which enables the initial cooking of garlic and spices to be done without burning. Vegetable ghee is made in factories by hydrogenising (pumping hydrogen into vegetable oil to solidify it – margarine is made in the same way). Vegetable oil (usually made from rape seed) or corn oil (from maize), or ground nut oil (from peanuts) are acceptable, and less saturated than ghee, having the advantage of being neutral in flavour. Polyunsaturated oils (such as soya and sunflower oil) are also acceptable, although their burning temperature is much lower. Specialist oils used in different regions of the subcontinent include sesame oil, coconut oil (see page 26) used in the south, and pure mustard oil (made from mustard seeds and used

particularly in the north-east). EU regulations compel manufacturers to blend mustard oil with another oil, due to claims that too much pure mustard oil is carcinogenic. Strongly flavoured oils, such as olive or walnut oil, are not used in Indian cooking because they impart the wrong sort of flavour into the spices.

Onion

This ancient bulb originated in central Asia, and by 3000 BC was strongly in evidence in Egypt and China alike. The onion, of which there are some five hundred varieties, is related to the chive, garlic and leek.

An onion consists of about 88 per cent water and 10 per cent carbohydrate. The process of browning onion (illustrated on page 43) is enabled by the reduction of this huge water content, which allows the onion to be slowly fried without it becoming incinerated. The process is also helped along by the carbohydrate which turns to sugar and caramelises. The onion's volatile oils, or disulphides, are neutralised, and the onion tastes savoury, yet sweet and delicious. Second to spices and along with garlic, this taste is the most important ingredient in curry cooking.

It is the onion which, when cooked and puréed, gives the base for the creamy sauce so essential to most curries. The pink onion is also useful in decorative terms for fresh chutneys and garnishing, as is the equally attractive white onion. The larger, yellow onion, also called the 'Spanish' onion, but which grows all over Europe, is very mild and with an average weight of around 225 g (8 oz), is easy to peel and prepare. The torpedo or red Italian onion is interesting for its shape.

Shallots are miniature relatives of onions, and probably originated in Israel. They were developed as bunches of bulbs in the Middle Ages by the French for gourmet purposes. Though fiddly to peel, they can be fun for dishes where onions predominate, such as the onion bhaji or pakora or dopiaza curry, and for garnishing.

The onion is an excellent source of vitamin C and has 70 calories per 100 g (3½ oz).

Rice
Chawal

Rice was domesticated in south India 9,000 years ago, in heavily irrigated 'paddy' fields. The plant is a slender grass, whose grain forms in thin 'ears'. The Tamils called this grain *arisi*, derived from their word to 'separate', referring to the process of splitting the grain from the husk, to produce 'brown rice' (not to be confused with the Parsee dish, Brown Rice). The brown bran is then removed, leaving the familiar white polished grain. The Tamil word *arisi* became the derivation for the ancient Persian word *w'rijza'h*, the Latin *oryza*, and the modern Italian *riso*.

Today, there are over 7,000 varieties of rice, and it is the staple of over two-thirds of the world's population. Basmati rice is paramount in Indian cooking. It grows mainly in the foothills of the Himalayas and the best is from Derha Dun. Basmati rice has an unparalleled flavour, and once cooked, it elongates enormously to create fluffy grains with a superb texture, especially if the grain is aged. A great tip is to lay basmati rice down (like fine wine) in an airtight container for one or more years (ten is not unheard of). Watch out for dirty rice (washed in muddy rivers), and 'cheap' brands, with broken grain or grit. Remember that with rice, as with most things, you get what you pay for.

Another major Indian variety is Patna rice. It is considerably cheaper than basmati, so it is widely used as the day-to-day rice in many households, while basmati is reserved for that special occasion. Patna is named after a city in north-eastern India, but the rice is used all over the country. Like basmati, Patna benefits from an airtight ageing process, although six months is sufficient. Patna rice is generally only available in the West at specialist Asian grocers.

All unpolished rice, Thai black rice included, takes considerably longer to cook, and results in a more chewy texture and a nuttier taste than the more refined polished versions.

Rose Water

Rose water is available in small bottles. It is distilled and transparent, like water, and its very subtle fragrance and flavour are very easily lost, particularly in cooking. Its use is thus confined to a few cold sprinkles on already cooked food. Certain rice dishes and desserts call for rose water. An alternative flavour is obtained from screwpine water (*kewra*) which is identical in all respects except that it is made from the pandanus or screwpine flower.

Salt
Namak, Kala Namak or Saindhar

Salt is the most important taste additive, or seasoning, in the world, as well as the most ancient. It is an inorganic mineral, whose taste comes from sodium chloride, and it is essential to life. References to salt appear throughout history. For example, it was so important to the Romans that they paid their troops and officials part of their remuneration in salt, hence the word 'salary'.

Pink salt is ground from black rock salt. It is found underground, inland, at sites which are now dried-out prehistoric lakes or seas. In India, the main source for black salt (*kala namak*) is in the Ganges district of central India. Other mines produce grey or even blue salt, which has an acquired, distinctive taste. Sea salt, or bay salt, is manufactured differently from rock salt, through a process of evaporating sea water. It has a fine flavour, although the best-tasting white salt is again a top-quality rock salt. Its natural, translucent, gleaming white crystals have a superb flavour, unmatched by ordinary

commercial free-flowing table salt, to which phosphates, magnesium carbonate and starch are added to assist flow and inhibit moisture build-up.

SUGAR
Palm Sugar and Molasses
Jaggery and Gur

True jaggery is a fructose found in the sap of tropical palm trees, hence it is also called palm sugar. Its colours range from pale gold to dark brown, and it is toffee, or fudge-like in taste and texture. It is collected in *chattees* (earthenware pots) which are placed high up in the trees by specialists (whose nimble tree-climbing requires no tools). If left for more than a few hours, the sugar ferments to become 'toddy' or *feni* (highly alcoholic brews), thus the tree-climbers are called 'toddy wallahs'.

Among aficionados, the very best jaggery comes from the city of Kolaphur. However a cheaper version which does not have quite the same fudge-like flavour, and is a sucrose (more intense than sugar) can also be made: sugar cane is crushed to obtain a liquid (molasses) which is dehydrated. It resembles jaggery in appearance although it is less vibrant in colour. Visitors to India will have observed street vendors, whose trolleys are fitted with a hand mangle – this is the press, and with some vigorous turning it yields sugar cane juice, which is sold on the spot as a drink.

Various grades of jaggery or gur are available from Asian stores, but good-quality molasses or brown sugar will substitute.

Tamarind

Tamarind, also known as the Indian date, is an important souring agent, particularly in southern Indian cooking. The tamarind tree bears pods of about 15–20 cm (6–8 inches) long which become dark brown when ripe. These pods contain seeds and pulp, which are preserved by compression into a rectangular block, weighing 300 g (10 oz) (see page 45).

Vinegar

There is little call for vinegar in Indian cooking, the main souring agents being lime or lemon juice, yoghurt and/or tamarind. One Indian state which does use vinegar, however, is Goa. There, they use a vinegar made from the toddy or sap extracted from palm trees. It is not available in the UK, but a very near substitute is Japanese rice vinegar.

Pots and Pans

Obtaining Pans

Curry can be cooked using conventional Western saucepans and frying pans, although I sincerely believe that much of the fun comes from the noisy clattering of a large chef's spoon in a karahi or wok! Such specialist equipment can be obtained at some Asian stores and by mail order.

Preparing Pans

Unless it is non-stick or stainless steel, a new wok or karahi needs to be cleaned with an abrasive sink-cleaning cream to remove the plastic lacquer or machine oil applied by the manufacturers to prevent rust. This is not at all easy, but do it you must. After that it should be rinsed several times in hot water, then placed on a heated ring on the stove for a minute or so. This dries it out for the next stage.

Seasoning pans

Place about 3 or 4 tablespoons cooking oil (used oil is acceptable) in the pan. Heat it to smoking point and swirl it around, then cool it. Pour it away and wipe the pan clean with kitchen paper. Repeat several times.

It is an extremely smoky process, so it is a good idea to do it outside if you can, say on a barbecue. This starts the build-up of a protective film on the pan, which, over time, provides a non-stick finish or patina.

Cleaning Pans

Ideally, your pan should never be scoured clean as this would mean losing the blackening patina that builds up over time, and which is also said to improve the flavour of the food being cooked. Indeed the Chinese say, 'the blacker the wok, the better the cook'. It is true that a blackened pan looks the part, but (sacrilege!) having said all this, I honestly cannot tell the difference between using a new well-scoured pan and my old well-blackened (and I'm sure less hygienic) one. However, the best tool to use to clean the pan without scratching it or losing the patina is a Chinese wok brush. This has a firm round handle and a number of stout bamboo bristles. It cleans the pan effectively, but it then takes a fair bit of cleaning itself!

Other Equipment

To cook the recipes in this book, you will, of course need a stove top (any type), a grill with tray and rack, and an oven and baking trays. In addition to your pans, you may find the heavy metal flattish tava useful for cooking chupattis and parathas, and omelettes, dosa and pancakes too. A nutmeg grater is really useful as can be a decorative mortar and pestle if you just need to grind a few spices.

You will also need the following common kitchen utensils and tools:

- Knives
- Chopping boards
- Mixing bowls – non-metallic in all sizes
- Large sieve
- Large chef's spoon for stir-frying
- Large frying pan
- Saucepans in all sizes with lids
- Bamboo steamer – 20 cm (8 inch) OR a metal steamer with a perforated inner pan and a tight-fitting lid (a colander or strainer over a pan with a lid will substitute)

Electrical Tools

For grinding spices, I recommend an electric coffee grinder (see page 38) or a spice mill attachment. To create the smooth texture needed in certain curry gravies, a blender or hand blender is really useful (see it in use on page 42). While food processors and blenders are essential to a few of the recipes in this book, they are expensive, and purées can be made just as effectively the old-fashioned way, by passing the mixture through a sieve.

A microwave oven is useful for blanching vegetables and for reheating leftover food.

Rice cooker

If you have a rice cooker that's fine, but if not, you'll find that my method for cooking rice (see page 50) gives you perfect results, and quicker.

Sizzlers

Tandoori and kebab dishes should be served to the table, very hot, smoking and sizzling as you see it done in restaurants. To do this you'll need a special heavy, cast-iron sizzler. There are two types: a flat oval tray and a small two-handled karahi dish. Each is made of cast iron and has a wooden base. They make for an attractive presentation, but be careful not to burn yourself or your guests with the excruciatingly fire-hot dishes, nor to splutter hot oil over their clothes.

How to use your sizzler:
1 The food is cooked to readiness in a separate pan.
2 Just prior to serving, place the dry cast-iron dish directly onto the stove over a ring set at its hottest. Let the dish get as hot as it can – this takes at least 5 minutes.
3 Turn off the heat (to prevent the oil from catching fire) and add a teaspoon or two of ghee or oil to the pan.
4 Carefully add a ½ teaspoon of water or lime juice. Take care, because the hot oil and water will splutter and steam. Add the food at once. Do not overload.
5 Warn your guests of your approach, then take your sizzler to the table, still hissing, using heavy gloves and table mats.

Keeping Curry

By definition vegetable curry should be freshly cooked. However, there are always surplus items or leftovers which it would be ridiculous to throw away.

- Always use a refrigerator to store cooked food.
- Always ensure that the food is cold before refrigerating. Putting warm food into the fridge raises the temperature inside while the heat exchange motor struggles to bring the temperature back down. This introduces the risk that food already in the fridge could go off.
- Refrigerated dishes should ideally be used within 24 hours. However, provided you know that the ingredients used to cook your food were absolutely fresh, not pre-frozen, and they were cooked immediately after purchase, and cooled rapidly after cooking, it is safe to store the dish in the fridge for up to 48 hours. Freezing is a much safer method of storing however.

Note: The texture and flavour of refrigerated curries will change: they will taste slightly blander, because the spices will have marinated into the ingredients, and vegetables will become softer.

Portions

Appetites vary enormously: a 'huge' plateful to one person, may leave another person hungry.

When I entertain or supply food for paying customers, I tend to provide enormous helpings. It is better to have fully satisfied diners than the other way round. But what is a generous portion?

My guide to the average serving per person is to use 175 g (6 oz) net of the principal ingredient before cooking (skinned, peeled, de-seeded etc.). The average curry dish will include a further 50 g (2 oz) of flavouring and thickening ingredients (spices garlic, ginger, onion, tomatoes, pepper etc.).

A curry meal is fun with a number of main dishes, and the more people who are eating the meal, the easier this is. With four people you might serve four or five vegetable dishes, plus rice, bread and chutneys. For each person allow approximately 50 g (2 oz) (uncooked weight) of each of the five dishes plus 50–75 g (2–3 oz) extra.

For rice allow 50 g (2 oz) dry uncooked weight per person for a smaller portion, and 75 g (3 oz) for larger appetites. For lentils, allow 25 g (1 oz) uncooked weight, minimum per person.

If all this sounds complicated it isn't really. As always, common sense should prevail.

Alcohol

There is a belief in the West that the people of the subcontinent do not drink for religious reasons. In fact, that applies only to Moslem populations, which, in the context of the curry lands, includes Pakistan, Bangladesh, most of Indonesia and parts of Malaysia. Indian non-Moslems enjoy a tipple, especially beer and whisky, both brought to India by the British, and there are numerous local brews, ranging from Indian gin, rum, brandy and whisky, to toddy from date, coconut and palm trees. Many Indians are, however, unable to afford alcohol and more traditional beverages are water, fruit juices, cordials (one of the most popular being freshly squeezed lemon or lime juice with ice and water) and lhassi (yoghurt with water, crushed ice, spices and salt or sugar). What is of note, is that generally, Indians do not drink anything with their food.

In the West, things are done differently, and curry restaurants, though mostly Moslem-run, are licensed, while most of those that are not, allow patrons to bring their own drink in at no charge. (In this way they do not themselves profit from the sale of alcohol and so they comply with the rules of the Koran.) A very few curry restaurants make it clear that no alcohol may be consumed on their premises.

Lager is still the most popular drink among curry eaters, with over 55 per cent of diners preferring it. During the 1990s all but the die-hard wine snobs have come to realise that many wines go well with spicy food – white or rosé, sparkling or still, the choice is up to you. Even fine reds work well with curry and it is fun experimenting.

Nutritional Information

All food supplies the body with fuel or nutrients in the form of carbohydrate, fat, protein, minerals and vitamins.

Carbohydrate is composed mainly of starch. It is a major energy source since the body converts it into sugar (glucose), also called blood sugar. Carbohydrate is also composed of dietary fibre, or roughage. This is not digested, but is very important to the digestion process.

Protein is one of the body's building blocks. Everything in the body is made up of proteins which continually replace themselves and the protein in food is used for this process. Meat and fish are both high-protein foods, and in the context of this book, proteins are found in eggs, dairy products, and particularly, legumes.

Vitamins are required in small amounts for general wellbeing – the word derives from the Latin *vita*, meaning life. There are a number of vitamins known by the letters A to E and K.

Minerals are important in very small amounts for healthy bones, teeth and body fluids. They include many metals and chemicals.

Fat is present in among other things oils, dairy products and nuts. The body does not need much fat as it can create the fat it needs from carbohydrate and protein and too high an intake of fat will create an excess of energy which the body then uses to create its own fat – hence too much fat can lead to obesity.

Neither does the body need an excess of sugar. Enough natural sugar (fructose) for the body's requirements is generally available from fruit and vegetables. Sucrose is mostly man-made. It is a carbohydrate with an energy value of 394 calories per 100 g (3½ oz).

The calorie is a method of expressing the body's energy requirements. The kilocalorie, or kilogram calorie (k cal), as it is correctly called, is 1,000 calories. The components of food can all be given calorific values. The sugar example above should, in fact, be expressed as 394 k cals per 100 g (3½ oz). Each person's calorie requirements vary according to sex, age, height and activity level: a small, sedentary woman may require just 1,800 calories per day, while a large, active man doing physical work will require at least twice that. Three and a half thousand calories over and above a person's normal intake will add 450 g (1 lb) to their body weight. Given that a single sugar lump has 10 calories, and that sugar is added to so many products, it is easy to see how weight problems arise.

Disasters

Every cook has a disaster at some point, and it always seems to come at the worst possible time. Here are some ideas for correcting common mistakes:

Burning

This is possibly the worst disaster, one that can happen all too easily. If it is very bad you will have no alternative but to dispose of the offending item. But prevention is the answer. If your dish is very dry keep stirring, if you are grilling watch it all the time. If the contents of a pan stick, do not stir, remove the pan from the heat, let it cool, then stir, when the sticking will release if it is minor. If it has actually burned, very gently turn out the contents when cool and carefully separate all burned food. If the whole dish tastes lightly of carbon (burnt taste), you may be able to rectify by adding sweetness, see ('Too Sour' below).

My own very first appearance on BBC TV's flagship daytime show of the 1990s, 'Good Morning', was marked with a pan fire. It happened because I was using a cast-iron frying pan which I heated just before my piece was due to begin. My start time was delayed, however, and the pan got too hot. When I started and put in some oil, followed by some wet garlic purée – whoof, it was on fire. All I could do was to place a lid over it with a damp tea towel, and the fire was out. I managed to cook the planned item and expected to get the sack. But the producers were delighted, and the next time, I had to demonstrate how to put out a pan fire, attended by five members of the Birmingham Fire Brigade, complete with fire engine!

Putting a pan fire out

Many home fires are caused by chip pans catching fire, and usually because they are left unattended. The first signal is smoking, then the oil vaporises and becomes a gas, after which it ignites explosively. If it is possible to do so, the secret is to cut off the pan's oxygen supply, by, as stated above, replacing the lid, and topping off with a damp tea towel. What you must never do is to fight the fire with water. It simply compounds the explosive effect. If things are too far gone, simply get out of the house and leave the work to the fire brigade.

Making a thick sauce thinner

In most cases simply add water – but just a little at a time. It may help to add oil as well, at a lower ratio – four times water to one of oil, for instance. This will retain the body of the dish. Cook for several minutes before serving to ensure blending.

Making a thin sauce thicker

Either ladle off the excess liquid into a reserve pan, or if there really is a lot of liquid, strain the entire dish. Continue to cook the drier dish until it blends, then add back some of the reserved liquid if needed.

If you are in a hurry you can quickly thicken a runny sauce using rice flour. It does not have the wheaty taste of ordinary flour but too much will alter the taste of your curry. Use in an emergency only.

Too oily

Remove the dish from the heat. Let it stand until the oil floats to the top. Ladle the oil off (keep it for subsequent cooking), stir well and reheat.

Colour

There is nothing less appetising than grey-looking curries and dhals. Your principal ingredients will define the dish's ultimate colour but you may want to enhance it. The simple trick is food colouring. Red, orange, yellow and green powder are immensely effective, and the merest pinch will do the trick. Try, for example, an eighth of a teaspoon of yellow in your next dhal. For those few people who dislike these additives or are allergic to them, you can use turmeric (yellow), paprika (red), ground spinach (green), or alkanet root (deep crimson). Although natural, these are less effective than powders and they do change the flavour of your dish. To go darker (browner) use gravy browning.

Too Sour

Add white or brown sugar, a sweetish sauce (tomato sauce for example), or puréed mango chutney. Just a spoonful or two should pull back the over-sour taste. Keep stirring and tasting the dish as you go.

Too Sweet

This is a trifle harder to rectify. You can add a souring agent such as lemon juice, vinegar or tamarind, but this will probably change the flavour of the dish. If you have time try adding something which will 'spread' the taste, such as frozen peas. You can then quickly fry up a second spicing with onions to add to the mix. If you have plenty of time, make a new batch omitting any sweet ingredients which may have caused the initial problem. Combine the two when cooked and freeze the surplus.

Too Salty

It is infinitely better to under-salt, or even to omit salt altogether. Diners can easily sprinkle their own at the table and it never affects the quality of the dish to do so. However, most of us like to add at least a little salt while cooking and it is then that mistakes can happen. If it is a big mistake – the salt pot burst and emptied into the dish! – do not stir; quickly ladle out the salt from the area in which it sits or gently spoon it off the top. If it has been stirred in and is just a case of slight over-salting, simply omit salt from everything else. If it is too late for that and the principal dish is the only problem, you can add quick items – frozen peas or other vegetables, tinned items like tomatoes etc. anything to bulk out the taste. If you have a little time to spare, you can fry some onions and spices to make a thick gravy and add it to your dish. If it is the day before make a second batch to combine iwith the first, freezing the surplus.

Curdling

All milk-based products – milk, cream, yoghurt – are prone to curdling when heated and added to acidic ingredients. Lightly beating the cream or yoghurt, or shaking the milk in its bottle or carton, ensures adequate mixing. When adding to ingredients already cooking, reducing the heat to cool also reduces the risk of curdling. If curdling does occur though, strain the contents of your pan, cool then add some more of the same ingredient (cream, yoghurt, milk), reheat, then add back the strained liquid as required. Stir continuously until you reach cooking heat.

When the meal is not ready

Always have appetisers on hand to amuse your guests and to allow yourself a breathing space.

HERBS

The main herb used in curry cooking is coriander, with mint in second place, and basil fundamental to Thai curries. However, with the herbal explosion that has taken place of late at the greengrocer and supermarket, one simply cannot ignore other herbs in curry cooking, even if their use is limited to garnishing. The French use the word *aromate* to describe any fragrant vegetable matter that is used for flavouring, and everyone enjoys the extra 'aromatic' dimension herbs bring to one's cooking, especially the non-meat eater. Accordingly we begin the **Ingredients File** with a look at herbs, lettuce and salad leaves. Feel free to use them as you like alongside the recipes in this book.

Basil
Tulsi

Basil was nominated 'king' of herbs in ancient times. Indigenous to east Asia, it had reached Europe by the time of the Greek empire. Its name reflects the esteem in which it was held (*basilikos* meaning 'royal'). Indeed some sources state that only the Greek sovereign (*basileus*) was permitted to eat it, and to discourage lesser mortals from trying it, rumours were put about that any association with basil would turn them into a scorpion. Today there are forty varieties of basil available worldwide, the most common in Britain being sweet basil (*Ocimum basilicum*).

Called *tulsi* in India, where it is used for non-culinary purposes, it is a really fragrant fresh herb. However, it makes a refreshing change used judiciously in certain dishes, where aromatics are paramount. Two varieties of European purple basil (purple ruffle and dark opal) are available. Overall they are a pretty beetroot colour, the leaves of the former being quite deeply serrated, and the latter less so, but its fragrance is more spicy, veering towards ginger. Basil is fundamental to Thai cooking, with three

main Thai varieties of basil being widely used. Thai sweet basil (*Ocimum basilicum horapha*) or *bai horapa* in Thai, is the most widely used. It is slightly spicier than the Western variety with a strong hint of fennel seed or aniseed. Its appearance is also different from that of Western sweet basil. Its leaves are a little smaller, with a pointed tip, and can have a slight purple tinge. It is often available with small edible purple flowers. Holy basil (*Ocimum sanctum*) is also commonly used in Thai cooking (called *bai grapao* in Thai, and *tulsi* in India, where it is used in Hindu religious ceremonies). Its leaves are larger than horapa's, and about the same size as our sweet basil, although the edges are serrated (whereas European sweet basil leaves are smooth) and they are less shiny, perhaps paler than Western basil. Grapao has a hot or peppery taste. For this reason it is sometimes called 'hot' basil and it is popular in Thai curries. The third variety is *bai manglak*, bush basil (*Ocimum canum*) or Greek basil. It is also sometimes called hairy basil because its leaves have tiny hairs. The leaves are the smallest of the three Thai varieties of basil, and are quite pointed. Manglak has a distinctively lemon flavour which makes it a gorgeous garnish. Its flavour can lead to confusion with lemon basil (*Ocimun citriodorum*).

Thai horapa basil

Sweet basil

Chervil

Resembles coriander in appearance, but is distinguished by its taste of aniseed.

Chive

These are slender, fine, long, tubular dark green leaves averaging about 2mm in diameter. They taste of onion, and are great as an elegant garnish.

A bigger member of the chive family, with flatter coarser leaves, they are depicted here in bud and flowering. The buds/flowers and the leaves are edible, and taste like chives with a hint of garlic.

Garlic chives, in bud and flowering

Coriander or Cilantro
Dhania

Coriander (*Coriandrum sativum*), known in the USA by its Italian name, *cilantro*, is now widely available in the West. Its musky candle-waxy flavour is decidedly an acquired, but once acquired, essential taste. Coriander leaves are mid-green and flat with jagged edges, and are also important, some say indispensable, in Indian cookery. They are indisputably India's most widely used herb. However, the flavour of the leaves bears absolutely no resemblance to that of the seeds, India's most widely used spice (see page 19). Soft stalks may also be used, but thicker stalks should be discarded (more of the coriander plant is used in Thai cooking than in most Indian). If you want the appearance of coriander, but not its flavour, use flat-bladed parsley (*Petro selinum sativum*). Since the two leaves are similar in appearance, the trick to identification at the greengrocer is to crush a leaf in your fingers. Only coriander has the musky smell.

Cress

Mustard and cress or mustard cress is the plant of the yellow mustard seed (see page 23). Used for its spicy taste, it was once the doyen of the British canteen, but it has been overshadowed by trendier new spices.

Winter cress originated as a marsh crop in central Europe. It was used by the Romans, and was first recorded in Britain in the early 1800s. It too has a spicy peppery taste, and it can be lightly cooked like spinach. Winter cress is undergoing a revival, having almost died out at one point in Britain. It is more slender in appearance than its close relative, watercress, but it has an intriguing flavour.

Mustard and cress

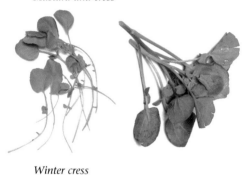

Winter cress

Watercress

Curry leaf
Kari Phuliq

See page 20.

Dill/Fennel
Sowa or Soua

Dill and fennel are almost identical leaves: bright, deep green, delicate and feathery, and redolent of aniseed. They make fine garnish leaves. The main difference between them is that fennel has an edible bulb growing above the surface (see page 20). The seeds of each are also different.

Fenugreek Leaves
Methi

Fresh fenugreek leaf is available at Asian stores, and is easy to use: carefully remove the leaf from the stalk, which is too bitter to be enjoyable, and add to a dish near the end of cooking to prevent it from turning black and bitter. Substitute about four times as much fresh as dried fenugreek leaf. (See also page 21.)

Lemon Grass

See page 21.

Mint
Podina

Mint grows prolifically as a herbaceous perennial, its bushy shrub reaching up to a metre (3 feet) in height. The most popular variety is spearmint. Like all mints, it is native to Europe, and was particularly popular with the Greeks and Romans, who distributed it throughout their empires. Spearmint's distinctive flavour comes from its volatile oil, consisting predominantly of menthol, with lesser amounts of carvone and limonene.

Other popular mint species are apple mint and peppermint. These, in common with all other mints, have less powerful aromatics (and less menthol), than spearmint, though all have interesting characteristics of their own.

Fresh mint grows in India, where it is called *podina*, but is little used in cooking, appearing here and there in chutneys and certain aromatic dishes. Dried mint is a useful store cupboard item.

Mizuna

This herb is native to Japan, where it is widely used. A herb with a delicate taste, mizuna has recently found its way into the British supermarket.

Parsley

Flat-bladed parsley resembles coriander, but is used as a garnish rather than in cooking as it rather lacks flavour.

Curly Parsley

Curly parsley once was king of the British herbal garnish. It has now lost this status, but it is an interesting and tasty herb, none the less.

Tarragon

Remove the stalk, and tarragon's long leaves make it an elegant and tasty garnish.

Step By Steps

Garam Masala

Garam means 'hot' and masala means 'mixture of spices'. Whole spices are cooked by dry-frying (with no oil or liquid) or 'roasting'. They are then cooled and ground. Garam masala is used in various ways. It can be sprinkled on finished cooking, or added to yoghurt dips, or to certain curries, towards the end of their cooking time (to retain the aromatics), particularly those curries from north India. It can also be used from the beginning of the cooking process, as in Balti curries. The example given here is a traditional Kashmiri garam masala.

MAKES ABOUT 250 G (9 OZ) WHEN
GROUND

60 g coriander seeds

50 g cummin seeds

40 g fennel seeds

25 g black peppercorns

15 g cloves

15 g brown cardamoms

3 pieces mace

25 g pieces cassia bark

4 bay leaves

5 g ginger powder

1 Omitting the ground ginger, mix the remaining nine whole spices together in your pan. Keeping it dry, stir the mixture continuously as it heats up.

2 Very soon the mixture will give off steam, rather than smoke. The process is called 'roasting'. The volatile oils, or aromas, are now being released into the air. Stir for a few seconds more, then transfer the spices to a cold pan or bowl, to stop them cooking. They must not burn. If they do, your cooking will have a bitter, carbonised taste. If they burn, discard the spices and start again.

3 Allow the garam masala to cool completely. This is for two reasons: firstly, it will go more brittle, so will grind more easily; secondly, if the mixture is hot when you grind it in an electric grinder, the blades could overheat the spices, and burn off the very volatile oil you are striving to capture.

4 Whether you use a mortar and pestle or an electric grinder (here it is a coffee grinder), work with small batches at a time to avoid overloading the machine.

5 Grind until the clattering noises change to a softer similar sound, then grind on until the mix is as fine as you want it, or as fine as the grinder will achieve.

6 Thoroughly mix all the ingredients together, including the ginger powder. Store in an airtight jar in a dark, dry place. Like all ground spices, although it will last for many months, it will gradually lose its fragrance until eventually it tastes of little or nothing. It is best to make garam masala freshly, in batches even smaller than this example.

Fragrant Stock

The subtler authentic Indian recipes often need water added at some stage in their cooking. More effective is a light fragrant stock, known in India as akhni or yakhni. It is really easy to make and any surplus can be successfully frozen in yoghurt pots.

MAKES ABOUT 700 ML (1¼ PINTS)

10–12 green cardamoms

10–12 cloves

5 or 6 bay leaves

6–8 pieces cassia bark

2 tablespoons dried onion flakes

1 tablespoon ghee

750 ml (1¼ pints) water

Simply simmer all the ingredients together for about 20 minutes, then strain the stock, discarding the solids. The stock can be frozen in small batches, in disposable moulds.

Note: Dried onion flakes (dehydrated onion) are much quicker to use than fresh onion.

Aromatic Salt

Recipes throughout this book call for aromatic salt. You can, of course, use ordinary salt, but aromatic salt adds a little more 'magic' to your cooking. The light version, shown on the right, is complete in itself, but it can be developed into a spicier version, shown top left. In each case, grind, and then store in an airtight jar.

Lightly Spiced Aromatic Salt

MAKES 100 G (3½ OZ)

100 g (3½ oz) coarse sea salt

1 teaspoon freshly ground allspice

1 teaspoon ground cinnamon

Spicier Aromatic Salt

MAKES 100 G (3½ OZ)

1 quantity lightly spiced aromatic salt

1 teaspoon dried mint

½ teaspoon ground fenugreek

1 teaspoon ground almonds

½ teaspoon turmeric

Panch Phoran

At the front left of the photograph of aromatic salt, above, is panch phoran, a Bengali mixture of five (panch) whole aromatic seeds, used alone in certain dishes. Celery and/or caraway seeds can be substituted for cummin. Simply mix together and store in an airtight container.

MAKES ABOUT 75 G (2½ OZ)

1 tablespoon cummin seeds

1 tablespoon aniseed

1 tablespoon wild onion seeds

1 tablespoon black mustard seeds

1 tablespoon fenugreek seeds

Curry Masala

Indians call any mixture of spices 'masala'. Its simplistic name, 'curry powder', helped give Indian food a poor reputation, and certain Indian foodies refuse ever to use it. Indeed, many of the recipes in this book do not need such a mixture. However, there are other recipes which can benefit from a ready-prepared, good-quality, home-made masala mix. It is easy to make, so do try to avoid factory-made alternatives, and use this well-tried and trusted masala of fifteen spices. If you cannot weigh these amounts precisely, 5 g is roughly equivalent to 1 teaspoon of ground spice.

MAKES ABOUT 250 G (9 OZ)

Top row, left to right:

60 g coriander

30 g cummin

20 g fenugreek

25 g gram flour (besan)

25 g garlic powder

Middle row, right to left:

20 g paprika

20 g turmeric

20 g garam masala (see page 38)

5 g bay leaf

5 g asafoetida

Bottom row, left to right:

5 g ginger powder

5 g chilli powder

5 g yellow English mustard powder

5 g black pepper

5 g cinnamon

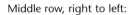

1 Put all the masala ingredients into a bowl (top left).

2 Mix well (top right).

3 Add just enough water to make a paste thick enough to drop sluggishly off the spoon (bottom right).

4 It goes rather darker in colour after being fried (bottom left).

Oil-based Masala Paste

5 Heat the ghee, then add the masala paste, and stir continuously (right).
6 Keep stirring until after a few minutes its colour has gone much darker, and the ghee separates and 'floats' (note the spoon, left) when the mixture is left to stand off the heat for a while.

Tandoori Masala

MAKES ABOUT 250 G (9 OZ)

40 g coriander

30 g cummin

40 g garlic powder

40 g paprika

20 g ginger powder

20 g mango powder

20 g dried mint

20 g beetroot powder (optional)

10 g anatto seed powder (optional)

10 g chilli powder

5 g red food colouring powder (optional)

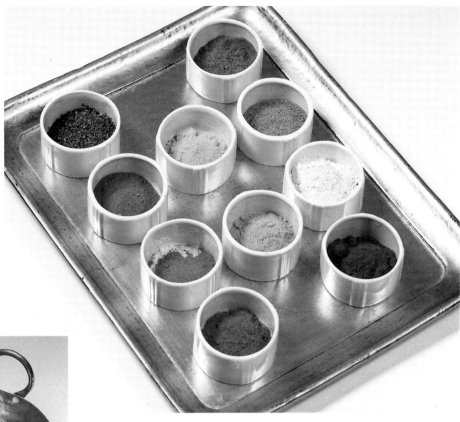

1 Put all the ingredients into a bowl.

2 Mix well.

3 Add just enough water to make a paste thick enough to drop sluggishly off the spoon.

Oil-based Tandoori Paste

1 Heat the ghee, then add the masala paste, and stir continuously.

2 Keep stirring until after a few minutes the colour is much darker, and the ghee separates and 'floats' (note the spoon) when the mixture is left to stand off the heat for a while.

Curry Masala Gravy

Like most restaurants, the Indian restaurant has found a foolproof method enabling it to produce, very rapidly, any amount of different dishes, in its case 'formula' curries. Every day, it pre-cooks meat, chicken and certain vegetables, then chills them. And it makes a large stock-pot of thick curry masala gravy. The next part of the process is to fulfil individual customers' orders, on a person-by-person, dish-by-dish basis, using these main ingredients, pinches of appropriate spices, and a ladleful or two of the gravy.

At home, we are unlikely to cook for a hundred diners or more each evening, so for the recipes in this book I have modified restaurant techniques to produce four-portion dishes, by, for example, oven casseroling some dishes, and stir-frying others.

However, in order to recreate the smooth texture of restaurant curries, some recipes do need a curry masala gravy. This recipe makes enough for about twelve individual curries, each of which requires about 110 g (4 oz) gravy. Since, as I say, most of my recipes are for four portions, this gravy will therefore make enough for about three recipes. I keep saying 'about' because the exact gravy content can be varied according to taste. To save on time, washing-up and smells, you may wish to make several batches of this gravy at once.

MAKES ABOUT 1.3 KG (3 LB) CURRY
MASALA GRAVY

110 g (4 oz) ghee

150 g (5¼ oz) cloves garlic, finely chopped

110 g (4 oz) ginger, finely chopped
(optional)

1 kg (2¼ lb) Spanish onions, chopped

600 ml (1 pint) water

250 g (9 oz) curry masala (see page 40)

1 Heat the ghee and stir-fry the garlic and optional ginger for the minute or two it takes for them to go translucent (front wok). Lower the heat and add the onions, bit by bit, as they reduce in size in the wok, stir-frying as needed until they have all become browned and caramelised (sweetened) (rear wok).

2 Add the water, then mulch the mixture down in a blender, or using a hand blender, until you achieve a smooth purée.

3 (Right wok) The cooked curry masala paste (see page 40) can either be added to the gravy or, to be more flexible, you can keep the paste and the gravy separate until needed. To preserve the finished gravy, fill three large yoghurt pots, cover and freeze.

Shown in the rear wok is onion tarka (see opposite page for recipe).

Slow-cooking Garlic and Onions – the Tarka

It is so important to get the first few minutes of every curry's cooking right, that I'm giving a very detailed method for it here. This technique is used in many recipes in this book. The spices and ingredients may vary, but the techniques do not, so it may be helpful to practice this recipe.

MAKES ENOUGH TO START
A 4-PORTION RECIPE

2–3 tablespoons ghee or corn oil

3–6 cloves garlic, finely chopped

2.5 cm (1 inch) cube ginger, thinly sliced

110 g (4 oz) onions, thinly sliced

3 or 4 spring onions, bulbs and leaves, chopped

2–3 tablespoons curry masala paste (see page 40)

1 tablespoon green masala paste (see page 45)

SPICES

1½ teaspoons cummin seeds

½ teaspoon lovage seeds

½ teaspoon coriander seeds

1 Heat the oil or ghee in a pan over a high heat until it is nearly smoking. Add the spices and stir-fry for about 20 seconds, keeping the seeds briskly on the move to prevent them from burning. Add the garlic and continue with the brisk stir-frying for a further 30 seconds. If using ginger, as we are here, add it now and continue the stir-fry for 30 more seconds.

2 Add the onions and mix them in well. Lower the heat to the point where you can hear the mixture sizzle calmly. Stir from time to time to turn the mixture over. Cook like this until the onions go brown. It is at this stage that it is called the tarka. What is happening here is that the onion, water content is being cooked out allowing the onions to become caramelised. Starch is turning to sugar. The process needs gentle heat and at least 12–15 minutes, maybe longer depending on the onion type and the heat level. The whole process is easy enough, but it is somewhat slow. It is however very important to the curry flavour. Curry pastes are added after the caramelisation is achieved.

You can, of course, make up a number of batches of tarka (onion only or onion with garlic or with ginger too), for the freezer. You can double up the quantity in the pan (but no more or it won't caramelise) or you can work with more than one pan at a time to make several batches.

Quick Method

If time is of the essence or you do not wish to spend 20–25 minutes browning onions as described in the previous recipe, here is an ultra-quick three-minute method using quick dried or dehydrated packet chopped onion flakes.

If the packet requires you to rehydrate the onions first, ignore that instruction. Simply add them to your stir-fry dry.

MAKES ENOUGH TO START
A 4-PORTION RECIPE

4 tablespoons sunflower oil or butter ghee

1 teaspoon white cummin seeds

2 or 3 cloves garlic, finely chopped
  OR 2 or 3 teaspoons garlic purée

2 teaspoons finely chopped ginger

40 g (1½ oz) quick-dried sliced onions

120 ml (4 fl oz) cupful cold water

1 Follow the first stage of the previous recipe until the ginger has had its 30-second stir-fry.

2 Now add the dried onions, stir-fry briskly and continuously. They will absorb the available oil like a sponge, then they will start sizzling. Keep a close watch because they will start to go brown almost at once, and could blacken and burn quickly after. So we must, at this browning stage, instantly cool them down by pouring in the cold water and removing the pan from the heat. As with the previous recipe you can make up extra batches and freeze them for later use.

Note: Remember that the quantities stated in the methods above are for a 4-portion curry, so if freezing, use containers which will yield the portion sizes you require.

Ghee

Ghee is clarified butter, is very easy to make and gives a distinctive and delicious taste. When cooled and set, it will keep for several months without refrigeration. If you want to make vegetable ghee, simply use pure vegetable block margarine instead of butter.

900 g (2 lb) butter, any type

1 Place the butter blocks whole into a medium-sized non-stick pan and melt over a very low heat.

2 When completely melted, a froth will form on top. Raise heat very slightly. Ensure it does not smoke or burn, but don't stir. Leave to cook for about 1 hour. The impurities will sink to the bottom and float on the top.

3 Carefully skim any impurities off the top with a slotted spoon, but don't touch the bottom.

4 Turn off the heat and allow the ghee to cool a little. When it cools it solidifies, although it is still quite soft. It should be a bright pale lemon colour and smell like toffee. Strain it through kitchen paper or muslin into an airtight storage jar. If it has burned it will be darker and smell different, but provided it is not too burnt it can still be used.

Tamarind Purée

MAKES ABOUT 450G (1 LB)

300 g (10 oz) block compressed
   tamarind
1.3 litres (2¼ pints) water

1 Bring half the water to the simmer in
a largeish saucepan. Break up the
tamarind block into the water.

2 Simmer and occasionally stir for 10
minutes, pulping it well with the back
of a spoon.

3 Strain through a metal sieve, again
pulping it well with the back of a
spoon, and keeping the husks in the
sieve. The brown liquid should be quite
thick, and there will be plenty of it.

4 Bring a second batch of fresh water
to the simmer in a saucepan. Add the
retained husks and repeat stage 2.

5 Mix the two batches together and
use or freeze in yoghurt moulds as
required.

Note: For a small portion, cut off about
an eighth of the block – a piece about
4 cm (1½ inches). Soak this in about
100 ml (3½ fl oz) water for half an hour
or more. Pulp and strain as above.
Lemon or vinegar, which can be used as
substitutes, will give completely
different flavours.

Green Masala Paste

*Depending on how spicy you want it, 1–2 tablespoons of this mix can be used for between
10 and 20 curries.*

MAKES ABOUT 450 G (1 LB)
1 teaspoon fenugreek seeds
6 cloves garlic, chopped
2 tablespoons fresh ginger, finely chopped
40 g (1½ oz) fresh mint leaves
40 g (1½ oz) fresh coriander leaves
120 ml (4 fl oz) vinegar
3 teaspoons salt
2 teaspoons turmeric
2 teaspoons chilli powder
½ teaspoon ground cloves
1 teaspoon ground cardamom seeds
150 ml (5 fl oz) vegetable oil

1 Soak the fenugreek seeds in water
overnight. They will swell and acquire a
jelly-like coating.
2 Next day, strain the fenugreek
discarding the water.
3 Mulch down all the ingredients,
except for the oil, in a blender or food
processor, to make a purée. Leave to
stand for at least 10 minutes.
4 Heat the oil in a large wok, then add
the purée, stirring continuously, until

after a few minutes its colour has gone
much darker. To check it is fully
cooked, leave the mixture to stand off
the heat for a while. The ghee separates
and 'floats'.
5 Transfer the paste to a sterilised
lidded jar.
6 Inspect after a day. Top up with hot
ghee or oil to cover the paste as needed.
The paste will keep indefinitely.

Paneer

Paneer is the only form of cheese made in India. It is really simple to make by heating and curdling milk, and then separating the solids. It is used in curries and sweetmeats, either crumbled or in its denser cubed form. It goes hard and rubbery if kept overnight so it should always be freshly made.

MAKES ABOUT 225 G (8 OZ)
2 litres (3½ pints) full cream milk
freshly squeezed juice of 1 or 2 lemons
OR 3–6 tablespoons white distilled vinegar

1 Bring the milk just up to boiling point, and be careful that it doesn't boil over!

2 Take the milk off the heat, and add lemon juice or vinegar (shown here) until the milk starts to separate. Stir to assist the separation.

3 Using a clean tea-towel and a large sieve, strain off the liquid (the whey). There is always a lot of whey, relative to the solids (the curds), and while you can use some for stock or soup, you will probably discard most of it.

4 Fold the tea-towel over the curds, and form them into a flat disc which must be compressed. The easiest way to do this is to fill a saucepan with water, and place it with a weight on its lid, on top of the disc.

5 For crumbled paneer, remove the weight after 15–20 minutes and crumble as shown. For cubes, leave the weight in place for at least an hour, maybe two, then the disc can be cut into cubes or chip shapes.

Rissoles

MAKES 8–12 RISSOLES, DEPENDING ON SHAPE

4 large potatoes, boiled in salted water,
   drained and mashed
85 g (3 oz) mixed vegetables from the
   freezer e.g. carrots, peas, beans,
   sweetcorn
1 tablespoon curry paste
2 tablespoons dried onions
2 tablespoons dried onions, fried
1 egg, beaten
breadcrumbs
oil for shallow frying

SPICES
1 teaspoon cummin seeds
½ teaspoon fennel seeds

1 Mix the mashed potato, mixed
vegetables, curry paste, onions and
spices together, making sure they are
well combined.

2 Divide the mixture into equal
portions (the number will depend on
how large or small you wish your
finished rissoles to be). For a starter or
main dish, make them about 7.5 cm
(3 inches) across; for canapés or koftas,
make them walnut shell size.

3 Break the egg into a shallow bowl
and beat for a few seconds. Dip the
rissoles in the egg making sure they are
well covered, then transfer to another
shallow dish containing the
breadcrumbs and roll well, again
making sure that they are well covered.

4 Remove and shallow-fry in a frying
pan with a little oil. Fry until golden
brown on both sides.

See page 63 for more rissole recipes.

Papadoms

There are three ways of cooking papadoms. Here we see how to deep-fry papadoms and achieve different shapes. See page 54 for other cooking methods.

1 Preheat the oil to 170°C/340°F.
2 Deep-fry one papadom at a time in the hot oil for about 5 seconds. It will whoosh up and expand.

3 Remove from the oil with tongs, shaking off the excess. Allow to cool, but keep in a warm, damp-free place for an hour or two, until each papadom is crispy and oil-free.

4 They will remain pliable for about 5 seconds so if you want to fold them into halves or quarters you must work fast and fold deftly with tongs. It takes practice and care, especially for safety with the oil.

Making a bowl-shaped papadom is fun, but again needs care and practice. Here we use a small pilchard tin, covered with foil, and a large mug (the handle is important). Put the hot papadom centrally over the tin, and ease the mug down over it. You may get a few breakages, but practice makes perfect.

 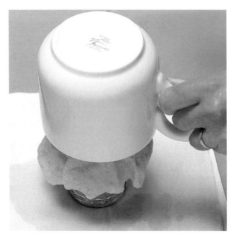 

Bhaji
(or Bhajee, Bhajia)

MAKES 8

clockwise from top:

225 g (8 oz) coarsely chopped onion

85 g (3o z) gram flour

1 teaspoon dried fenugreek leaves

1 tablespoon curry masala paste (see
   page 40)

2 garlic cloves, finely chopped

½ teaspoon lovage seeds

½ teaspoon cumin seeds, roasted

1 teaspoon aromatic salt (see page 39)

1 teaspoon garam masala (see page 38

1 tablespoon fresh mint, chopped

2 tablespoons fresh coriander leaves,
   chopped

1 tablespoon lemon juice

vegetable oil for deep-frying

1 Mix all the ingredients except the onion together, adding sufficient water to achieve a thickish paste which will drop sluggishly off the spoon. Mix in the onion, then leave to stand for at least 10 minutes, during which time the mixture will fully absorb the moisture.

2 Meanwhile, heat the deep-frying oil to 190°C/375°F. This temperature is below smoking point and will cause a drop of batter to splutter a bit, then float more or less at once.

3 Inspect the mixture. There must be no 'powder' left, and it must be well mixed.

4 Scoop out an eighth of the mixture and place it carefully in the oil. Now add the other portions, allowing about 15 seconds between each one so that the oil will maintain its temperature.

5 Fry for about 10 minutes each, turning once. Remove from the oil in the order they went in and drain well on kitchen paper. Serve with salad garnishes, lemon wedges and chutneys. Or allow to cool and then freeze. To use, reheat in deep hot oil for about 2 minutes, but don't let them get too brown. Serve hot.

Variation Restaurant Bhaji Method

1 Mix the batter as above but use less water to achieve a drier, mouldable texture. Add the onion and leave to stand, as above.

2 Heat the deep-frying oil, as above.

3 Roll the mixture into smooth balls of about 5 cm (2 inches) in diameter. You will need to wash your hands frequently while doing this.

4 Deep-fry the bhajis for 2–3 minutes to set the batter firmly, then remove them to go cold for later cooking. Alternatively, continue cooking.

5 The part-cooked bhajis can be left spherical, or when cool enough they can be flattened into discs with the heel of your hand.

6 When required, reheat the deep-frying oil, fry them for 5–7 minutes and serve hot.

Pullao Rice by Absorption

See pages 168–9 for more information about cooking rice. You can omit some of the spices listed below if you don't have them to hand. If you don't like chewy spices omit or remove the cloves, bay leaves and cassia.

300 g (10 oz) basmati rice

1 tablespoon butter ghee

SPICES

(clockwise from top of plate, above right)

2 or 3 bay leaves

5 cm (2 inch) piece cassia bark

4 green cardamoms

4 cloves

1 brown cardamom

(clockwise from the butter ghee)

½ teaspoon black cummin seeds

1 teaspoon fennel seeds

2 star anise

25–30 strands saffron

600 ml (20 fl oz) boiling water

1 Soak the rice in cold water for at least 10 and at most 20 minutes, then rinse until the water is more or less clear. Strain.

2 Measure the water and bring it to the boil. (The difference is shown in the picture. The washed rice is on the right in the picture top right.)

3 Choose a lidded saucepan or casserole pot whose capacity is at least twice the volume of the strained rice.

4 Heat the ghee in it, then add all the spices except the saffron, and stir-fry for 30 seconds.

5 Add the rice and stir-fry, ensuring the oil coats the rice and it heats up.

6 Add the boiling water and stir in well.

7 As soon as it starts bubbling put the lid on the pan and reduce the heat to under half. Leave well alone for 6 minutes, but turn the heat off after all the water has disappeared, which, to save you looking is after 3 minutes or so.

8 Inspect after 6 minutes. If all the liquid has not been absorbed, replace the lid and leave for 2 minutes. Otherwise, stir well, ensuring that the rice is not sticking to the bottom. Now taste. If it is brittle in the middle, add a little more water and return to high heat.

9 Gently fork in the saffron, then place the saucepan or casserole, lid on, in a warming drawer or oven preheated to its very lowest setting. This should be no lower than 80°C /175°F and no higher than 100°C / 210°F /Gas ⅛.

You can serve the rice at once, but the longer you leave it, the more separate the grains will be. Thirty minutes is fine, but it can be left for up to 90 minutes. Prior to serving fluff it up with a fork, gently, so as not to break the grains.

Naan Bread

See pages 175–9 for more information about bread cooking.

MAKES 4

25 g (1 oz) fresh yeast

450 g (1 lb) strong white flour

warm water

1 batch leavened dough, see page 175

2 teaspoons sesame seeds

½ teaspoon wild onion seeds

1 tablespoon melted ghee

1 Dissolve the fresh yeast in a small bowl containing a little lukewarm water.

2 Place the flour in a large ceramic or glass bowl at room temperature.

3 Make a well in the centre and pour in the yeast and sufficient warm water to combine the mixture into a lump.

4 Turn the lump out onto a floured board, add the seeds, and knead with the heel of your hand.

5 Return the dough to the bowl and leave in a warm, draught-free place to ferment and rise (this is called proving).

This can take an hour or so, during which the dough should have doubled in size and should have stretch marks.

6 Turn out the dough. It should be bubbly, stringy and elastic. Knock it back to its original size by rekneading it. Use fairly soon, or else it will prove again.

7 Divide the dough into four equal parts and, on a floured work surface, roll out each piece into a teardrop shape at least 5 mm (¼ inch) thick. Add more seeds if needed.

8 Preheat the grill to three-quarters heat, cover the rack pan with foil, put the naan on to it, brush it with melted ghee, and set it in the midway position.

9 Watch it cook (it can easily burn). As soon as the first one develops brown patches, remove it from the grill. Turn it over and return it to the grill and cook until it is sizzling, then remove.

10 Repeat with the other three naans, then serve at once.

Vegetable Curry Starters

There is perhaps no better start to a meal than that of the Indian meal. Enjoy an aperitif with Bombay mix, India's tasty spicy nibble, the equivalent of the potato crisp or chip as the Americans call it. Follow this with a basket of papadoms, the world-class nibble which, served with chutneys, are a starter in themselves. Present them with a new look, as illustrated, and they become a talking point.

Starters as such are not served in the traditional Indian meal. Such items are served as snacks at any time of day, often prepared and sold by street vendors whose prices are really cheap. The great advantage of cooking at home is that you too can make great price savings and you can serve these items as snacks or with the main meal. Whichever way you choose to serve them, this chapter provides you with a wonderful and varied selection of recipes. Soups and salads, rissoles of various kinds, served cold or hot. Stuffed vegetables make excellent starter subjects, as does Bombay's favourite pavement snack, bhel puri, with its sister food, gol goppa and the refreshing savoury chilled drink that goes with it, jal jeera. Tandoori need not be confined to meat and chicken and here you will find tandoori ways with vegetables. You will find three simple, spicy cold starters perfect for entertaining – red beans, aloo archar, and chestnuts – and finally, there is no way I could omit the nation's favourite, the onion bhaji. Have fun trying them all.

The papadom basket, with ribbons and red salad; in the foreground are garam masala raita, tomato chutney and green chilli chutney

PAPADOMS

Whichever way you spell 'papadom', and there are many ways, from 'papard' to 'puppuddum', it is an unparalleled piece of south Indian culinary magic which has been around for a long time. Each is made by hand, from a lentil flour dough ball, which is slapped by hand, in a trice, into a thin flat disc, and laid out on huge trays to dry in the sun. This is usually done by women who have spent a lifetime learning their skill. When the papadoms are hardened, they are put in dozens or twenties into packets and it is in this form that most people buy them. At this stage, the papadoms are about as edible as a disposable plastic plate. The magic comes about when they are cooked, whereupon they become light, crisp, crunchy wafers. At the restaurant, they are served as an appetiser, in much the same way as the Anglo-French bread roll, Italian grissini, or Chinese prawn cracker, to fill a gap while customers place their orders.

Papadoms come in many sizes, from mini to large, and their flavours vary from plain and unspiced, to those spiced with black pepper, cummin seed, chilli, whole lentils, and so on. There are three ways of cooking them.

Deep-frying

See page 48 for step-by-step method. Note also the folding technique and bowl-shape ideas. Alternatively, before cooking your papadoms you can cut them with scissors to achieve diamonds or squares or ribbons for interesting presentation ideas. Fried papadoms need to stand for an hour or so for the oil to disappear (see note below).

Grilling

Preheat the grill to about medium-high. Grill one or two papadoms at a time, for about 10 seconds, with the grill tray in the midway position. Ensure that the edges are cooked. Being oil-free, grilled papadoms can be served at once or stored until ready.

Microwaving

Papadoms can also be microwaved, though their flavour is not as good as when they are grilled. This method also creates strong smells. Most microwaves are power-rated at 650 watts. Place a papadom on a plate and cook for about 30 seconds on full power. Inspect and apply more heat if necessary. Serve at once or store.

Note: papadoms should be cooked a couple of hours in advance if possible. They should then be stored in a warm, non-humid place (they easily absorb moisture in the air), ideally near the warm stove, to prevent them from losing their crispness.

SPICY SNACKS

Examine a packet of Bombay mix and you will find an array of ingredients within it, all of which have been deep-fried to make them crunchy and crispy. There are spices, nuts such as peanuts and cashews, lentils such as chana dhal, kabli chana, rice and green peas. Biscuit-coloured squiggles of different shapes and sizes, called 'murukus', are made from a spicy gram flour dough called 'ompadi'. A special hand tool called a murukus mould press is used to squeeze the dough through flat perforated discs known as ompadi plates. Each plate is perforated with circular holes or star shapes of different diameters, from tiny ('sev') through medium ('ganthia') to large ('teeka sev'). Many of these ingredients can be purchased separately in 100 g (3½ oz) packets. It is fun to make your own mixture. Try the example which follows, and try your own combinations too. Stored in an airtight tin, your mix, if fresh to begin with, will last for months. Incidentally, Bombay mix has never been heard of in Bombay; there it is simply called murukus.

Murukus Mixture

For your home-made Bombay or savoury mix, simply use proprietary 100 g (3½ oz) packets of mixes plus spices.

MAKES 600 G (1 LB 5 OZ)
100 g (3½ oz) ganthia
100 g (3½ oz) thick teeka sev
100 g (3½ oz) chana dhal
100 g (3½ oz) chick peas
100 g (3½ oz) green peas
100 g (3½ oz) peanuts

SPICES
1 tablespoon garam masala (see page 38)
1 tablespoon roasted cummin seeds
1 teaspoon lovage seeds
1 teaspoon roasted coriander seeds
1 teaspoon chilli powder to taste
aromatic salt to taste (see page 39)

Mix together all the ingredients including the spices. Store and use as required.

Colours in Vegetables

The yellow pigmentation predominant in carrot, and in mango, pumpkin, red potato, swede, melon, and peach comes from carotene. This is also present in seafood, causing it to go pink when cooked. Carotene converts to vitamin A in the body. The green colour in vegetables comes from chlorophyll. The green colour dulls rapidly during cooking, although the gentler and quicker the cooking, the less dull it becomes.

Lettuce and Salad Leaves

Lettuce probably originated in the Caucasis and eastern Asia. It was certainly cultivated by the Egyptians, and much later by the Romans who brought it to Britain. In those days it was very bitter and used medicinally as a sleeping draught. Its use as a vegetable came much later.

The familiar crisp white or pale green leaves of the cos, romaine, iceberg and crisphead have graced salads and sandwiches for decades. Recent breeding, however, has given the lettuce a new status, as much as a herb and garnish as for anything else. The leaves come now in all shapes and sizes, with colours ranging from white or yellow to dark green, and red to purple, and the range of flavours is equally vast. The easiest way to sample these delights is to buy packets of fresh mixed leaves, now on offer at the supermarkets. This is an economical, effortless way to enjoy small quantities of different leaves at one time. Here are some lettuce and leaf examples:

Baby Cos

Iceburg

Lamb's Lettuce

Lollo Bondo

Radicchio

Lollo Rosso

Red Mustard

Escarole

Endive

Red Chard

Royal Oak

Roquette or Rocket

Onion Rasam

Spicy Consommé

In south India, rasam – a piquant, sour (tamarind) spicy (chilli) consommé served hot, is a sort of national dish. This rasam uses plenty of onions. It can be made a day or two in advance and can also be frozen.

SERVES 4

2 tablespoons sesame oil

1 teaspoon mustard seeds

1 teaspoon sesame seeds

½ teaspoon turmeric

4 or 5 cloves garlic, sliced

1–3 fresh chopped red chillies (optional)

225 g (8 oz) onion, thinly sliced

900 ml (1½ pints) water or stock

12 dried or fresh curry leaves

1 tablespoon tamarind purée (see page 45)

1 tablespoon red lentils

1 teaspoon chilli powder

1 teaspoon chopped dried red chilli

2 tablespoons chopped fresh coriander leaves

salt to taste

chopped chives to garnish

1 Heat the oil. Fry the seeds for 10 seconds. Add the turmeric, garlic, chillies (if using), and onion and stir-fry for about 3 minutes.

2 Bring the water or stock, the curry leaves, tamarind, lentils, chilli powder and dried chilli to the simmer in a 2.25-litre (4-pint) saucepan. Simmer for about 20 minutes.

3 Add the stir-fried ingredients, the fresh coriander leaves, and salt to taste. Simmer for 5–10 minutes more. Optionally strain and discard the solids. Put into serving bowls (or Florentine cups) garnished with the chives.

Onion Rasam

Mulligatawny Soup

Mulligatawny soup – a thick meat-based potage – was perhaps the most famous of dishes to come out of the Raj. It had been modified from an authentic, age-old Tamil recipe – a fiery hot consommé called 'milagu-tannir', meaning 'pepper-water'. My version here is a thin, meat-free soup, spicy, but not fire-water, which can be served hot or cold.

SERVES 4

1 litre (1¾ pints) fragrant stock (see page 39)

2 tablespoons blended mustard or sunflower oil

2 teaspoons curry masala dry mix (see page 40)

2 or 3 cloves garlic, finely chopped

110 g (4 oz) onion, finely chopped

1 or 2 fresh red chillies, shredded

1 tablespoon dry basmati rice

1 tablespoon polished split red lentils

2 tablespoons tamarind purée (see page 45)

2 tablespoons chopped fresh coriander leaves

some fresh or dry curry leaves, if available

salt to taste

1 Bring the stock to the simmer in a 3-litre (5¼-pint) saucepan.

2 Meanwhile, heat the oil in the wok and stir-fry the masala for 30 seconds. Add the garlic, onion and chillies, and stir-fry for a further 3 or 4 minutes.

3 Add the fried items, the rice and the lentils to the simmering stock, stirring at first to ensure that nothing sticks to the bottom of the pan.

4 Simmer for some 10 minutes, then add the tamarind purée and the leaves.

5 Give the soup a final 3 or 4 minutes simmering, then salt to taste. Serve hot or cold.

Sabzi Shorba Soup

Lentil and Vegetable Soup

Potatoes and lentils form the basis of this thick tasty soup. It needs other vegetables of your choice (here I am using frozen mixed vegetables – peas, sweetcorn, diced carrot and beans) which can be added as required.

SERVES 4

2 tablespoons vegetable oil

½ teaspoon turmeric

1 teaspoon cummin seeds

½ teaspoon fennel seeds

2 cloves garlic, finely chopped

4 oz (110 g) onion, finely chopped

1 tablespoon curry masala paste (see page 40)

750 ml (1½ pints) fragrant stock (see page 39) or water

4 tablespoons red lentils

6 tablespoons mashed potatoes

110 g (4 oz) frozen mixed diced vegetables, thawed

1 teaspoon garam masala (see page 38)

aromatic salt to taste (see page 39)

chopped fresh coriander leaves

1 Heat the oil in a karahi or wok and stir-fry the turmeric and seeds for 30 seconds. Add the garlic, onion and curry paste and stir-fry for 2 more minutes.

2 Transfer the stir-fry to a 2.25-litre (4-pint) saucepan. Add the stock or water and lentils and bring to the boil. Reduce the heat and simmer for about 15 minutes. Remove any frothy scum.

3 At the end of that time, test to ensure that the lentils are cooked. Add the potatoes and vegetables and simmer for about 5 more minutes.

4 Add the garam masala and salt to taste. Add more water if you wish to thin the soup, bringing it back to a simmer. Serve garnished with a sprinkling of fresh coriander.

Bengali Tamarta Shorba

Tomato Soup

Quite how the ancient world managed without tomatoes until Columbus 'discovered' them in the Americas, I cannot imagine. Of course, they are now as much a part of the Indian repertoire as everything else. Here we can use various commercial tomato products, plus typical Bengali spicing, to achieve a tasty soup, which can be served piping hot on a cold day, or cold with crushed ice on a hot day.

SERVES 4

2 tablespoons vegetable oil
1 teaspoon mustard seeds
½ teaspoon nigella seeds
4 cloves garlic, finely chopped
110 g (4 oz) onion, finely chopped
300 ml (½ pint) water or fragrant stock
   (see page 39)
800 g (1½ lb) canned tomatoes and their juice
juice of one fresh lemon
1 tablespoon tomato ketchup
1 tablespoon tomato purée
1 teaspoon garam masala (see page 38)
aromatic salt to taste (see page 39)
chopped fresh coriander leaves

SPICES

½ teaspoon coriander
½ teaspoon cummin
½ teaspoon chilli
½ teaspoon paprika

1 Heat the oil in a karahi or wok and stir-fry the spices and seeds for 30 seconds. Add the garlic and onion and stir-fry for 2 more minutes.
2 Transfer the stir-fry to a 2.25-litre (4-pint) saucepan. Add the stock or water and the tomatoes and bring to the boil. Reduce the heat and simmer for about 15 minutes.

3 Break up the tomatoes with a whisk or electric hand blender. Add the lemon juice, tomato ketchup, tomato purée and garam masala and stir in. If you wish you can add water to thin the soup. Salt to taste, and simmer on for a while longer.
4 Garnish with the fresh coriander and serve.

INDIAN SALADS

In all of India's long history of cooking, there has never been a salad culture, apart, that is, from the celebrated Cachumber salad (see page 183). This may be because salads do not keep well in India's hot climate. As we see on page 55, we in the West have gorgeous salad ingredients and, if you are anything like me, a regular craving to eat them. Here are four salads, coloured green, red, orange and white. One or more is particularly apt served with snacks and starters. Try the Goan salad dressing with all of them.

Hare Salat

Green Indian Salad

SERVES 4

200 g (7 oz) prepared mixed green salad
   leaves
4–6 spring onion leaves
2 tablespoons fresh coriander leaves, chopped
2 cloves garlic, very finely chopped
aromatic salt to taste (see page 39)

SPICES

1 teaspoon sesame seeds
½ teaspoon mustard seeds
½ teaspoon lovage seeds

1 Heat a karahi or wok. Dry-roast the spices for 1 minute. Remove from the heat to cool.

2 Coarsely chop the leaves and spring onions and mix them in a bowl with the spices, garlic and salt.
3 Chill in the refrigerator for 2 hours prior to serving.

Laala Salat

Red Indian Salad

SERVES 4

1 medium-sized cooked beetroot
1 red bell pepper
1 medium-sized red onion
4 fresh red chillies (optional)
16 cherry tomatoes, halved
20 black seedless grapes, halved
1 teaspoon brown sugar
2 tablespoons sesame oil
4 tablespoons red wine
aromatic salt to taste (see page 39)
1 radicchio (red chicory)

SPICES

3 teaspoons sesame seeds
1 teaspoon mustard seeds
1 teaspoon fennel seeds

GARNISH

finely chopped parsley
4 wedges of lemon or lime

1 Heat a karahi or wok. Dry-roast the spices for 1 minute. Remove from the heat and cool.
2 Chop the beetroot, pepper, onion and chillies (if using) into thin julienne strips. Place in a large bowl and mix in the tomatoes, and grapes.
3 Mix together the spices, sugar, oil and wine. Mix into the salad, salting to taste
4 Put the bowl in the refrigerator and chill for 2–4 hours.
5 Serve in a nest of radicchio leaves, garnished with parsley and lemon or lime wedges.

Lobia Chana Salat

Orange Bean Salad

SERVES 4

2 tablespoons sesame oil

2–4 cloves garlic, finely chopped

2.5 cm (1 inch) cube fresh ginger, shredded

110 g (4 oz) onion, finely chopped

up to 2 fresh orange or red chillies
   (optional)

1 orange bell pepper, in thin slices

110 g (4 oz) carrot, shredded

225 g (8 oz) Chinese leaves, shredded

110 g (4 oz) canned black-eyed beans

110 g (4 oz) whole chick peas

16 tangerine wedges

black salt to taste

SPICES

2 teaspoons panch phoran

½ teaspoon mango powder

½ teaspoon turmeric

½ teaspoon paprika

GARNISH

2 tablespoons chopped fresh coriander
   leaves

lime or lemon juice

1 Heat the oil in a karahi or wok and stir-fry the garlic, ginger and onion for about 2 minutes. Add spices and stir-fry them for a further couple of minutes. Allow to cool.

2 Chop the chillies and bell pepper into thin slices. Shred the carrot and Chinese leaves. Stir these items into a large bowl with the white wine. Add the cold stir-fry, the beans, chick peas and tangerine wedges and salt to taste.

3 When completely cold, transfer to a bowl and refrigerate for between 1 and 4 hours. To serve, garnish with the coriander and a squeeze of lime or lemon juice.

Sufaid Khumbi Salat

White Indian Salad

SERVES 4

4 tablespoons walnut or hazelnut oil

2 teaspoons black mustard seeds

110 g (4 oz) desiccated coconut

200 ml (7 fl oz) coconut milk

2–3 red or green chillies

200 g (7 oz) white button mushrooms

1 bulb fennel

200 g (7 oz) white radish

110 g (4 oz) onion

salt to taste

GARNISH

fresh lemon or lime juice

sprigs of fresh coriander or parsley

walnuts

1 Heat the oil in a karahi or wok and stir-fry the seeds for about 30 seconds. Add the coconut and briskly stir-fry for 2 minutes. Add the coconut milk and allow to cool.

2 Chop the chillies, mushrooms, fennel, radish and onion into thin slices and stir together in a large bowl. Mix in the cold coconut stir-fry and salt to taste.

3 Refrigerate for between 1 and 4 hours.

4 Serve cold on a nest of Chinese leaves. Squeeze on the lemon or lime juice and garnish with the fresh coriander and walnuts.

Goan Salad Dressing

Just as there are not really any traditional Indian salads, there is not a traditional Indian salad dressing. However, Goan vinegar, made from coconut, has a remarkable flavour, and makes a great base for a spicy salad dressing. Goan vinegar is nigh on impossible to obtain outside Goa, but I have found that Japanese rice vinegar is a good substitute, and works well in this simple combination.

MAKES MANY SERVINGS

150 ml (5 fl oz) bottled rice vinegar

30 ml (1 fl oz) olive oil

2 teaspoons fennel seeds, ground

Simply combine everything in a screw-top bottle. Shake well and serve.
Note: this dressing improves as it matures, and will keep indefinitely.

VEGETABLES

Artichoke

Hattichak

The artichoke is native to Europe and North Africa. To use, cut off the stem where it joins the head, and discard any tough and scaly leaves. Using scissors, trim any tough tips off the remaining leaves. After steaming or boiling, remove any further tough leaves and eat the hearts. Artichoke is a good source of vitamin C, dietary fibre and potassium, and yields 5 calories per 100 g (3½ oz).

Asparagus

Sootimolee

Native to Siberia and the Mediterranean, the asparagus is a member of the lily family. The Greeks cultivated it from wild plants centuries before Christ. Indeed, the word asparagus originated from the Greek word meaning to 'stalk' or 'shoot'. Asparagus is known to have been in Britain since the sixteenth century, when it grew wild on the shores. Within a hundred years it was being cultivated in a village outside London called Battersea (now SW11), which became famous as much for its bundles of asparagus, as for its cockney rhyming slang: 'sparrow grass'. Today there are some 300 species

worldwide, British asparagus having a particularly good flavour because the climate allows the stems to grow slowly.

The tips and tops of the asparagus stalks are the delicacy; discard the stalk at the point where it becomes tough. Asparagus is a good source of fibre, potassium and iron, and vitamins C and B. Raw, it has 18 calories per 100g (3½ oz).

Aubergine

Baigan, brinjal

The aubergine originated in South-east Asia and belongs to the nightshade family, as do tomatoes and potatoes. When first introduced to Europe, aubergine earned the name 'mad apple' due to its deadly family connection, and it was believed to cause insanity.

Oblong, pear or egg-shaped (hence its alternative name, eggplant), the aubergine is a fleshy berry fruit, generally deep purple in colour, and between 6 and 30 cm (2½–12 inches) long. It can be grilled or baked whole until it burns slightly (for a gorgeous smoky

taste), then the flesh may be scooped out and puréed. Alternatively omit the grilling, and slice into bite-sized pieces (retaining the skin) and cook. Either way discard the pith and seeds in the centre. Aubergine is a good source of fibre and iron, and vitamins A and C. It yields 14 calories per 100 g (3½ oz).

Avocado

Aguacate

Also known as the avocado pear, because of its shape, it was originally native to Latin America. By 300 BC it was featured in the picture writings of the Mexican Mayans, and in the twelfth century the Aztecs considered it sacred and used it as an aphrodisiac. Only Aztec high-born males were permitted to eat avocado, whose name derives from the Aztec words *ahuacatl* ('testicle') and *cuahuitly* ('tree'). 'Guacamole' also derives from these words.

The avocado grows on a medium-sized tree with dense, pointed leaves. The fruit is

10–15 cm (4–6 inches) long, with a single stone or pit. The edible greenish-yellow pulp is neither sweet nor juicy, and as smooth as butter, hence the avocado's alternative name, 'butter fruit'. Technically, the avocado is a fruit, not a vegetable, although it has an unusually low water content of 70 per cent. It does also, however, contain a high level of fat, which explains its high calorific value (196 per 100 g/3½ oz). Avocado is a good source of protein, vitamins B, C and E, and potassium.

Bamboo Shoot
Karail, Kirlu

The bamboo shoot grows prolifically in China alongside all the main rivers. It is the tender, cone-shaped top part of the shoot that is eaten. Bamboo shoots can be obtained fresh in the West from time to time but you are more likely to be served the canned version in your local Chinese restaurant. These come in two forms: whole shoot tips or sliced. The flavour of fresh bamboo shoots is, of course, better, and they yield 32 calories per 100 g (3½ oz).

Bean
Sem

The bean is a member of the legume or pulse family. The thin green (French) bean with its edible pod and smallish seeds originated in the Americas and was taken eastward post-Columbus. Before that, bean varieties had large seeds and virtually inedible scaly casings (e.g. the broad bean, still the

favourite of Arabia and the western Mediterranean countries). To distinguish the two types the term green bean is used to describe the runner bean, snap bean, French or Kenyan bean, and the Indian long bean. They are usually green but sometimes purple or yellow, and all have fleshy pods and soft seeds. The largest are long beans growing up to a metre (over 3 feet) in length; runner beans reach 25 cm (10 inches) in length; and the smallest, the snap bean, is about 10cm (4 inches) long. All are suitable for currying. Top, tail and string them (if necessary), then use whole, sliced or diced. Beans are a good source of fibre and vitamin C, and yield 28 calories per 100 g (3½ oz).

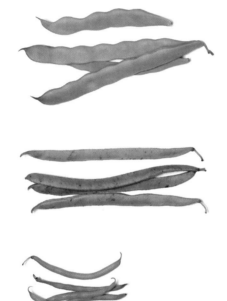

Bean sprouts
Moong sem

Bean sprouts (or bean shoots) have always been an important Chinese vegetable. They are added to many dishes or may simply be steamed and served as an accompaniment. They are also one of nature's wonders: more or less any dried bean or lentil will sprout when water is applied under the correct conditions. The Chinese commonly use soya

beans for sprouting. In India they commonly use the green moong bean. Bean sprouts are a good source of protein and fibre and contain 21 calories per 100 g (3½ oz).

Beetroot
Chukander

Beetroot is a member of the beet family, which also includes sugar beet, mangold (cattle fodder) and chard (leaf). Table beet, also known as garden beet or red beet, as well as beetroot, is an edible tuber which has been cultivated since ancient times (the Romans ate only the leaves). Sugar beet was used as an alternative to sugar cane in the manufacture of sugar after the Napoleonic wars, when the British blockaded the delivery of sugar cane to Europe. But it was beetroot, with its wonderful colour, that became a favourite table vegetable, whether boiled and eaten hot like potato, puréed for soup, or pickled in vinegar and eaten cold in salads. Beetroot is a good source of vitamin C and potassium, and yields 28 calories per 100g (3½ oz).

RISSOLES

Rissoles are excellent subjects for spicing. They make great snacks at any time, and are almost as good cold as hot. Try them on a picnic. They are easy to cook, as is shown in the step-by-step recipe on page 47. Rissoles can be served hot or cold, and are excellent with a salad. Alternatively, try them as a sandwich filler. Rissoles can be frozen, then reheated as required. Here is a selection of rissoles from India.

Mattar Kebab
Pea Rissoles

MAKES 8 RISSOLES

225 g (8 oz) cooked or thawed frozen peas, partly mashed
225 g (8 oz) mashed potatoes
1 teaspoon aromatic salt (see page 39)
vegetable oil for deep-frying
breadcrumbs for rolling

SPICES
1 teaspoon ground cummin
1 teaspoon ground coriander
1 teaspoon garam masala (see page 38)
½ teaspoon lovage seeds
1 teaspoon chilli powder

1 Mix the cold peas, mashed potatoes, salt and spices together to create a mouldable mixture.
2 Divide the mixture into 8 equal-sized portions and mould them into sausage shapes.
3 Heat the deep-fryer to 190°C /375°F.
4 While the oil is heating, roll each rissole in ample breadcrumbs.
5 Deep-fry the rissoles for about 10 minutes.

Various rissoles and a green salad (right); here I've added avocado and capsicum to the recipe on page 58

Aloo Kebab
Spicy Potato Rissoles

MAKES 8 RISSOLES

450 g (1 lb) mashed potatoes
50 g (2 oz) almonds and/or cashew nuts, chopped
1 teaspoon aromatic salt (see page 39)

SPICES
2 teaspoons garam masala (see page 38)
1 teaspoon ground coriander
½ teaspoon cummin seeds
1 teaspoon chilli powder

1 Follow the method for the previous recipe, substituting the nuts for the peas and forming the kebabs into disc shapes.

Mustard Blend Oil

Mustard seed has been distilled for thousands of years to make oil in certain areas of the subcontinent, where it imparts a delicious flavour in cooking. However, to comply with EU legislation, mustard oil is diluted with vegetable oil, to form a product known as 'blended mustard oil' or 'mustard blend oil', which is not as flavoursome as the undiluted version. Sesame, or another oil, may be substituted.

Aloo Tarka Chop
Potato Rissoles with a Spicy Centre

These are mashed potato rissoles, at the centre of which is buried a filling of cooked spicy tarka dhal. They are then breaded and fried.

MAKES 8 RISSOLES

8 tablespoons cold cooked tarka dhal (see page 138)
450 g (1 lb) mashed potatoes (salted)
2 egg yolks
150g (6 oz) breadcrumbs
6 tablespoons vegetable or corn oil

1 Mould the cooked tarka dhal into 8 equal size balls.
2 Take a ball of salted mashed potatoes, about 6.5 cm (2½ inches) in diameter. Flatten it to a disc shape. Make a depression in the top side. Insert the tarka dhal ball. Press the potato over it.
3 Glaze it with the egg yolk, then dab it in the breadcrumbs to cover generously. Repeat with the other rissoles.
4 Heat the oil in the large frying pan to 190°C/375°F. Fry the rissoles until golden, about 3 or 4 minutes a side. Remove from the oil and shake off any excess.
5 Serve hot or cold.

Dahi Wada

Dahi is natural yoghurt and wada, pronounced 'vardar', are spicy rissoles, in this case made from lentil flour (urid dhal), which is mixed with chilli and spices, then made into a dough which is either steamed or deep-fried. It is then cooled before being immersed in the pre-spiced yoghurt. The distinctive feature of the spicing is the use of tart mango powder and black salt, both an acquired taste. Chaat masala, available in packets from Asian stores, contains these and other spices, and you could use 1½ teaspoons of it in place of the mango, black salt and chilli peppers.

MAKES 4 WADAS

100 g (3½ oz) polished lentils
1 teaspoon chopped green chillies
⅓ teaspoon cummin seeds, crushed
⅓ teaspoon ground black pepper
⅓ teaspoon salt
1 tablespoon finely chopped onion
6 fresh curry leaves, chopped
vegetable oil for deep-frying

YOGHURT MASALA

225 g (8 oz) natural yoghurt
½ teaspoon mango powder
½ teaspoon black salt
½ teaspoon chilli powder
OR 1 teaspoon chaat masala (see above)

1 Grind the lentils (dry) into a flour (in a coffee grinder, small quantities at a time), and put in a bowl with the chillies, cummin, pepper, salt, onion and curry leaves.
2 Mix to a stiff dough with a little water, and allow to stand for 20 minutes.
3 Roll the dough into 4 equal-size balls or shape into rings. Heat the deep-fry oil to 180°C/350°F, and fry the wadas

Dahi Wada – lentil rissole in yoghurt

for 10 minutes, or until golden. Remove from the oil and allow to go cold.
4 Mix the yoghurt with the mango powder, black salt and chilli powder, add the cold wadas and leave in the fridge for an hour or two. To serve, sprinkle a little chilli powder on the dish.

Samosas

It is worth making a largish batch of samosas. Make the filling first and freeze any left over for future use. Here are two filling options.

EACH MAKES 20–24 SAMOSAS
SAMOSA FILLING

900 g (2 lb) mashed potatoes
1 teaspoon salt
450 g (1 lb) frozen peas
1 teaspoon ground black pepper
2 teaspoons chilli powder
2 teaspoons ground coriander
1 teaspoon ground cummin
2 tablespoons dried fenugreek leaves

SAG PANEER SAMOSA FILLING

450 g (1 lb) spinach, fresh, frozen or canned
2–4 cloves garlic, finely chopped
110 g (4 oz) spring onions, finely chopped
1 tablespoon curry masala paste (see page 40)
110 g (4 oz) crumbly paneer (see page 46) or cottage cheese
4 tablespoons chopped fresh coriander
4 tablespoons chopped fresh mint
1 tablespoon garam masala (see page 38)
½ teaspoon aromatic salt (see page 39)
up to 4 green chillies, finely chopped (optional)

1 To ensure the filling will be dry enough, strain off any excess liquid from the ingredients. Keep for use elsewhere.

2 Mix together the ingredients.
3 Use up any spare mixture in curries or soup.

SAMOSA PASTRY

2 tablespoons vegetable oil
450 g (1 lb) strong white plain flour
vegetable oil for deep-frying

1 Mix the oil, flour and enough water to make a dough which, when mixed, does not stick to the bowl. Leave it to stand for about an hour.
2 Divide the dough into four pieces, then shape each piece into a square. Roll out each square and cut it into four rectangles measuring 7.5 x 20 cm (3 x 8 inches). Remember, the thinner you roll the pastry, the crispier the samosas will be.
3 Take one rectangle and place a teaspoon of filling on it. Make the first diagonal fold, then the second and third.
4 Open the pouch and top up with some more filling. Do not overfill or the samosa will burst during frying.
5 Brush some flour and water on the remaining flap, and seal. Trim off excess pastry.
6 Preheat the deep-frying oil to 190°C/375°F. Put one samosa into the oil, and after a few seconds add the next, until about six are in. This maintains the oil temperature. Fry for 8–10 minutes, then remove, shake off excess oil, and drain on kitchen paper.
7 Serve hot or cold with tamarind chutney (see pages 66 and 183).

Note: You can substitute ready-made sheets of spring roll or filo pastry or samosa pads for home-made pastry at stage 2.

Gol Goppa ke Jal Jeera

Potato Snack with Crunchy Wafers and a Spicy Drink

This is eaten with the small crispy biscuits (gol goppa) which, if you are lucky, have puffed up into crispy spheres. Traditionally, the potato is placed onto or into the biscuit, and it is popped whole into the mouth. This is then chased down with a spicy cummin-flavoured drink (jal jeera), served in individual tumblers.

SERVES 4

POTATO CURRY

450 g (1 lb) potatoes, peeled and boiled

2 tablespoons curry masala paste
  (see page 40)

1 tablespoon chopped fresh coriander leaves

1 tablespoon chopped fresh or dried mint

1 Allow the potatoes to cool after cooking, then dice into 8-mm (¼-inch) cubes.

2 Mix in the other ingredients and chill in the refrigerator until required.

THE DRINK (JAL JEERA)

300 ml (½ pint) water

1 teaspoon black salt

1 teaspoon brown sugar

1 teaspoon ground cummin

½ teaspoon chilli powder

shake of Worcestershire sauce

crushed ice

1 Mix together all the ingredients except for the ice. Put into a jug and chill in the refrigerator until required.

2 Add the crushed ice prior to serving.

THE WAFERS (GOL GOPPA)

450 g (1 lb) strong white flour

3 tablespoons vegetable oil

1 teaspoon salt

1 Mix the wafer ingredients into a pliable dough.

2 Take a marble-sized piece of dough and roll it into a thin disc about 3.75 cm (1½ inches) in diameter. Repeat until all the dough is used up.

3 Heat the deep-fryer to a minimum of 190°C/375°F.

4 Place a wafer into the oil. If the oil is hot enough, it will puff up like a mini flying saucer. Add the next wafer and continue until the fryer can take no more. Turn each disc once then after a couple of minutes remove them from the oil, if possible in the order in which they went in.

5 Drain them and place on kitchen paper to cool.

6 Repeat stages 4 and 5 until all the discs are cooked.

7 When cold the wafers will become very crispy and crunchy. Serve at once or store in an airtight container.

Batata Pava

Gujarati Potato Snack

This is a subtly spiced potato curry, given a crunchy texture by the use of crispy puffed rice, available from the Asian store. The accompanying chutneys, and plain raita (see page 181) are mandatory.

SERVES 4

2 tablespoons vegetable oil

225 g (8 oz) potatoes, peeled, boiled and
  diced into 8 mm (¼ inch) cubes

juice of 1 lemon

1 tablespoon chopped fresh coriander leaves

1 teaspoon brown sugar

1–2 green chillies, chopped

1 tablespoon grated fresh or desiccated
  coconut

salt to taste

100 g (3½ oz) puffed basmati rice

SPICES

½ teaspoon mustard seeds

½ teaspoon turmeric

½ teaspoon asafoetida

1 Heat the oil in a karahi. Stir-fry the spices for 1 minute, then add all the other ingredients except for the puffed rice. Stir-fry until hot. Remove from the heat and allow to go cold.

2 Toss in the puffed rice at the last minute to keep it crisp. Serve cold, accompanied by the two sauces in separate serving bowls.

Imli Chutney

Brown Sauce – Sweet and Sour

MAKES ABOUT 330G (12 OZ)

110 g (4 oz) tamarind purée (see page 45)

110 g (4 oz) golden sultanas

110 g (4 oz) brown sugar

1 teaspoon ground cummin

salt to taste

1 Mix together the ingredients in a blender or food processor, using water as necessary, to achieve a thick, smooth purée. It is ready to serve.

Dhania Chutney

Green Sauce – Hot

MAKES ABOUT 275G (10 OZ)

110g (4oz) fresh coriander leaves

25g (1 oz) fresh green chillies, chopped

110g (4oz) onion, chopped

4 tablespoons coconut milk powder

1 teaspoon salt

1 Mix the ingredients in a blender or food processor, using water as needed, to achieve a thick, smooth purée.

Left, Gol Goppa and, right, Batata Pava

Bell Pepper
Badi mirch

This highly flavoured vegetable goes under a number of names, including paprika, pepper, sweet pepper, pimento and capsicum. None of these names is particularly accurate. In fact, the bell pepper is unrelated to pepper, and is just one member of the massive Capsicum family, to which chillies also belong (see page 18). The fleshy, hollow fruit capsule is approximately bell or heart-shaped, and measures up to around 11 cm (4 inches) in length. Unlike chilli, the bell pepper contains no capsaicin, the 'heat-giving' agent, but it does have a distinctive flavour, and is now bred in white, yellow, orange and purple, as well as red and green. The red, orange and yellow colours stand up better to prolonged cooking than do the green, which go rather grey if cooked for some time, although this does not affect their taste. To counter this, you can blanch, steam or microwave the pre-cut bell pepper, softening it and heating it enough that it can be added at a relatively late stage of cooking. Roasting the bell pepper, then removing its skin, gives it a whole new taste dimension. Discard the stalk, pith and seeds. Bell pepper is one of the richest sources of vitamin C (red more than green), and it is a good source of fibre and potassium and vitamin A. Raw, it yields 14 calories per 100 g (3½ oz).

Bitter Gourd
Karela

This is a knobbly, long, cylindrical pointed green vegetable, about the size of a banana. It is native to and greatly enjoyed in the subcontinent, and is now also available in the West. The *karela* (in Hindi/Urdu; *korola* in Bengali) was named after India's southernmost state, Kerela, by seventeenth-century Dutch governor Draaksteen, in his book *Hortus Inicus Malabaricus*. It is a very bitter vegetable, and as such it is an acquired taste. It is high in water content but low in nutrients and yields 21 calories per 100 g (3½ oz).

Broccoli or Calabrese
Hare ghobi

Belonging to the Brassica family, broccoli has short fleshy buds, clustered in a single head and was developed in Italy in the 1500s (*brocco* meaning 'arm' or 'branch' in Italian). It resembles cauliflower, for which it can be

substituted, although it is mostly dark green, inside and out. There are also varieties which are maroon/purple, blue-green and lime green. To use broccoli, cut it into small florets having discarded the leaves and tougher stalks. Boil, steam or microwave to tender. Broccoli is a particularly good source of vitamin C and also contains fibre, potassium and iron, and vitamins B and E. It yields 25 calories per 100 g (3½ oz).

Brussels Sprout
Chotee ghobi

A tiny member of the cabbage (Brassica) family, the Brussels sprout could be the original miniature vegetable. It is believed to have originated in Brussels in the 1200s, from wild cabbage. First records of the cultivated version date back to the 1700s in Brussels, and they first came to England at the end of that century. Brussels grow one above the other on an erect stem to an average of 3–4 cm (1¼ inches) in diameter. They are made up of tiny green (though some varieties are purple), tightly wrapped cabbage-like leaves. The stem is inedible but all of the sprout itself can be eaten. Brussels sprouts are a good source of fibre and protein and yield 41 calories per 100 g (3½ oz).

Cabbage
Bandghobi

Cabbage is another member of the Brassica family and one of the most ancient of vegetables. It originated in Asia minor and the eastern Mediterranean, and grew wild as far north as Britain, originally as loosely packed, dark green edible leaves, growing from a stubby stalk on a low plant. The first recorded cultivation of cabbage was in ancient Greece as early as 600 BC. 'Modern' cultivation, credited to medieval Germany, created crisp, tightly packed leaves, whose colours range through all hues of green to white and beetroot red. Most, but not all are spherical. Relatives include broccoli, cauliflower, kale and kohlrabi. Cabbage is good for fibre, potassium and iron, and vitamins B, C, and E. It yields 18 calories per 100 g (3½ oz).

Carrot
Gajar

The carrot is one of the most important members of the hugely prolific *Umbelliferae* family, of which parsnip, celery, parsley, coriander and several spices are also members. Originally native to Persia, Afghanistan and Pakistan the wild carrot is thought to have spread naturally to the eastern Mediterranean. It may have been first cultivated by the Romans, though this is not certain. By the 800s the Arabs brought it to western Europe. Its arrival in Britain was

in the 1500s. The carrot is a long tapering root similar in shape and size to parsnip, although modern breeding has resulted in other shapes. In the West, we are most familiar with bright orange-coloured carrot, although yellow, red and purple varieties are found in the Third World. The Indian variety, for example, is a deep, almost beetroot red. The colour comes from large amounts of carotenoid present (also found to some extent in many other vegetables, and in shellfish). Carrot can be eaten raw, so needs minimal cooking. For a large carrot, discard top and tail, wash then pare, and cut into strips, rounds or cubes. Baby carrots are best left whole. The carrot is an excellent source of vitamin A and also has fibre, potassium and iron, and vitamins B and E. The carrot yields 21 calories per 100 g (3½ oz).

Cassava
Yuca

We know from preserved Peruvian picture writings dating from 1000 BC that the cassava is native to that part of the Americas. Also known as yuca or manioc, it is a nutritious tuber. Once discovered (post-Columbus), and given that it was easy to store on board ship, cassava was used to feed the slaves traded by the Portuguese – and was taken to Africa and Asia. The cassava is a shiny brown, tapered cylindrical root, resembling the carrot in size and shape.

However, its acrid milky sap contains poisonous prussic acid which means that it (like the potato) must be cooked before eating. Casava chips are a popular product in the Caribbean. Cassava is high in carbohydrates and protein and yields 60 calories per 100 g (3½ oz).

Cauliflower
Phool ghobi, kovippu

This member of the cabbage (*Brassica*) family originated in northern Europe. The cauliflower is round and grows to between 12 and 25 cm (1.8–9.8 inches) in diameter, surrounded by tough inedible green leaves. The edible part is made up of short stems with numbers of florets, which are usually creamy white, although they can be green, yellow or maroon. Miniature varieties are bred. The two illustrated are both 7 cm (2.7 inches) in diameter, one, a regular (but small) full-grown white cauliflower, the other, the speciality variety, Romanesco, whose lime green florets have been bred to grow in conical shapes. Cauliflower is an excellent source of vitamin C and is also good for fibre, potassium and iron, and vitamin K. It yields 14 calories per 100 g (3½ oz).

TANDOORI AND TIKKA

There are as many delicious tandoori tikka-style vegetable dishes as there are vegetables. You can apply the technique to any vegetable(s) of your choice, such as white yam, red sweet potato (American yam), white sweet potato, parsnip, swede, turnip and even uncooked beetroot.

Tandoori Potato

SERVES 4
4 large baking potatoes
juice of 1 lemon

THE MARINADE
180g (6 fl oz) natural yoghurt
3 tablespoons mustard blend oil
   (see page 63)
1 teaspoon finely chopped garlic
1 teaspoon finely chopped ginger
1 tablespoon fresh mint, finely chopped
OR 1 teaspoon bottled vinegared mint
3 tablespoons chopped coriander leaves
1 teaspoon cummin seeds (roasted, ground)
1 teaspoon garam masala (see page 38)
1 tablespoon curry masala paste
   (see page 40)
2 tablespoons tandoori masala dry mix
   (see page 41)
1 teaspoon aromatic salt (see page 39)

1 Mix all the marinade ingredients together thoroughly.
2 Scrub and optionally peel the potatoes, then poke them deeply with a small thin-bladed knife to assist penetration of the marinade.
3 Rub each potato with lemon juice. This adds flavour and helps the marinade to adhere.

4 Coat each potato well with the marinade, then wrap carefully in foil.
5 Preheat the oven to 170°C/340°F/ Gas 3.
6 Place the potatoes in the oven and bake for 45 minutes–1 hour
7 Removing them from their foil, optionally put the potatoes under the grill at medium heat to finish them off. Just cook them until they blacken slightly, turning once.
8 Optionally you can scoop out the centre of each potato, retaining the shell for refilling (see below).
9 Serve hot, on a bed of salad, with chutneys and Indian breads.

Tandoori Potato Filling

SERVES 4
4 scoops of cooked potato, see above
2 teaspoons tandoori masala paste
   (see page 41)
4 teaspoons peas
2 teaspoons chopped fresh coriander leaves
4 tablespoons yoghurt
1 teaaspoon garam masala (see page 38)

1 Mix together the potato, tandoori paste, peas and leaves, and fill each scooped-out potato with the mixture.
2 Top off with a mixture of the yoghurt and garam masala.

Tikka Dry Stir-fry Vegetables

SERVES 4 (AS AN ACCOMPANIMENT)
450 g (1 lb) prepared vegetables of your
   choice

2 tablespoons vegetable ghee or oil
2 cloves garlic, sliced
2.5 cm (1 inch) cube ginger, sliced (optional)
110 g (4 oz) onion, sliced
2 teaspoons tandoori masala paste
   (see page 41)
3 or 4 tablespoons yoghurt
2 or 3 tomatoes, chopped
few pieces green and/or red pepper, chopped
up to 2 fresh chillies (red and/or green),
   chopped
salt to taste
1–2 teaspoons garam masala (see page 38)

MASALA
1 teaspoon white cummin seeds
½ teaspoon black cummin seeds
   (optional)
½ teaspoon wild onion seeds
½ teaspoon black mustard seeds

1 Heat the ghee or oil in a large karahi or wok.
2 Fry the masala for 20 seconds then add the garlic and stir-fry for 30 seconds more. Add the ginger (if using) and continue for 30 seconds more then add the onions and lowering the heat, fry for about 5 minutes to allow them to begin to go golden, stirring occasionally.
3 Raise the heat and add the tandoori paste and the yoghurt and stir-fry the mixture for a couple of minutes, until it changes colour (goes darker) which means it is cooked.
4 While the onions are cooking, blanch the vegetables (or steam or microwave them) just to heat and soften them. Add them to the pan with the tomatoes, peppers and chillies and stir-fry for just a few minutes until they are as crisp or tender as you want them. If at any time the dish starts sticking, add a little water to 'release' (but not swamp) it. Salt to taste, sprinkle with the garam masala and serve at once.

Tandoori potato with filling, tandoori sweet potato, tandoori cauliflower and broccoli and, bottom left, a chutney with carrot and whole green chillies in mustard oil

Mushroom Tikka Stir-fry

SERVES 4 (AS AN ACCOMPANIMENT)
450 g (1 lb) mushrooms, any type
remaining ingredients as in the Tikka Dry
    Stir-fry Vegetables recipe on page 71

1 No need to blanch or soften the mushrooms, simply clean and peel them if required.
2 Add mushrooms after the marinade has changed colour (see stage 3 above), and follow the rest of the recipe above.

Chestnut Tikka Stir-fry

SERVES 4 (AS AN ACCOMPANIMENT)
450 g (1 lb) peeled and cooked chestnuts, canned and drained or vacuum packed
remaining ingredients as in the Tikka Dry
    Stir-fry Vegetables recipe above

1 Simply add the chestnuts to the karahi after the marinade has changed colour (stage 3 above) and follow the rest of the recipe above.

Pineapple Tikka

SERVES 2 (AS A STARTER)
2 tablespoons tandoori paste (see page 41)
200g (7 oz) yoghurt
8–10 chunky pieces fresh pineapple, cut into
    4-cm (1½-inch) cubes

1 Mix the tandoori paste and yoghurt in a non-metallic bowl. Add the pineapple.
2 Cover and refrigerate for 2–12 hours.
3 Just prior to cooking, thread the pineapple pieces onto two skewers. (Use any spare marinade in a curry.) Preheat the grill to medium.
4 Place the skewers on a rack above the foil-lined grill tray and place this in the midway position. (Alternatively use a barbecue.) Cook for 5 minutes, turn and repeat.
5 When fully cooked, raise the tray nearer to the heat and singe the pieces to achieve a slight blackening. Serve on a bed of salad with lemon wedges, naan bread and tandoori chutney.

THREE COLD STARTERS

These are three of my favourites. I often serve them together as a starter at dinner parties. All three are quick and easy to prepare (virtually instant in fact), tasty and popular. Served cold, they can be prepared well in advance. They improve with marination, kept in the fridge.

Spicy Chestnuts

SERVES 4 AS PART OF A STARTER
350 g (12 oz) cooked, peeled chestnuts
4 tablespoons aubergine pickle
1 tablespoon curry paste
1 teaspoon brown sugar

GARNISH
1 tablespoon chopped fresh coriander

1 Mix all the ingredients together in a pan and warm through.
2 Garnish with the fresh coriander and serve.

Dahi Rajma
Red Beans in a Sour Sauce

SERVES 4 (AS PART OF A STARTER)
400 g (14 oz) canned red kidney beans
150 g (5½ oz) yoghurt
2 tablespoons double cream
2 tablespoons tandoori masala paste (see page 41)
1 tablespoons chopped fresh mint
salt to taste

1 Rinse the beans thoroughly.
2 Mix all the ingredients together in a non-metallic bowl.
3 Chill and serve cold.

Aloo Archar
Potato in a Pickle Sauce

SERVES 4 (AS PART OF A STARTER)
4 tablespoons proprietary garlic pickle
400 g (14 oz) canned peeled baby potatoes
1 teaspoon curry masala paste (see page 40)
1 tablespoon chopped fresh coriander leaves
1 fresh red chilli, chopped (optional)
1 tablespoon natural yoghurt
salt to taste

1 Chop the large pieces of pickled garlic into smaller ones.
2 Open and strain the canned potatoes, keeping the liquid for soup or stock.
3 Put them into a bowl, add the curry masala paste, the chopped pickle, leaves, chilli (if using) and yoghurt and gently stir to mix well. Salt to taste. Chill and serve.

Spicy chestnuts (top), Dahi Rajma (left) and Aloo Archar garnished with peanuts

Imasha or Mahasha
Stuffed Tomatoes

MAKES 8 IMASHA

4 firm beefsteak tomatoes, about 9 cm
    (3½ inches) in diameter
1 cupful fresh coriander leaves, with stalks
vegetable oil for deep-frying
50 g (2 oz) thawed frozen or cooked fresh
    peas
1 tablespoon curry masala paste
    (see page 40)
4 fresh green chillies
225 g (8 oz) mashed potatoes
aromatic salt to taste (see page 39)

SPICES

2 teaspoons cummin seeds
1 teaspoon mustard seeds
1 teaspoon garlic powder
½ teaspoon mango powder

1 Halve the tomatoes and, keeping the
case intact, carefully scoop out and
reserve the seeds and pulp.
2 Heat the oil in the deep-fryer to
190°C/375°F and deep-fry the fresh
coriander for a few seconds. It will
whoosh and cook fast. Remove from
the oil, drain, then crumble it up.
3 Mix the peas, spices, curry masala
paste, chillies (if using), tomato pulp
and the crumbled fried coriander leaves
with the mashed potatoes. Add salt to
taste. The mixture should be soft and
mouldable.
4 Preheat the oven to 160°C/325°F/
Gas 3. Spoon the potato mixture into
the tomato cases and place them on a
sheet of foil on an oven tray. Bake for
15–20 minutes. Serve hot.

*You can used the same stuffing in
aubergines, chillies and peppers that have
been charred first by baking or grilling*

Bhare Avocado Ka Sootimolee
Stuffed Avocado with Asparagus

SERVES 4

16 asparagus shoots
50 g (2 oz) Cheddar cheese
200 g (7 oz) pre-cooked plain rice
50 ml (2 fl oz) soured cream
1 tablespoon mayonnaise
2 tablespoon tandoori paste
aromatic salt to taste (see page 39)
2 ripe avocado pears

GARNISH

salad leaves
lemon or lime wedges
paprika or chilli powder
finely chopped parsley
4 pieces red capsicum pepper

1 The asparagus must be cooked in
advance. As the tips are delicate,
steaming is best. If you do not have a
steamer, place a strainer above a
saucepan of boiling water. Steam for
about 10 minutes, remove and cool.
Chill in the fridge for 2 hours.
2 Grate the cheese.
3 Mix the rice with the cheese, soured
cream, mayonnaise and tandoori paste.
This attractive pink mixture should be
stiff enough to shape. Add salt to taste
and keep chilled until required.
4 No more than 1 hour before serving,
halve and stone the avocados.
5 Press them down slightly on a work
surface, so that they will not roll when
stuffed.
6 Carefully place enough filling on to
an avocado half to fill the hole, cover
the surface completely, and build it up
to a rounded mould.
7 Repeat with the other 3 halves.
8 Return the loaded avocados to the
refrigerator until required.

Badami Dum
Potato Stuffed with Almonds and Topped with a Spicy Gravy

SERVES 4

4 large baking potatoes, scrubbed but not
    peeled
vegetable ghee (not melted)
2 or 3 tablespoons fresh coriander leaves,
    finely chopped

THE STUFFING

100 g (3½ oz) almonds, coarsely chopped
2 tablespoons garam masala (see page 38)
vegetable ghee

THE GRAVY

450 g (1 lb) curry masala gravy (see page 42)

1 Preheat the oven to 180°C/
350°F/Gas 4.
2 Smear each potato with ghee and
scatter the fresh coriander all over.
Wrap in foil and lace on an oven tray
in the oven. Bake for about an hour.
3 During this time, prepare the stuffing
and the gravy.
4 For the stuffing, simply mix the
chopped almonds with the garam
masala and a little ghee. Set aside.
5 At the end of the hour, test that the
potatoes are cooked by poking into the
centre with a small knife. It should slide
through without resistance. If there is a
little uncooked portion in the centre,
return to the oven.
6 When cooked, unwrap the potatoes,
slit along the long side to the mid-
point. Carefully scoop out some potato
(use it in another recipe) and replace it
with the stuffing. Return the potatoes
to the oven for 10 more minutes.
7 Gently heat the gravy and pour it
over the potatoes. Serve as a snack or as
an accompaniment to a main meal.

Celeriac

Celeriac is a large spherical root or tuber of about 20 cm (8 inches) in diameter, very closely related to celery (see below). It must be pared and cooked, and has a similar taste but interesting texture variation to celery. Celeriac is high in water content but low in nutrients and it yields 32 calories per 100 g (3½ oz).

Celery
Shalari

Celery is a herbaceous plant and a member of the *Umbelliferae* family, its closest relative being parsley. Celery's wild ancestor was certainly known to the Egyptians, since celery seeds have been found in some of their tombs. Celery was grown in ancient Greece and Rome for medicinal purposes, and was first cultivated in Italy and France in the 1500s, at which time celeriac (see above) was defined as a separate species. Celery has long white or green fleshy, slightly stringy stems which can be eaten raw or with minimal cooking. Celery is a good source of vitamin C and potassium and yields 7 calories per 100 g (3½ oz).

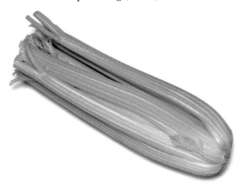

Chayote or Chokoes (Christophene)

This Latin American vegetable is a type of squash. It is also called *mirliton* in the deep south of the USA, and *christophene* in the Caribbean. It is the *laboe siam* in the Far East, and *hop jeung kwa* in China, where it is also now cultivated. Buddhists revere it for its shape which is reminiscent to them of a praying Buddha. The chayote is usually pear-shaped and grows to an average of 10 cm (4 inches) in length, although some varieties grow much larger. Its pale green case reveals a single discardable stone and white flesh with an insipid, sweetish watery taste – a cross between courgette and melon. Chayote is a good source of Vitamin C and yields 30 calories per 100g (3½ oz).

Chestnuts, sweet and water

The sweet chestnut grows as a hard nut, encased in a hard rich brown shell, on trees indigenous to Europe. It has its day, it seems, just once a year at Christmas as part of the traditional dinner, but it deserves better use. It is available all year round, ready-cooked in vacuum-packs, jars or cans, and fresh in the West at Christmas time. Fresh, it can be pricked and roasted then shelled, or shelled and boiled. (See Index for recipes.) The sweet chestnut is good for starch, sugars and dietary fibre and yields 170 calories per 100 g (3½ oz).

There are two types of water chestnut grown in Asia, the most common being *pi-tsi*. It is an aquatic tuber with a crunchy, crisp texture and bears no resemblance to the sweet chestnut. The Chinese water chestnut is usually only available canned in the West.

Chicory

Chicory is often confused with endive. Although they both belong to the lettuce family they are two different species, with different attributes and appearance. *Chicorium endivia*, the pale green curly salad leaf, known simply as endive (see page 55) goes back to Greek times. So too does the broad leaf variety, *Chicorium intybus*, known simply as chicory, and also called Brussels chicory or witloof. Pictured here, chicory leaf grows to about 15 cm (6 inches) long, and several are tightly wrapped to form a sort of torpedo shape. The leaves are white with yellow tops, and taste slightly bitter. They can be eaten raw or lightly cooked. Chicory roots are used to make a type of 'coffee'. Chicory has a high water content but is low in nutrients and yields 17 calories per 100 g (3½ oz).

Chilli

The hot member of the Capsicum family (see also page 18). The chilli should be washed and de-stalked, then chopped into narrow rings or slices, or kept whole. You may discard the seeds if the chilli is pithy, but that's a bit like throwing the baby out with the bath water, as the seeds provide heat. Contrary to popular belief, chillies do not cause indigestion if one is used to them. Chilli needs no pre-cooking of any kind; simply add it to the recipe of your choice after the spices, garlic and onion are fried, or as individual recipes direct. Fresh chilli, like onion and garlic, actively helps to reduce blood pressure and cholesterol. It is one of the richest sources of vitamin C (red chillies more than green) and is also a good source of fibre and potassium, and vitamin A. Chilli yields 21 calories per 100 g (3½ oz).

Chinese Leaf or Cabbage
Chino ghobi

There are many different types of cabbage used extensively in Chinese cooking and some are readily available in the West. A member of the cabbage (*Brassica*) family,

Chinese leaf or pe-tsai (*Brassica pekinensis*) is long, firm and lettuce-like in appearance. The leaves can vary from pale to dark green. Both the stem and the leaves can be eaten raw or lightly cooked. (See also Pak choi, page 102.)

Courgette

Also called zucchini, courgette is a kind of mini marrow and a member of the squash family. A good source of Vitamin C, it yields 15 calories per 100g (3½ oz).

Cucumber
Kakari, Kheera, Ssasha

Cucumber belongs to the gourd family, native to northern India at least by 1000 BC, and thought to be taken to the West following Alexander the Great's incursion into India in 325 BC. High in water content, cucumber does not respond well to cooking or freezing. It is a good source of vitamin C and yields 10 calories per 100 g (3½ oz).

Drumstick
Sejan, saijna danta

A member of the gourd family, native to south India. It is long and thin, growing up to half a metre (over 16 feet). Its ribbed tough outer casing contains soft juicy tasty flesh. To cook the drumstick is chopped into pieces, then boiled or curried; to eat it is halved, and the flesh sucked off. Only then is the inedible skin discarded. The drumstick yields 20 calories per 100 g (3½ oz).

Fennel Bulb
Soonf phul

Fennel is a member of the hugely prolific *Umbelliferae* family, of which carrot, parsnip, celery, parsley, coriander and several spices are also members. Native to the Mediterranean, and known in Italy as Florence fennel or *finocchio*, it was brought to Britain by the Romans. It grows as a bright white tuber visible above ground on top of which are feathery green leaves. Its distinctive feature is the aroma and fragrance of aniseed which comes from the plant's oil in which anethole is present. This makes it an ingredient in such specialities as chartreuse and pastis. Fennel bulb is edible raw or lightly cooked, the leaves are a fragrant herb, and the seeds are an aromatic spice. It is a good source of vitamin C, with some potassium and dietary fibre. Fennel bulb yields 10 calories per 100 g (3½ oz).

Indian Restaurant Top 16

A visit to the Indian restaurant leaves us in no doubt as to which dishes are the favourite among diners. It also leaves many non-meat/chicken eaters believing that Indian dishes were not designed for them. In fact nothing could be further from the truth. Each dish is fundamentally a sauce, modified from a master sauce, and made independently of the main ingredient which can just as easily be vegetables as anything else. But can this be an authentic application of traditional dishes? Surely each masala must be individually ground and cooked? For example, dhansak is a traditional Parsee meat dish cooked with lentils and vegetables; patia is seafood cooked in a hot, sweet and sour sauce; and roghan josh is a dish where meat is marinated with yoghurt and aromatic spices, followed by slow-cooking. And surely, vegetables require anything but slow cooking? The fact is that 'authenticity' is not necessarily a term one would apply to standard curry-house dishes. Most of us who are not born to curry in the subcontinent are introduced to it at the Indian restaurant. As our palate develops, we may well want more authentic dishes, but notwithstanding that, most of us enjoy falling back on curry-house tastes provided they are done well. So here are curry-house-style recipes for the Top 16 restaurant dishes, cooked with any single vegetable (or combination) of your choice. As for authentic dishes, you will find them aplenty in the subsequent chapters.

Dhansak

Gourd, Marrow and Squash

Kaddu, Kandam, Mulam, Shadai

Curcurbitacae (curcurbits) from which the word gourd derived, is the botanical name of this family of ancient vegetables whose soft flesh, with its high water content, is encased in a harder rind-like inedible casing, which in some species is smooth, in others knobbly and still others, ribbed. The family is thought to have originated in the Bengal area of India, but they may go back as far as 7000 BC in both Asia and America. However this occurred there are widely different curcurbits in both continents: anything called squash is native American, including butternut, snake, custard and spaghetti squash, as well as curcurbits as large as the pumpkin or as small as the patty pan. Also native American is the courgette (zucchini). In the old world, the native gourd family includes the cucumber, gherkin and the marrow which originated in Persia and grows to around 30 cm (12 inches), and a whole range of exotic gourds from India (including the ribbed gourd (*looki*), bottle gourd (*doodi*), round gourd (*papdi*), drumstick (*sajjar*), bitter gourd (*karela*) and snake gourd (see separate entries for the last three). The soft flesh has a high water content so requires minimal cooking, and supplies relatively few nutrients. Depending on the species, the gourd yields between 7 and 25 calories per 100 g (3½ oz).

Jerusalem artichoke

Hattichak

This tuber was discovered in the Americas and brought to the old world by the early 1600s. It has nothing to do with Jerusalem, and got its name, in fact, from the Spanish *girasol*, because it is heliotropic, meaning it turns towards the sun. It also has nothing to do with the true artichoke, apart from its flavour. The Jerusalem artichoke yields 74 calories per 100 g (3½ oz).

Kale

Kale (above right) is a member of the cabbage (*Brassica*) family. It is distinctive for its intensely curled, separate leaves as opposed to the cabbage's packed sphere of smooth leaves. Varieties of kale include: curly kale (dark green and very curly); blue curly kale (similar, but a gorgeous blue-green); ornamental kale (such as the beautiful 'coral queen', dark green with a deep red centre); and the purple and red Russian kale. Good for fibre, potassium and iron, and vitamins B, C and E, kale yields from 40 calories per 100 g (3½ oz).

Kantola (Kakrul)

This ovoid fruit is rarely seen in the West where it is known as the spring or spiny bitter cucumber (kantola or kakrul in the subcontinent, and pak khao in Thailand and China). It is grows to about 6 cm (2.3 inches) in length. Its skin has short, soft, spiny spikes, and turns from bright green to yellow as it ripens. The skin is discarded and the creamy flesh with its numerous seeds has the texture of an orange when raw, but is transformed when cooked. As its English name suggests, it is bitter, but not as much as the bitter gourd (see page 68). Kantola has a high water content but is low in nutrients and it yields 21 calories per 100 g (3½ oz).

Balti Mixed Vegetable Curry

Being of Kashmiri origin. Balti is aromatic and herby, using garam masala spices and plenty of coriander and/or mint to accompany freshly cooked main ingredients. A quick trick is to use canned vegetables.

SERVES: 4

2 tablespoons vegetable oil

200 g (7 oz) canned ratatouille

200 g (7 oz) canned sweetcorn

200 g (7 oz) canned chick peas

2 tablespoon chopped Brinjal pickle

200 g (7 oz) baby leaf spinach

6 cherry tomatoes, halved

1 or 2 fresh red chillies, chopped

1 teaspoon garam masala (see page 38)

2 or 3 tablespoons fresh coriander leaves, finely chopped

aromatic salt to taste (see page 39)

SPICES

⅓ teaspoon whole aniseeds

½ teaspoon fennel seeds

⅓ teaspoon whole allspice seeds

1½ teaspoon garam masala (see page 38)

1 teaspoon curry masala dry mix (see page 40)

½ teaspoon garlic powder

⅓ teaspoon ginger powder

⅓ teaspoon chilli powder

1 Roast and grind the aniseed, fennel seeds and allspice (see page 38 for method).

2 Mix with the other spices.

3 Add just enough water to the masala mix to make a paste.

4 Heat the oil and stir-fry the above paste for a couple of minutes.

5 Combine with all other ingredients. Heat it right through, salt to taste, garnish and serve hot accompanied by a Balti karak naan and Balti chutney.

Bhoona

Bhoona is the process of cooking a wet ground masala paste in hot oil. In the case of a vegetable bhoona, the result is a mild, dryish curry.

450 g (1 lb) mixed frozen vegetables, thawed

3 tablespoons vegetable ghee or oil

2 cloves garlic, finely chopped

2.5 cm (1 inch) cube ginger, thinly sliced into matchsticks

1 tablespoon curry wet masala paste (see page 40)

200 g (7 oz) onion, thinly sliced

2 tablespoons fresh coriander leaves, chopped

aromatic salt to taste (see page 39)

1 Clean and prepare the vegetables as necessary.

2 Heat the ghee or oil in a karahi or wok. Stir-fry the garlic and ginger for 20 seconds. Add the masala mix and stir-fry for a further minute. Add the onion. Stir-fry for around 5 minutes.

3 Add the vegetables and the coriander and mix in well. Simmer for a couple of minutes more. Salt to taste and serve.

Dhansak

The most popular of all Parsee dishes is dhansak. This recipe is a simplified version of the traditional method, adapted for vegetables.

SERVES 4

60 g (2 oz) red lentils, split and polished

200 g (7 oz) canned chick peas

2 tablespoons butter ghee

225 g (8 oz) onions, finely chopped

2 cloves garlic, finely chopped

200 g (7 oz) canned tomatoes, strained

3 or 4 pieces red or green bell pepper

1 tablespoon jaggery or brown sugar

200 g (7 oz) canned ratatouille

110 g (4 oz) fresh baby spinach leaves

2 tablespoons fresh coriander leaves, chopped

1 tablespoon Brinjal pickle, finely chopped

1 tablespoon coconut powder

2 teaspoons garam masala (see page 38)

1 teaspoon dried mint

sugar to taste

lemon juice to taste

aromatic salt to taste (see page 39)

MASALA 1

1 teaspoon cummin seeds

1 brown cardamom

5 cm (2 inch) piece cassia bark

½ teaspoon black mustard seeds

MASALA 2

1 teaspoon turmeric

1 teaspoon coriander, ground

1 teaspoon cummin, ground

¼ teaspoon fenugreek seeds, ground

½ teaspoon chilli powder

1 Rinse the lentils and soak them for up to 20 minutes, then drain.

2 Cook the lentils in twice their volume of water for about 20 minutes, add the chick peas and their liquid, then coarsely mash them inside the pan.

3 During stage 2, heat the ghee in the wok, and fry the ingredients of masala 1 for about 30 seconds. Use just enough water to make a paste of masala 2, which you add to the wok and stir-fry for about a minute. Add the onions and garlic and continue to stir-fry for about 10 minutes or until golden.

6 Add the stir-fry to the mashed lentils and the remaining ingredients except for the seasoning (sugar lemon juice and salt).

7 Stir until hot, season and serve.

Brinjal Bhajee

SERVES 4

225 g (8 oz) aubergine, chopped and
   blanched
4 tablespoons mustard blend oil
1 teaspoon panch phoran (see page 39)
½ teaspoon celery seeds
2 bay leaves
200 g (7 oz) onion tarka (see page 43)
2 tablespoons curry masala paste
   (see page 40)
110 g (4 oz) celery, finely chopped
110 g (4 oz) spring onion finely chopped
1–2 red chillies, freshly chopped
1 tablespoon red pepper, chopped
½ tablespoon green pepper, chopped
½ tablespoon yellow pepper, chopped
1 tablespoon coriander leaves, finely
   chopped
1 teaspoon jaggery or brown sugar
juice of 1 lemon
aromatic salt to taste (see page 39)

1 Heat the oil in a karahi, stir-fry the
panch phoran, celery seeds and bay
leaves for 30 seconds.
2 Add the onion tarka and the masala
paste and stir-fry for about 2 minutes.
3 Add about 175 ml (6 fl oz) water, and
stir to the simmer. Add the celery,
spring onion, chillies and peppers, plus
the aubergine, and simmer for about
6 minutes.
4 Add the coriander, sugar and lemon
juice. Simmer for a while longer. Add
salt to taste and serve at once.

Mushroom Bhajee

SERVES 4

450 g (1 lb) mushrooms, washed and thinly
   sliced
3 tablespoons vegetable ghee
2 teaspoons garlic, finely chopped
6–8 green cardamom pods
3 teaspoons curry masala dry mix
   (see page 40)
2 tablespoons green bell peppers, finely
   chopped
2 teaspoons fresh red chilli, chopped
4 cherry tomatoes, quartered
1 tablespoon fresh coriander leaves, finely
   chopped
salt to taste

1 Heat the ghee and fry the garlic and
cardamoms at quite a high heat for just
1 minute. Add the masala mix, with
just enough water to make a paste in
the pan, and stir-fry for a couple more
minutes.
2 Add the peppers, chilli and tomatoes,
and when sizzling, add the mushrooms
and briskly, but carefully, so as not to
break them, stir them around just to
coat them. Throw in the coriander, salt
to taste and serve.

Vegetable Bhajee

*Bhajee, or bhaji, means literally 'a dryish
vegetable curry'.*

SERVES 4

3 tablespoons sunflower oil
225 g (8 oz) onion, thinly sliced
4 cloves garlic, finely chopped
2–3 fresh green cayenne chillies, chopped
2 tablespoons green pepper, chopped
4 large potatoes, peeled, cooked and
   quartered
4 large carrots, cooked and chopped into
   roundels
110 g (4 oz) frozen peas, thawed
110 g (4 oz) frozen Kenyan beans, thawed
2 tomatoes, chopped
1 tablespoon sugar
2 teaspoons garam masala (see page 38)
1 tablespoon freshly squeezed lemon juice
salt to taste

MASALA
½ teaspoon turmeric
½ teaspoon coriander
4 cloves, crushed
5cm (2 in) piece cassia bark
2 green cardamom pods, crushed

1 Heat the oil in a karahi or wok, stir-
fry the masala ingredients for about a
minute. Add the onion, garlic, chilli
and pepper and continue to stir-fry for
about 3 minutes. Add the potatoes and
continue to stir-fry for a couple of
minutes to coat them with the mixture.
2 Add the carrots, peas, beans and
tomatoes. Stir in enough water to keep
things mobile. Simmer for 2 more
minutes.
3 Add the sugar and garam masala and
stir and simmer for a final minute.
7 Stir in the lemon juice, salt to taste
and serve.

Brinjal Bhajee

Keema ke Rajma Mattar Curry

Soya Mince Curry with Beans and Peas

Keema means 'minced meat'. But using soy granules, we can create an excellent vegetarian keema curry, enhanced with peas and red kidney beans. You can also use this keema as a samosa filling.

SERVES 4

225 g (8 oz) soya mince granules

2 tablespoons butter ghee

½ teaspoon turmeric

1 teaspoon fennel seeds

½ teaspoon cummin seeds

4 cloves garlic, finely chopped

5-cm (2-inch) cube fresh ginger, finely chopped

225 g (8 oz) onion, finely chopped

1 or 2 green chillies, chopped

1 tablespoon red bell pepper, chopped

6 canned plum tomatoes

1 tablespoon tomato ketchup

150 ml (5 fl oz) canned tomato soup

150 g (5½ oz) frozen peas, thawed

200 g (7 oz) canned red kidney beans, drained and rinsed

1 tablespoon fresh coriander leaves, chopped

1 tablespoon fresh mint leaves, chopped

1 tablespoon dry fenugreek leaves

1 tablespoon garam masala (see page 38)

aromatic salt to taste (see page 39)

4 eggs, hardboiled and halved

MASALA

2 teaspoons coriander, ground

1 teaspoon cummin, ground

1 teaspoon chilli powder

4 cloves

6 green cardamoms

½ teaspoon mango powder

½ teaspoon lovage seeds

1 Soak the soya granules in an equal quantity of cold water for 30 minutes, then drain.

2 Heat the ghee in a karahi and fry the turmeric and seeds for about 20 seconds. Add the garlic and ginger and stir-fry for about 30 seconds more, then add the masala ingredients, with just enough water to make a paste, and stir for a further minute.

3 Add the onion, chillies and peppers and continue to stir-fry for a minimum of 5 more minutes, or longer, until golden. Add a little water if it dries up too much.

4 Add the tomatoes, ketchup and soup, and the drained soya granules, peas and beans. Stir until it all is hot.

5 Mix in the leaves and garam masala and salt to taste.

6 Garnish with the eggs and serve with plain rice and/or puris or parathas.

Dopiaza

Do means 'two' and piaza means 'onions', and this north Indian dish gets its name from the double batch of onions used in its preparation.

SERVES 4

675 g (1½ lb) cooked vegetables of your choice

3 tablespoons ghee

225 g (8 oz) onion, thinly sliced

2 tablespoons mustard blend oil

3–4 cloves garlic, finely chopped

110 g (4 oz) onion, finely chopped

200 ml (7 fl oz) fragrant stock (see page 39) or water

2 or 3 fresh red chillies, shredded (optional)

2 tablespoons fresh coriander leaves, finely chopped

2 teaspoons garam masala (see page 38)

aromatic salt to taste (see page 39)

MASALA

2 teaspoons coriander, roasted and ground

½ teaspoon cummin, roasted and ground

1 teaspoon turmeric

1 teaspoon chilli powder

1 Heat the ghee in a karahi or wok on a lowish heat and stir-fry the sliced onions until they are brown (it will take at least 15 minutes – see page 43). Then set aside in a bowl.

2 Add just enough water to the masala ingredients to make a thin paste.

3 Using the same karahi or wok, heat the mustard oil and stir-fry the garlic for 1 minute. Add the masala paste and continue to stir-fry for another couple of minutes, until the oil 'floats'.

4 Add the chopped onions, stock or water, and chillies (if using), and simmer for about 5 more minutes.

5 Add the onions cooked at the beginning, the coriander leaves, garam masala and the vegetables of your choice.

6 Simmer for about 5 more minutes. Salt to taste and serve with tarka dhal and parathas.

Asparagus, Potato and Carrot Dopiaza

Bindi Bhajee

Stir-fried Okra Curry

Okra, also known as 'ladies' fingers', are appalling if cooked badly, when they ooze an unpleasantly sticky, yet tasteless, sap. This can easily be prevented by cooking them in the briefest possible time, without cutting them, and immediately prior to serving them.

SERVES 4
450 g (1 lb) okra
6 tablespoons mustard blend oil
2 teaspoons black mustard seeds
½ teaspoon black cummin seeds
4 tablespoons pink onion, chopped
2 tomatoes, finely chopped
1 tablespoon green pepper, sliced lengthways
2–3 fresh green chillies, sliced lengthways
1 tablespoon sugar
juice of 1 lemon, freshly squeezed
1 tablespoon coriander leaves, chopped
salt to taste

MASALA
½ teaspoon turmeric
1 teaspoon cummin, ground
1 teaspoon coriander seeds, ground
½ teaspoon chilli powder
1 teaspoon cassia bark, ground
½ teaspoon green cardamom seeds, ground

1 Carefully wash the okra.
2 Heat the oil in a karahi or wok, stir-fry the seeds for 30 seconds, then add the masala ingredients and onion and stir-fry for 5 minutes.
3 Add the tomatoes, pepper, chillies and sugar and stir-fry for 5 minutes.
4 Add the uncut okra to the karahi and stir-fry for 5 minutes. Stir gently. If the okra gets bruised or cut it will go very sappy. Add water by the spoonful to keep things mobile.
5 Add the lemon juice and the chopped coriander leaves.
6 Stir-fry for 5 minutes more. If the okra were tender to start with they are now cooked perfectly. Add salt to taste and serve at once. Do not refrigerate or freeze this dish – it will go sappy and mushy.

Kofta

Kofta simply means 'balls'. In this vegetarian version, the balls are coated in gram flour batter, then deep-fried. Making the sauce first enables you to get the balls hot and ready to serve in the pre-cooked sauce.

SERVES 4
SAUCE
2 tablespoons butter ghee or vegetable oil
225 g (8 oz) onion, finely chopped
OR 350 g (12 oz) onion gravy (see page 43)
150 ml (5 fl oz) fragrant stock (see page 39)
aromatic salt to taste (see page 39)

SAUCE MASALA
1 teaspoon garlic powder
1 teaspoon turmeric
¼ teaspoon asafoetida
1 teaspoon garam masala (see page 38)
1 teaspoon dry fenugreek leaves
¼ teaspoon caraway seeds

KOFTA MASALA
1 teaspoon coriander, ground
½ teaspoon mango powder
¼ teaspoon chilli powder
2 teaspoons cummin seeds
2 teaspoons gram flour

KOFTAS
450 g (1 lb) mashed potatoes
4 tablespoons peas
2 tablespoons cashew nuts, coarsely ground
1 or 2 red chillies, finely chopped
1 teaspoon sugar
½ teaspoon aromatic salt (see page 39)
oil for deep-frying

GARNISH
swirls of double cream
chopped almonds, toasted

1 To make the sauce, heat the ghee and fry the sauce masala ingredients for a minute, then add the onion and stir-fry for about 10 minutes, or until golden. If using onion gravy, it just needs to be brought to the simmer.
2 Simmer for the next 10 minutes or so, adding the stock or water until it starts to thicken. The sauce should be neither too thick nor too runny. Keep simmering, or allow to cool then reheat; add it to the balls at stage 6.
3 To make the balls, mix together all the kofta and kofta masala ingredients except the gram flour. The mixture should be glutinous enough to form into balls. Roll into balls about 2 cm in diameter.
4 Mix the gram flour with enough water to make it thin enough to coat the balls, but still adhere to them. Coat the balls.
5 Heat the oil in a deep-fry pan to 190°C/375°F and fry the koftas until they are hot throughout and golden in colour (about 3 minutes).
6 To serve, place the balls in a serving dish. Pour the warm sauce over them and garnish with cream and nuts.

Vegetable Jalfrezi

Jal, or jhal, in Bengali means 'spicy', and frezi means 'stir-fry'.

675 g (1½ lb) cooked vegetables, of your
choice
4 tablespoons ghee or vegetable oil
½ teaspoon turmeric
1 teaspoon white cummin seeds
1 teaspoon mustard seeds
4 garlic cloves, finely chopped
5-cm (2-inch) piece fresh ginger, finely
chopped (optional)
2 tablespoons curry masala mix (see page 40)
1 large Spanish onion, peeled and chopped
2 or more green chillies, sliced
½ green pepper, seeded and coarsely chopped
½ red pepper, seeded and coarsely chopped
2 tablespoons coriander leaves, freshly chopped
2 or 3 fresh tomatoes, chopped
2 teaspoons garam masala (see page 38)
salt to taste
lemon juice

1 Heat the ghee or oil and fry the
turmeric and seeds for about 30
seconds. Add the garlic and ginger and
stir-fry for about 30 seconds more, then
add the masala mix, with just enough
water to make a paste, and stir for a
further minute.
2 Add the onion, chillies and peppers
and continue to stir-fry for about 2
more minutes.
3 Add the coriander, tomatoes and
garam masala, and stir-fry for a further
2 minutes on medium heat. Add the
cooked vegetables and a little water if
needed.
4 Salt to taste, and serve with a
squeeze of lemon juice.

Korma

SERVES 4
675 g (1½ lb) cooked vegetables of your
choice, chopped
3 tablespoons vegetable oil
1–3 teaspoons garlic, finely chopped
200 g (7 oz) onion, finely chopped
150 ml (5 fl oz) single cream
65 g (⅓ block) creamed coconut
1 tablespoon fresh coriander leaves, very
finely chopped
2 teaspoons ground almonds
2–3 teaspoons garam masala (see page 38)
1 teaspoon white sugar
salt to taste

MASALA
2 teaspoons ground coriander
2 teaspoons curry masala dry mix
(see page 40)
½ teaspoon cummin, ground
½ teaspoon turmeric
½ teaspoon chilli powder

1 Mix the masala ingredients with
enough water to achieve an easily
pourable paste.
2 Heat the oil in a karahi or wok until
it is nearly smoking. Add the garlic and
stir-fry briskly for 20–30 seconds. Add
the spice paste and keep on stirring for
about another minute.
3 Add the onion, reduce the heat, and
stir-fry for at least 10 minutes (at most
20), until the mixture has thoroughly
softened and caramelised.
4 Take the pan off the stove and purée
the mixture using an electric blender.
5 Add the cream and coconut. When
melted, add the vegetables and simmer
until hot, adding just enough water to
keep a thickish texture.
6 Add the remaining ingredients,
including salt to taste, and continue
cooking and stirring for a final minute
or so. Serve with pullao rice.

Madras

*Curries called 'Madras' at the British Indian
restaurant indicate a fairly hot curry, i.e. hot
but not the hottest.*

SERVES 4
675 g (1½ lb) overall weight mixture of
cauliflower, broccoli, beans, peas, carrot,
tomato, sweetcorn, etc., weighed after
peeling and preparing
½ teaspoon turmeric
½ teaspoon cummin, ground
1 teaspoon black pepper, freshly milled
1–3 teaspoons chilli powder
3 tablespoons vegetable oil
½ Spanish onion, peeled and thinly sliced
450 g (1 lb) curry masala gravy (see page 40)
4 plum tomatoes, fresh or canned and
strained
2 teaspoons garam masala (see page 38)
½ teaspoon dry fenugreek leaves
2 tablespoons ground almonds
1 tablespoon lemon juice, freshly squeezed
aromatic salt to taste (see page 39)

1 Add just enough water to the
turmeric, cummin, pepper and chilli
powder to make a paste.
2 Heat the oil in a wok or karahi, then
add the paste and stir-fry for a minute
or so. Add the onion and stir-fry for a
further couple of minutes. Add the
curry gravy, and the tomatoes.
3 Continue to simmer on low heat,
stirring from time to time, for around
10 minutes, until everything is
cohesively cooked – it should turn
darker and thicker.
4 Meanwhile, cook the vegetables and
keep them hot
5 At the end of stage 3, add the
remaining ingredients, including the
vegetables and salt to taste, adding a
little water if it needs loosening. Cook
for a couple of minutes more and serve.

Patia

This Parsee dish patia, meaning 'fish curry', is sour (tamarind), hot (chilli) and sweet (from jaggery, or honey or brown sugar). This non-fishy vegetable version is untraditional. 'Demi-vegetarians' may like to add cooked prawns at stage 4.

SERVES 4

500 g (1 lb 2 oz) cooked vegetables of your choice

3 tablespoons yoghurt

150 g (5½ oz) onion, roughly chopped

4 cloves garlic, chopped

2.5 cm (1 inch) cube fresh ginger, chopped

2 tablespoons mustard blend or vegetable oil

½ red pepper, very finely chopped

1–3 fresh red chillies, chopped

2 tablespoons jaggery or brown sugar

2 or 3 tomatoes, finely chopped

1 tablespoon tomato purée

1 tablespoon tomato ketchup

2 tablespoons tamarind purée (see page 45)

aromatic salt to taste (see page 39)

MASALA 1

½ teaspoon mustard seeds

½ teaspoon fennel seeds

½ teaspoon cummin seeds

½ teaspoon fenugreek seeds

MASALA 2

2 teaspoons paprika

1 teaspoon chilli powder (optional)

1 teaspoon coriander, ground

½ teaspoon cummin, ground

1 Pound or blend the yoghurt, onion, garlic and ginger, plus 4 tablespoons water, to a paste.

2 Heat the oil, and fry the ingredients of masala 1 until the seeds start to pop, for about 30 seconds. Add the masala 2 ingredients and cook for a further minute. Lower the heat and add the yoghurt blend, red pepper and chillies, and stir-fry for about 10 minutes.

3 Add the jaggery, tomatoes, purée, ketchup and tamarind purée to the fried mixture, and simmer until you have a thick, dark gravy (at most 5 more minutes).

4 Add the vegetables and salt to taste. Simmer until hot right through then serve with rice, chupatti and chutneys.

Roghan Josh

The word 'roghan' means 'red' in Kashmiri, while in Persian, where the dish originated, it means 'clarified butter'. Traditionally the dish becomes red by frying alkanet root in ghee.

SERVES 4

350 g (12 oz) root vegetables such as sweet potato

325 g (11½ oz) other cooked vegetables of your choice

130 g (4½ oz) plain yoghurt

2 teaspoons beetroot, mashed

225g (8 oz) onion, finely chopped

5 cm (2 inch) piece fresh ginger, roughly chopped

2 cloves garlic, finely chopped

400 g (14 oz) canned tomatoes, strained

4 tablespoons butter ghee

5 or 6 flakes alkanet root (optional)

1 tablespoon fresh coriander leaves, chopped

2 teaspoons garam masala (see page 38)

aromatic salt to taste (see page 39)

MASALA 1

6 green cardamoms

1 brown cardamom

6 cloves

3 or 4 pieces cassia bark

4 bay leaves

20–25 saffron strands

MASALA 2

2 teaspoons paprika

½ teaspoon chilli powder

1 teaspoon coriander, roasted and ground

1 teaspoon allspice, freshly ground

1 Peel and chop the sweet potatoes and bring them and the ingredients of masala 1 to the boil in just enough water to cover them. Cook until tender. Retain the potatoes, aromatic water and spices for use in stage 6.

2 Mix the yoghurt with the cooked vegetables.

3 Put the onion, ginger, garlic and tomato into a blender, and pulse to a purée.

4 Heat the ghee in a wok. Add the alkanet root (if using). As soon as the ghee turns red, strain the root though a metal strainer, discarding it and keeping the ghee.

5 Reheat the ghee. Stir-fry the ingredients of masala 2 with a spoon or two of water for a couple of minutes, until the ghee 'floats'. Add the purée and continue to stir-fry for 3 or 4 more minutes.

6 Add the cooked vegetables including the sweet potato with its aromatic liquid, and bring to the simmer

7 Add the fresh coriander leaves, garam masala, and once simmering again, salt to taste, then serve.

Roghan Josh with peanuts, tomato and karela gourd.
Note the red oil (see alkanet root, page 16)

Phal

Phal, a creation of the British Indian restaurant, is the hottest curry their cooks can create.

SERVES 4

675 g (1½ lb) cooked vegetables of your
   choice
2 tablespoons ghee
4 teaspoons chilli powder, extra hot
3 cloves garlic, finely chopped
450 g (1 lb) curry masala gravy
   (see page 40)
175 g (6 oz) tomatoes, chopped
4–8 fresh red and green chillies, chopped
salt to taste

1 Heat the ghee in a karahi or wok. Stir-fry the chilli powder for 2 minutes until the ghee 'floats'. Beware it can be choking so open a window! Add the garlic and continue to stir-fry for 30 seconds.

2 Add the curry gravy and bring to the simmer. Add the tomatoes, fresh chillies and salt to taste. When simmering add the vegetables and when they are hot through, serve.

Tikka Masala

The world's most popular curry is tikka masala. The concept is simple: make a tandoori or tikka item and make a typical curry-house rich, creamy, tangy, mild gravy to go with it, but colour it red.

SERVES 4

675g (1½ lb) cooked vegetables of your
   choice
2 tablespoons ghee
3 cloves garlic, finely chopped
225 g (8 oz) onion, very finely chopped
1½ tablespoons curry masala paste
   (see page 40)
1½ tablespoons tandoori masala paste (see
   page 41)
6 canned plum tomatoes
1 tablespoon white spirit vinegar
1 tablespoon tomato ketchup
175 ml (6 fl oz) canned tomato soup
½ green pepper, chopped
4 green chillies, chopped
100 ml (3½ fl oz) single cream
2 tablespoons coconut milk powder
1 tablespoon garam masala (see page 38)
1 tablespoon dried fenugreek leaves
1 tablespoon fresh coriander leaves,
   chopped
aromatic salt to taste (see page 39)

1 Heat the ghee in a large karahi. Stir-fry the garlic for 30 seconds, then add the onion and stir-fry for 8–10 minutes until golden brown.

2 Add the pastes and stir-fry for 2 minutes. Add the tomatoes, vinegar, ketchup, soup, green pepper and chillies.

3 Stir-fry for 5 minutes or so, then add the cooked vegetables, cream, coconut milk powder, garam masala and leaves. Simmer for a further 5 minutes, adding a little water if needed. Salt to taste and serve.

Vindaloo

This dish was brought to India by the Portuguese, when they first arrived in Goa in 1498. Called 'vino d'ahos' it consisted of pork, marinated in wine vinegar and garlic (ahos), and is still found in Portugal today. At the curry-house vindaloo bears no resemblance to its Goan namesake. Here is a vegetable adaptation of the classic dish.

SERVES 4

675 g (1½ lb) cooked vegetables of your
   choice
3 tablespoons ghee
1 teaspoon cummin seeds
6 cloves garlic, chopped
225 g (8 oz) onions, chopped
4 fresh green cayenne chillies, chopped
2 tablespoons lemon juice, freshly squeezed
1 tablespoon fresh coriander leaves,
   chopped
2 teaspoons garam masala (see page 38)
aromatic salt (see page 39)

MASALA MIX

50 ml (2 fl oz) red wine
2 tablespoons red wine vinegar
6 cloves garlic, crushed
3 tablespoons red chilli, finely chopped
1 teaspoon aromatic salt
10 cloves
6 green cardamoms
5 cm (2 inch) piece cassia bark

1 Peel and chop the vegetables and bring them and the masala mix ingredients to the boil adding just enough water to cover them. Cook until tender. Retain with the resultant aromatic liquid and spices for use in stage 3.

2 Heat the ghee in a karahi. Stir-fry the seeds and garlic for a minute, then add the onions and chillies and continue to stir-fry for 5 minutes.

3 Add the cooked vegetables and aromatic liquid from stage 1, and bring to the simmer.

4 Add the lemon juice, fresh coriander leaves and garam masala. Once simmering again, salt to taste and serve.

Tikka Masala with okra, avocado and sweet potato

Kohlrabi

Kohlrabi is a member of the cabbage (*Brassica*) family but instead of having crisp tightly packed leaves it grows as a single spherical bulb (it is, in fact, a tuber, though it grows above ground) up to the size of a grapefruit. It has been recorded as being cultivated in northern Europe by the 1400s, although it may have been used by the Romans. The two main varieties grown are a pale green (Vienna white) and beetroot red (purple Vienna). Kohlrabi is a good source of fibre and protein and yields 18 calories per 100 g (3½ oz).

Leek
Vilayaiti, lasson

A member of the onion family, native to the Mediterranean, and introduced to Britain by the Romans, the leek is now an important symbol to the Welsh. To prepare, cut off the roots and the tops of the leaves, discard any damaged outer leaves and ensure there is no gritty soil between the remaining leaves. Slice lengthways or into roundels. These, incidentally, make great decorative rings for garnishing. Leek is an excellent source of vitamin C and is also good for vitamins A, B, and E, potassium, fibre, iron and magnesium. Leek yields 30 calories per 100 g (3½ oz).

Legumes
Dhal

Legumes include beans, lentils and peas. In certain cases the pods (see Mangetout) as well as the seeds (called pulses) are edible, and they are eaten fresh. The seeds can also be dried, in which form they can be stored for months or years. This process has been practised for thousands of years, and is a simple one: the pulses are picked, podded and spread out to dry in the hot sun for a few days. (That is why pulses in general, and chick peas in particular, should be carefully picked over before using, as it is not uncommon to find small stones and pieces of grit among the seeds. Bigger producers now use convection ovens to dry the pulses, but they should still be examined first.) To reconstitute dried pulses it is necessary to soak them; the larger and harder the pulses, the longer the soak (chick peas and red kidney beans, for example, need twelve hours or more). The soaking and subsequent rinsing removes minor toxins called lectins, present to a lesser or greater degree in all pulses. The greatest carrier of lectins is the red kidney bean, which must always be soaked, then fast boiled for ten minutes at the start of the cooking process to rid them of toxins. The range of pulses is enormous. Not only are they remarkable for their nutritional value being high in protein, fats, carbohydrates, minerals and vitamins, but they are filling and, with spices and other flavourings added, extremely tasty. The calorie content of raw legumes varies between 100 and 380 calories per 100 g (3½ oz).

Lotus Root
Ambal, bhen

A rather extraordinary perforated aquatic root, indigenous to, and very popular in China, Pakistan and Kashmir. Lotus root is available canned and occasionally fresh at specialist Asian greengrocers in the UK. To prepare, peel the fresh root, and cut it into roundels. Keep it immersed until you cook it. Boil, steam or microwave until tender, or blanch and stir-fry. Lotus root yields 70 calories per 100 g (3½ oz).

Maize
Makka, bhutta

Maize is a member of the grass family, and is more commonly known as sweetcorn. It is native to the Americas, where it has been used dried to make flour, and fresh as a vegetable since long before the time of Columbus. It is a cereal crop, providing many well-known dried breakfast products, and popcorn at the cinema! As a vegetable it is eaten 'on the cob' with its hundreds of golden, soft, tasty grains. They are very high in starch and sugar and excellent for protein. Boiling converts the starch to sugar, but try slowly frying them, and allowing them to caramelise. Miniature cobs (baby corn, about 5–7.5cm/2–3 inches long) have been developed and are popular in oriental cookery. These are readily available in supermarkets everywhere, both fresh and canned. 'On the cob', maize is high in starch, low in protein and yields 123 calories per 100 g (3½ oz); unsweetened, canned it yields 76 calories per 100 g (3½ oz).

Mangetout

Val

Mangetout is a member of the pea (legume) family, hence its alternative names, snow pea or sugar pea). It grows on thin vines (the leaves of which are also eaten by the Chinese and are occasionally available from Chinatown). Mangetout are flat, bright, fleshy, green young pea pods, containing miniature peas. The mangetout is in fact a pulse, but is eaten before it matures and, like the green bean, both pod and seeds are eaten after topping and tailing. It gets its name from the French *mange tout*, meaning 'eat all'. Mangetout contains small amounts of lectin, the toxin present in all pulses, so should ideally be cooked before eating. Being flat and relatively small, it makes a perfect stir-fry subject, its brief cooking enhancing and retaining the green colour. Mangetout is an excellent source of vitamin C and is also good for fibre, magnesium, iron, and vitamin B. Raw mangetout yields 56 calories per 100 g (3½ oz).

Mango

Am

Mango is mostly enjoyed as a fruit (see page 152), but is also used as a vegetable, particularly for pickling. The varieties used for these purposes are small and green when ripe. They are also very sour. It is these mangoes which when dried are ground into the very sour mango powder, *am chur*.

Mushroom

Khumbi

Technically, the mushroom is not a vegetable but an edible fungus. The French were the first to cultivate them. Now there are literally hundreds of edible species to choose from, the most familiar of which include field, cup, button and flat. Other less familiar cultivated varieties, each with its own distinctive flavour, include beefsteak fungus, parasol, cep, blewit, pleurotte and oyster. To prepare them (they are all handled in the same way) wash and dry them, peeling only if necessary, then cut as required, and add without further cooking to the curry of your choice. Mushrooms are a good source of vitamin B, potassium and fibre. They yield 14 calories per 100 g (3½ oz).

Dried mushrooms

For as long as can be remembered the Chinese have preserved their mushrooms by drying them in the sun so that they then keep more or less indefinitely. To reconstitute them, place in a large bowl and pour in enough boiling water to fill the bowl. Leave to soak for 30 minutes then drain. Dried mushrooms give a distinctive flavour, colour and texture to Chinese cooking.

Dried black or brown mushroom (*dong-gu*) have a thick cap and a fairly strong fragrance. The larger ones with a pale colour and cracked skins have the best flavour. Cloud ears or wood ears (*mu-er*) are grown on trees and are used mainly for texture. They are brown and have a curly leaf shape. Silver fungus, snow ear or white wood fungus are similar to cloud or wood ears and whitish in colour. They are crunchy and pretty but rare, and so are extremely expensive. They are available dried or canned. Straw mushrooms are small and teardrop shaped. They are very flavourful but are rarely available in the West in any form other than canned. Other types occasionally available over here are golden needle mushrooms and the enormous Hunan umbrella mushroom.

Restaurant Vegetable Favourites

Here are such popular restaurant curries as Achari, Afghani, Ceylon, Kashmiri, Malai, Malaya, Methi, Mughlai, Korma and Niramish, each with their own distinctive features, described in the introduction to each appropriate recipe. As in the previous chapter, they can be adapted to a single vegetable, or a combination. The remaining recipes are intended for specific named vegetables, for example the highly adaptable potato. Aloo ghobi, potato with cauliflower, and Bombay potato are restaurant favourites, and great dishes. Nothing can be simpler than jeera aloo, potato cooked with just four ingredients. Rather more complex to prepare, but just as versatile as the potato, in that it can be cut into any shape, fried, and crumbled is paneer (Indian cheese). Recipes here include paneer curry with peas, spinach, and sweet potato, plus a novel paneer tikka kebab, where cubes of the cheese are tandoori-marinated before being grilled on skewers. Also in this chapter is a seriously hot recipe – naga curry, made from the hottest chillies.

Achari Sabzi, here using soya chunks (top right) and plenty of garlic

Achari Sabzi
Vegetables Curried with Pickle

Achar means 'pickle', and achari means 'curried in a pickle base'.

SERVES 4

500 g (1½ lb) soya chunks, weighed after
  stage 1

4 tablespoons ghee or vegetable oil

½ teaspoon turmeric

1 teaspoon white cummin seeds

1 teaspoon mustard seeds

8–10 cloves garlic, finely chopped

2 tablespoons curry masala dry mix
  (see page 40)

3 tablespoons lime pickle, puréed

2 tablespoons garlic pickle, puréed

225 g (8 oz) onion, chopped

2 or more red chillies, sliced

½ green pepper, coarsely chopped

½ red pepper, coarsely chopped

2 tablespoons fresh coriander leaves,
  chopped

2 or 3 fresh tomatoes, chopped

2 teaspoons garam masala (see page 38)

lemon juice and salt to taste

1 Soak the soya chunks in ample water
for 20 minutes. Drain and press the
chunks to remove excess water.

2 Heat the ghee or oil and fry the
turmeric and seeds for about 30
seconds. Add the garlic and stir-fry for
about 30 seconds more, then add the
masala mix and puréed pickles, with
just enough water to make a paste, and
stir for a further minute.

3 Add the onion, chillies and peppers
and continue to stir-fry for about 5
more minutes.

4 Add the soya chunks, the coriander,
tomatoes, and garam masala, and stir-
fry for about 5 minutes on medium
heat. Add a little water if needed.

Aloo Ghobi Methi

5 When everything is hot, salt to taste,
and serve. It's nice with a squeeze of
lemon juice over the top.

Afghani Sabzi
Vegetables in the Afghan Style

*Afghanistan food is simple fare. Dairy
products, especially yoghurt, are important.
Pulses, wheat and root vegetables grow in
the brief summer and are then dried and
stored for the hard winters.*

SERVES 4

175 g (6 oz) sweet potato

175 g (6 oz) carrot

175 g (6 oz) marrow

175 g (6 oz) leeks, chopped into discs

4 tablespoons vegetable oil

20 peanuts, shelled and peeled

6–8 walnuts

4 cloves garlic, sliced

2 tablespoons tomato juice

4 tablespoons yoghurt

1 tablespoon sultanas (optional)

1 teaspoon aromatic salt (see page 39)

CHAR MASALA – ALL ROASTED AND
GROUND

½ teaspoon green cardamom seeds

½ teaspoon cummin seeds

1 or 2 pieces couch bark

½ teaspoon cloves

1 Cook the sweet potato, carrots and
marrow separately until tender.

2 Wash then slice the leeks into discs,
then press out discs into rings.

3 Heat the oil in a karahi or wok. Stir-
fry the nuts. Remove them from the oil
and set aside.

4 Reheat the oil. Stir-fry the garlic for
30 seconds. Add the char masala and
the tomato juice and continue to stir-
fry for 30 seconds more. Add the leek
rings and continue to stir-fry for about

3–4 minutes, until they become
translucent.

5 Add the yoghurt and the nuts and
sultanas, and when sizzling, add the
cooked vegetables.

6 Stir-fry just long enough for
everything to be hot right through,
then salt to taste and serve with bread
or plain rice and/or with another curry.

Aloo Ghobi Methi
Fenugreek-flavoured Potato and Broccoli Curry

*This simple dish comes from the Punjab.
The food is robustly spiced, with the
intensely savoury fenugreek playing an
important role.*

SERVES 4

225 g (8 oz) broccoli florets, cooked

225 g (8 oz) cauliflower florets, cooked

2 large potatoes, cooked and quartered

4 tablespoons vegetable ghee

110 g (4 oz) onions, sliced

2 cloves garlic, finely sliced

2 or 3 fresh tomatoes, halved

1 green chilli, chopped

salt to taste

fresh lemon wedges

MASALA

1 teaspoon mustard seeds

1 teaspoon curry masala dry mix (see page
  40)

½ teaspoon ground fenugreek seeds

½ teaspoon dry fenugreek leaves, ground

½ teaspoon chilli powder

½ teaspoon garam masala (see page 38)

1 Heat the ghee in a karahi or wok,
and stir-fry the onions and garlic for
about 3 minutes.

2 Add the masala ingredients with a
spoon or two of water, and continue
stir-frying for a couple more minutes.

3 Add the tomatoes and chilli, and stir-fry for 5 minutes.

4 Add the florets, and just enough water to keep things mobile. Simmer for about 5 minutes, or until the florets are fully tender.

5 Add the potato, squeeze in the lemon juice, and salt to taste. Mix well, heat through, and serve.

Bombay Potato

A curry-house classic, and yet another British restaurant invention.

SERVES 4

500 g (1 lb 2 oz) new potatoes, cooked and
   optionally peeled

4 tablespoons vegetable oil

150 g (5½ oz) onion, thinly sliced

1 tablespoon green bell pepper, chopped

8 tablespoons curry masala gravy
   (see page 40)

2 tomatoes, halved

1 tablespoon fresh coriander leaves, chopped

salt to taste

MASALA

½ teaspoon turmeric

½ teaspoons chilli powder

¼ teaspoon mango powder

¼ teaspoon wild onion seeds

1 Heat the oil, and stir-fry the masala ingredients for 30 seconds.

2 Add the onion and the pepper, and continue to stir-fry for a further 3 minutes, adding small amounts of water as necessary.

3 Add the curry gravy. Stir-fry for 2 minutes then add the potatoes,

The brilliant natural red of the large chillies sets off the browns of the Jeera Aloo. In the foreground are some ultra-hot Naga chillies (see page108)

tomatoes and the leaves and simmer for 5 minutes.

4 Salt to taste and serve.

Ceylon Curry

A hot, creamy, tangy curry, with coconut milk, dried chillies and lemon.

SERVES 4

675 g (1½ lb) cooked vegetables of your
   choice

3 tablespoons mustard blend oil

1–3 cloves garlic, finely chopped

200 g (7 oz) finely chopped onion

1–4 dried red chillies

6–10 fresh or dried curry leaves

milk for thinning

65 g (⅓ block) creamed coconut, chopped

150 ml (5 fl oz) single cream

1 tablespoon freshly squeezed lemon juice

salt to taste

MASALA

2 teaspoons curry masala dry mix
   (see page 40)

1 teaspoon ground coriander

½ teaspoon turmeric

1 Cut the vegetables into bite-sized cubes.

2 Mix the masala ingredients with enough water to achieve an easily pourable paste.

3 Heat the oil in a karahi or wok until it is nearly smoking. Add the garlic and briskly stir-fry for 20–30 seconds. Add the above paste, and keep on stirring for about another minute.

4 Add the onion and reducing the heat, stir-fry for at least 5 minutes until the mixture has thoroughly softened.

5 Optionally, take the pan off the stove and purée the mixture, using the electric hand blender.

6 Return the pan to the stove adding the chillies, curry leaves, and purée, and add a little milk if it looks dry, and achieve a simmer.

7 Add the coconut and the cream, and stir thoroughly until the coconut is melted. The sauce should be quite runny (add more milk if necessary).

8 Add the cooked vegetables, and when everything is hot right through, add the lemon juice.

9 Salt to taste and serve with lemon rice (see page 169).

Jeera Aloo
Potato Cooked with Cummin

Just five ingredients make this one of the simplest dishes in this book. It works equally well as a starter, or as a main course dish.

SERVES 4 (AS A STARTER)

450 g (1 lb) cooked baby new potatoes,
   optionally skinned

50 g (2 oz) salted butter

1 tablespoon white cummin seeds

2 tablespoons ground cummin

salt to taste

4 large red chillies (optional)

1 Melt the butter in your karahi to quite a high heat, but be careful not to burn it. Add the seeds and stir-fry for about 30 seconds. Lower the heat, add the ground cummin and continue to stir-fry for a further 30 seconds, then add 3 or 4 tablespoons of water and stir-fry for about a minute more.

2 Add the potatoes and briskly stir-fry for about 2 minutes. Salt to taste and serve.

3 If you wish to serve in a large red chilli or red bell pepper, soften it first by grilling it until it blackens a little. Then slit it open carefully, and scoop out the pith and seeds before stuffing.

Kashmiri Curry

Kashmir was the cool summer home of the Moghul emperors. Their chefs perfected the most aromatic of all the food of the subcontinent, three examples of which are korma, roghan josh, and Balti. For reasons known best to itself, the curry house has its own interpretation, wide of the real Kashmiri mark, but popular in its own way, particularly with those who enjoy fruity curries. Tinned lychees, pineapple, banana, cream and coconut, are featured here, combined with curry gravy.

SERVES 4
675 g (1½ lb) cooked vegetables of your
   choice
1 tablespoon ghee
2 or 3 cloves garlic, finely chopped
3 or 4 tablespoons onions, finely sliced
225 g (8 oz) curry masala gravy
   (see page 40)
½ tablespoon red/green pepper, finely
   chopped
½ tablespoon yellow pepper, finely chopped
4 pineapple cubes
4 tinned lychees
2 tablespoons juice from the lychees
1 tablespoon dark muscovado sugar
   (optional)
50 ml (2 fl oz) single cream
50ml (2 fl oz) coconut milk
aromatic salt to taste (see page 39)

GARNISH
sliced banana

1 Heat the ghee in a karahi or wok, and stir-fry the garlic for 30 seconds. Add the onions and stir-fry for a further 2 or 3 minutes.
2 Add the peppers, and continue to stir-fry for a couple of minutes more.
3 Bit by bit, over about 5 minutes, add the gravy and briskly stir-fry it so that it thickens.

4 Add the remaining ingredients, including the salt to taste. Simmer until it is hot right through.
5 Garnish with the banana slices and serve with a rice dish.

Malai

Malai means 'cream' so whenever you see a malai curry in India, you know it will be a rich, mild dish. The sauce can be richer even than korma, and milder too unless you add the optional dried chillies. A celebrated favourite is malai kofta, where vegetable rissoles are served in a light, creamy sauce. You can use vegetables of your choice here.

SERVES 4
675g (1½ lb) cooked vegetables of your choice
   OR kofta balls (see pages 86)
2 tablespoons curry masala dry mix
   (see page 40)
3 tablespoons vegetable oil
2–3 cloves garlic, finely chopped
225 g (8 oz) onion, very finely chopped
½ green bell pepper, finely chopped
4 dried red chillies (optional)
125 ml (4 fl oz) single cream
aromatic salt to taste (see page 39)

1 Mix the curry masala with just enough water to make a paste.
2 Heat the oil in a karahi and stir-fry the garlic for 30 seconds. Add the masala paste and stir-fry for a couple of minutes, until the oil 'floats'.
3 Add the onion and green pepper and optional chillies, and briskly stir-fry for about 5 minutes.
4 Add the cream and bring to the simmer. Add the vegetables and simmer until everything is hot right through.
5 Salt to taste. Garnish and serve with rice and breads.

Malaya

Malaya curries show their Indian, Chinese and Thai influences. Thin fragrant gravies, based on coconut milk, are flavoured with chillies, ginger, and lemon grass.

SERVES 4
600 g (1 lb 4 oz) cooked vegetables of your
   choice
6 tablespoons mustard blend oil
225 g (8 oz) onion, chopped
3 cloves garlic, finely chopped
1 teaspoon yellow mustard seeds
1 teaspoon black mustard seeds
4 dried red chillies
2 green chillies, chopped
300 ml (½ pint) canned coconut milk
2 stalks lemon grass (optional)
8–12 dried or fresh curry leaves.
8–12 cubes fresh pineapple
salt to taste
lemon juice, freshly squeezed

1 Heat half the oil in a saucepan or small wok and stir-fry the onion and garlic until golden to make a tarka, then set aside (see page 43).
2 Heat the remaining oil in the wok or karahi. Stir-fry the mustard seeds for a few seconds until they pop. Add the chillies, coconut milk, lemon grass (if using) and curry leaves.
3 Simmer and stir for at least 3 minutes to allow the flavours to exude.
4 Add the vegetables and the pineapple.
5 Cook until everything is hot and keep the sauce fairly thick but fluid while cooking by adding a little water as required.
6 Salt to taste. Sprinkle with the lemon juice, and serve with lemon rice (see page 169).

Methi

Methi, pronounced 'may-tee', is fenugreek. The leaf is very savoury and very spicy, and is one of the tastes of the Punjab.

SERVES 4

675 g (1½ lb) cooked vegetables of your
　choice
4 tablespoons butter ghee
2 teaspoons ground coriander
450 g (1 lb) curry masala gravy
　(see page 40)
4 tablespoons dried fenugreek
OR 100 g (3½ oz) fresh fenugreek leaves,
　chopped
2 teaspoons garam masala (see page 38)
2 tablespoons fresh coriander leaves,
　chopped
salt to taste

1 Cut the vegetables into bite-sized cubes.

2 Heat the ghee in a wok or karahi and stir-fry the ground coriander for 3 minutes, then add the gravy and simmer for about 5 more minutes to thicken it a little.

3 Add the fenugreek, garam masala and coriander. Simmer for another 5 minutes, adding a little water if needed to loosen it.

4 Add the vegetables and when hot, salt to taste. Serve with lachadar parathas and raita.

Mughlai Sabzi Korma

Exotic Vegetables Aromatically Spiced in Cream

This creamy dish incorporates saffron and fresh fennel, and makes an interesting comparison with the restaurant-style vegetable korma on page 87. Note the use of edible silver, and proving that not all kormas are mild, please don't omit the traditional chillies!

SERVES 4

600g (1 lb 4 oz) cooked vegetables of your
　choice
20–30 saffron strands
100 ml (3½ fl oz) milk
6 cloves garlic
5-cm (2-inch) cube ginger
85 g (3 oz) fresh fennel
1–3 red chillies
225 g (8 oz) onion
2 tablespoons pistachio nuts
4 tablespoons butter ghee
150 ml (5 fl oz) single cream
4 tablespoons natural yoghurt
3–4 tablespoons fresh coriander leaves,
　finely chopped
aromatic salt to taste (see page 39)

MASALA

seeds from 6 green cardamom pods
4 or 5 cloves
2.5 cm (1 inch) piece cassia bark
1 teaspoon white cummin seeds
1 teaspoon ground coriander
1 teaspoon fennel seeds
⅓ teaspoon ground cinnamon

GARNISH

2 tablespoons onion tarka (see page 43)
edible silver leaf (optional, see page 193)

1 Cut the vegetables into bite-sized cubes.

2 Add the saffron to the milk and bring it to the simmer. Turn off heat and let it stand for 10 minutes, from time to time gently massaging the saffron strands with a spoon to release their colour.

3 Coarsely chop the garlic, ginger, fennel, chillies, onion and nuts, then putting them in the blender, mulch into a pourable purée, using water as needed.

4 Heat the ghee in a wok or karahi. Stir-fry the masala ingredients for 1 minute, then add the purée and most of the fresh coriander. Continue to stir-fry for 3–4 minutes, adding water as needed to prevent sticking.

5 Add the cream and yoghurt, the saffron and milk, and the vegetables and stir-fry until well mixed.

6 Stir-fry until all is heated through. Salt to taste.

7 Serve hot, garnished with the silver leaf (if using), tarka, and the remaining fresh coriander. Serve at once with pullao rice and parathas.

Okra
Bhindi

Green, tapering, seed capsule, with a pointed tip and longitudinal grooves, okra is native to Africa and Asia. Its size ranges from about 6.25 cm (2½ inches) to as much as to 25 cm (10 inches). Select soft not scaly specimens, no more than 11.25 cm (4½ inches) long. Okra, also known as gumbo, bindi or ladies' fingers, can be eaten raw. Once cut it oozes sap, so cut just before a light stir-fry and eat at once. Okra is a good source of vitamin C, potassium and fibre and yields 17 calories per 100 g (3½ oz).

Pak Choi

Pak choi (*Brassica chinensis*) is a member of the cabbage (*Brassica*) family, and is one of many varieties of similar Chinese leaf. Also known as paksoi, bok choi, or celery cabbage, pak choi is increasingly available at supermarkets and greengrocers. Pak choi resembles chard, and grows to about 30 cm (12 inches) as a group of dark green leaves around a bright white stem. All parts are edible lightly cooked, and the stem is delightful raw, being not unlike delicate celery. A variety of pak choi is Chinese flowering cabbage, choy-sum or gai-lan (*Brassica rapa*). This is eaten when young complete with its yellow flowers.

Parsnip

Parsnip is a native European cream-coloured vegetable. It is a long tapering root similar in shape and size to a carrot. Parsnip was almost certainly cultivated by the Greeks and Romans. The high sugar content of parsnip results in a pleasant sweet flesh. To prepare, peel and cook as potato. Parsnip is high in starch, and provides some sugar, fibre and protein. It yields 56 calories per 100 g (3½ oz).

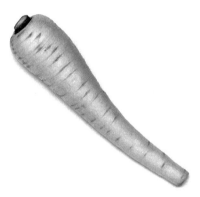

Pea
Mattar

The pea is a member of the legume or pulse family, and is one of mankind's oldest vegetables. Archaeological evidence of the pea has been found in various sites in Europe and the Middle East, dating back some eight thousand years. It is recorded as being in the Indian diet at the time of Christ. It reached China, having been traded down the silk route, and was recorded there by the seventh-century T'ang dynasty. The pea was probably brought to Britain by the Romans, but did not survive their departure, and was re-introduced during the reign of that great gourmet Henry VIII. The small green sphere, several of which grow in a green pod, is called the garden pea, and though it can be dried, it is generally eaten fresh. Unless the pod is very juvenile, it is inedible (see Mangetout). Fresh peas are available in season, and they make a

refreshing change from the ubiquitous frozen version, although it should be said that the frozen pea, being low in water content, is one of the best frozen products on the market. The pea is an excellent source of protein, sugar and starch and it contains numerous minerals. It contains small amounts of lectin, the toxin present in all pulses, so should ideally be cooked before eating. Peas yield 52 calories per 100 g (3½ oz).

Peppercorns
Mirch, milagu

We saw on page 23 that the peppercorn grows as a climbing vine which produces berries, called 'spikes', in long clusters. Green peppercorns are immature when picked, and fresh spikes are occasionally available in the UK. They are quite delicious used as a vegetable to accompany others. To use, remove the peppercorns from the vine and put into any appropriate recipe at virtually any stage. Although prolonged cooking will not hurt them, the berries do not need it, indeed they are delicious raw. Keep refrigerated and use sooner rather than later, as they will start to turn black. The calorie and nutritional content of peppercorns is negligible.

Plantain

Kela

Bananas bred for cooking as vegetables are referred to as plantains, their green skin being generally tougher than that of the banana. Their much firmer, starchier flesh can be sliced or diced and cooked, curried or fried as crisps. Banana flour is made from dried plantains. The plantain is an excellent source of vitamins C and B6, is good for fibre, carbohydrate and potassium, and yields 120 calories per 100 g (3½ oz).

Pointed Gourd

Parwal, potola

This is the slightly larger oval version of the tindoora (see page 107). It grows to between 7.5 and 15 cm (4–6 inches) in length, but in all other respects, the two are similar. A member of the marrow family, called *parwal* in Hindi and *potol* in Bengali, it has a similar flavour to marrow, though it has a slightly bitter after-taste. Like courgettes, its smooth outer case is also edible. Cook whole by

boiling until tender, or curry. The pointed gourd yields 15 calories per 100 g (3½ oz).

Potato

Aloo, batata

The potato was said to have been introduced to England by Francis Drake, following his voyage to Virginia in 1584, and eventually found its way as a 'newcomer' to India and her cooking. The potato is a tuber, round or oval, varying in diameter from 1.25 cm (½ inch) to 10 cm (4 inches). It belongs to the nightshade family, as do aubergine and tomato. No other vegetable is as versatile as the potato which can be boiled, baked, roasted, fried, cut into shapes or mashed. There are numerous varieties of potato, but in general terms: most large red potatoes are best for roasting; most large whites are best for frying and boiling (ergo currying); new potatoes are best scrubbed, not peeled, and boiled whole, and are superb in curries. Potatoes should be stored in the dark. They are high in starch, sugar, fibre and protein and the newer they are, the more vitamin C they have. A word of warning. Old potatoes can develop the toxin solanine in the form of sprouts or green patches, and should be discarded. The berries and any green on a potato is poisonous and should not be eaten. Boiled or baked potatoes are 80 calories per 100 g (3½ oz).

Naga Curry

Naga chillies are the hottest you can get in Bangladesh and India. They are similar to habañeros and Scotch bonnets. Using these chillies makes a seriously hot curry.

SERVES 4

675 g (1½ lb) cooked vegetables of your choice

3 tablespoons oil

4 cloves garlic, finely chopped

225 g (8 oz) onion, finely chopped

1 tablespoon curry masala paste (see page 40)

6 or more fresh green cayenne chillies

2 or more fresh naga, red habañero or Scotch bonnet chillies (see page 98)

1 tablespoon garam masala (see page 38)

salt to taste

MASALA

1 teaspoon cummin seeds

1 teaspoon coriander seeds

1 teaspoon mustard seeds

½ teaspoon lovage seeds

⅓ teaspoon fennel seeds

1 Chop the chillies, removing the stalks and in the case of the habañeros or Scotch bonnets, the seeds and pith. Handle them with care while preparing them, using disposable gloves if necessary: their capsaicin (heat agent) can be really painful in the eyes.

2 Heat the oil in a large karahi or wok. Stir-fry the masala ingredients for 20 seconds then add the garlic. Thirty seconds after that add the onion and stir-fry for 5 minutes.

3 Add the curry paste and stir-fry for another minute. Add a cupful of water and when that is simmering add the chillies.

4 After about 5 minutes, add the vegetables and the garam masala. Once hot, they are ready. Salt to taste, and serve at once.

Mattar Paneer ke Rangaloo

Fried Cheese with Peas and Sweet Potato or Yam Curry

Mattar (peas) paneer is another classic combination, the green of the peas contrasting with the golden colour of the deep-fried paneer. It is taken one step further here by using deep-fried potatoes – cooked as potato chips. For an interesting taste, use sweet potato or yam.

SERVES 4

225 g (8 oz) paneer (see page 46)
225 g (8 oz) sweet potatoes or yams
4 tablespoons butter ghee
2–4 tablespoons garlic, finely chopped
110 g (4 oz) onion purée (see page 43)
150 ml (5 fl oz) milk
2 tablespoons tomato purée
110 g (4 oz) frozen peas, thawed
aromatic salt to taste (see page 39)
vegetable oil for deep-frying

MASALA

2 tablespoons ground coriander
1 teaspoon ground cummin
1 teaspoon turmeric
1 teaspoon garam masala (see page 38)
1 teaspoon paprika
2 teaspoons dried fenugreek leaves

1 Make the paneer, then after a minimum of 1 hour, cut it into potato chip shapes.
2 Scrub the sweet potatoes or yams, removing unwanted matter, and scrape or peel them. Cut into the same shape and size as the paneer.
3 Heat the ghee in a wok or karahi and stir-fry the garlic and onion purée for about 5 minutes. Add the masala and continue for another 2 or 3 minutes,

adding the milk bit by bit. It will give a good creamy gravy consistency if done slowly. Then stir in the tomato purée. Set aside.
4 Heat the deep-fryer to 190°C/375°F and immerse the paneer in the hot oil, piece by piece to prevent the cubes sticking together, and fry for about five minutes, until evenly golden. Remove them from the oil and rest on kitchen paper.
5 Follow with the potato or yam cooked for the same length of time or until tender (like chips). Remove them from the oil and rest on kitchen paper. Take the deep-fryer off the heat.
6 Add the peas to the gravy, and reheat it to simmering. Add the still-hot deep-fried paneer and potato or yam to the gravy. Adjust the thickness of the sauce by adding a little water as needed. Salt to taste and serve when hot.

Paneer Tikka on Skewers

This interesting variation on the paneer theme tandooris the cubes, first by marinating them, then by skewering and grilling them.

SERVES 4

225 g (8 oz) paneer (see page 46)
200 g (7oz) red tandoori marinade
   (see page 41)
8 squares green pepper (same size as the
   paneer)
8 squares onion (same size as the paneer)
salad
lemon wedges

1 Make the paneer, then after a minimum of 1 hour, cut it into cubes. The number of cubes you get will depend on the type of milk you use and the size you cut to, but I suggest cutting it into 16 cubes.
2 Using a non-metallic bowl combine the marinade with the cubes, cover and refrigerate for 6 hours.
3 To cook, preheat the grill to medium. Intersperse eight pieces of paneer on a skewer with the green pepper and onion pieces. Repeat with the second skewer.
4 Place the skewers on a skewer rack or oven rack above an oven tray lined with foil. Place this in the midway position under the grill. Cook for 3 or 4 minutes.
5 Turn the skewers and cook for a further 3 minutes. Serve with lemon wedges and mint raita on a bed of salad.

You can use your paneer tikka in tikka masala curry (see page 90).

Paneer Tikka on skewers with Mint Raita

Radish
Mooli, mougri, mulaka

Radish originated in China as a herbaceous plant with a thick tap root. The varieties favoured in European salads are small round or oval specimens with a bright red skin and brilliant white flesh. The version favoured in the Orient, and now available in the West, is the white radish known in Chinese as *loh baak*, in Japanese as *daikon*, and in Hindi as *mooli*. The white radish grows long (10–40 cm/4–16 inches) and thin. Its colour is overall white. It has a high water content and few nutrients. Its attributes are its crispy texture and appealing light peppery taste. It can be eaten raw, or briefly stir-fried in curries. It is low in nutrients and yields 15 calories per 100 g (3½ oz).

Snake Gourd
Chichinga, poda langai

One of nature's oddities, the *chichinga* or snake gourd (not to be confused with the Orient's snake gourd, which is yellow, squat and curled-up, with a thin tail) grows hanging down from its indigenous Indian tree until maturity, when it is long and thin and up to a metre (39 inches) in length. The picture reflects the reason why it is known locally as the snake gourd. To use, pare off the skin after cooking, eating only the flesh. The snake gourd yields 20 calories per 100 g (3½ oz).

Spinach
Palak, sag

Spinach is a member of the goosefoot family, which includes beet. Spinach is a herbaceous plant, whose dark green leaf gets its unique flavour from its oxalic acid content. Thought to have originated in Iran, it had reached England by the 1500s and is today very popular in the subcontinent. Thorough rinsing is important when preparing spinach, to remove gritty soil. It should then be lightly cooked, not boiled to death. Indeed, baby spinach leaves can be stir-fried straight into the pot, merely after washing. It is an excellent source of fibre and also good for iron and potassium. Lightly cooked, it yields 30 calories per 100 g (3½ oz).

Spring Onion
Hare piaz

Spring onions are not used in traditional Indian cooking, but are excellent where a fresh taste is required such as in Jalfrezi or Balti, and for garnishing.

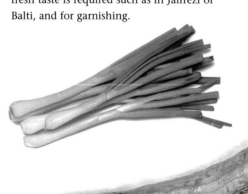

Swede

Yellow-fleshed swede is a natural cross between turnip and cabbage. It arrived in England from Sweden (hence the name) in the late 1700s. Cook as potato. It is high in starch, provides some sugar, fibre and protein, and yields 11 calories per 100 g (3½ oz).

Sweet Potato
Sharkarkand, rataloo

There is debate about whether the sweet potato originated in eastern Asia or South America. It is evidently so ancient, that wild species may have developed before continental drift caused the tectonic plates to separate. Sweet potato appears in Chinese recipes dating from before 1492, and is on record as having been 'discovered' in 1500 in Brazil by the Portuguese who brought it to Africa to feed slaves. By the mid-1500s it had become popular in Britain (Shakespeare makes potato references which predate the true potato's arrival in Britain). Although it yields an edible potato-like flesh, it is not related to the ordinary potato. The sweet potato is the thick root of a tropical plant. There are a number of varieties, with smooth skin, whose colours vary from light yellow to reddish-violet, giving rise to their general names, red and white sweet potato. The skin of the red sweet potato is maroony-pink. Some varieties have orange flesh, others have white flesh, all are very sweet. The flesh of the white sweet potato is yellow, drier and less sweet. Cook all types as potatoes – they make an excellent and colourful potato substitute. The sweet potato is sometimes erroneously called yam. Sweet potatoes are high in starch, sugar, fibre and protein. Boiled or baked sweet potatoes yield 85 calories per 100 g (3½ oz).

for thousands of years in rice-type paddy fields, for taro requires plenty of water in which to thrive. Here are illustrated small taro, also called 'sons of Taro' or *eddo*. To prepare, peel them, then boil until tender and add to any curry. The taro leaves are also edible, known in the Caribbean as callalloo greens or Caribbean greens, and in India, as *patra*. They can be cooked in the same way as cabbage, or they can be used for the appropriately named dish, Patra (see page 17).

Both taro leaves and roots are available at Asian shops. Another similar root is called tannia, and has the same qualities as taro. Known in Bengal as kocchu, it makes an interesting soup. Taro provides carbohydrate and protein and yields 61 calories per 100 g (3½ oz).

Tindoora or Tindla
Dilpasand

The tindoora resembles a gooseberry in colour, markings, and size, though not in shape (it is oval), nor in taste. Tindoora is a tiny member of the marrow family. It has a similar flavour to marrow, but like courgette, its outer case, which is bright green or yellow with longitudinal white stripes, is also edible. It has no English name, though its bigger brother is called pointed gourd (see page 103). Cook whole by boiling until tender, or currying. Tindoora yields 15 calories per 100 g (3½ oz).

Taro Roots and Leaves (Colcasia)
Arbi and patra

Roots or tubers are far more popular in the Third World than in the West (see also Cassava, Sweet Potato and Yam). One of the most popular in the subcontinent is *Colcasia esculenta* also known as *taro*, *dasheen*, and *arbi* in Hindi. Varieties of this root can grow to huge dimensions. They are native to the subcontinent, where they have been grown

Authentic Specialities

There is an almost limitless number of recipes suitable for this book and I have been fortunate enough to have collected many on my travels. Narrowing them down to the small selection needed for this and the subsequent chapters has not been easy, and in the end I have made a selection from all over India, using as great a variety of ingredients as possible.

Spicing methods and ingredients vary from region to region, indeed from town to town. Many a time I have sat in on discussions between townspeople from neighbouring villages about the way a particular dish should be made and never once is there agreement – the same dish can apparently be made a thousand different ways, with a change of spice here and there making the difference between how one village does it and another. Such subtleties are perhaps beyond the scope of this book, but I have tried to reproduce an end result as close as possible to the original recipe. My selection includes such classic dishes as avial from Malabar, kootoo from Mysore, thoran, porial and kari from south India, patra, undui and karhi from Gujarat, caldine and foogath from Goa, and kalia from Bengal. There are also two less well-known recipes: ottakuddi porial uses bamboo shoots, an ingredient rarely found in Indian cuisine, and gass dhotti is an equally rare recipe, which can be described as potato parathas. Ingredients range from pineapple to pumpkin, artichoke to aubergine, bitter gourd to banana flower, cabbage to carrot, and kohlrabi to celeriac.

Pakari, pineapple with peanut, presented in a scooped-out pineapple. Top right is red chilli sambol chutney

Pakari

Pineapple and Peanut Curry

Sweet and savoury combinations.

SERVES 4

2 small pineapples

4 tablespoons vegetable or coconut oil

110 g (4 oz) raw peanuts

2–4 cloves garlic, finely chopped

110 g (4 oz) onion, finely chopped

200 ml (7 fl oz) coconut milk

1–4 green chillies

aromatic salt to taste (see page 39)

MASALA

2 teaspoons coriander, ground

1 teaspoon cummin, ground

½ teaspoon cassia bark or cinnamon, ground

½ teaspoon turmeric

½ teaspoon black pepper, ground

1 tablespoon sugar

GARNISH

desiccated coconut

1 Halve both pineapples lengthways, keeping some leaves on each. Carefully scoop out the flesh and cut into small cubes. Set aside.

2 Heat the oil in a karahi or wok and stir-fry the peanuts for a couple of minutes. Strain them and set aside, retaining the oil.

3 Reheat the same oil in the karahi or wok and stir-fry the garlic for 1 minute. Add the onion and continue to fry for a further 3–4 minutes. Add the masala ingredients and stir-fry for another 2–3 minutes.

4 Add the coconut milk and the chilli and briskly stir-fry until simmering.

5 Add the pineapple chunks and the peanuts and bring back to the simmer. Salt to taste. Serve garnished with the desiccated coconut. Alternatively, garnish with shreds of fresh coconut.

Hathichowk Chettinad

Stir-fried Artichoke

Chettinad is a dish which hails from the southern Indian state of Tamil Nadu, where a community called Chetiyars have been resident since the earliest times.

SERVES 4

675 g (1½ lb) Jerusalem artichokes

6 tablespoons mustard oil

225 g (8 oz) onion, finely sliced

2–6 fresh red or green chillies, chopped

1 tablespoon curry masala paste
   (see page 40)

50 g (2oz) cashew nuts, deep-fried

1 tablespoon fresh coriander, chopped

aromatic salt to taste (see page 39)

MASALA

1 teaspoon black pepper, ground

12 dried curry leaves, ground

3 star aniseed

½ teaspoon whole fennel seeds

1 Trim and peel the artichokes and dice into about 2.5 cm (1 inch) cubes. Boil them until tender, then drain.

2 Heat the oil in a karahi or wok, stir-fry the masala ingredients for 1 minute, add the onion and chillies and continue stir-frying for about 5 more minutes.

3 Add the curry paste and when sizzling add the cooked artichokes and stir-fry for about 5 minutes. Add sprinklings of water to prevent the ingredients from sticking.

4 Add the cashew nuts and fresh coriander and when these are hot, salt to taste and serve at once.

Avial

Yoghurt, Coconut and Mango Curry

Avial is prepared at festival time at the great temples of Malabar in vast brass urns, 1.5 metres (5 feet) high and 3 metres (10 feet) wide, to feed the entire local population. This tradition goes back to the tenth century, when the Cholas built the temples.

SERVES 4

675 g (1½ lb) exotic mixed vegetables

the flesh of a fresh coconut and its water

2–4 fresh green chillies, roughly chopped

1 small sour mango, skinned, stoned and
   chopped

2 teaspoons cummin seeds

1 teaspoon turmeric

50 g (2 oz) natural yoghurt

10–12 curry leaves

salt to taste

4 tablespoons coconut oil

coconut milk powder if required

1 Prepare and trim the vegetables, as appropriate. The tradition is to cut them into fairly thin diamond-shaped pieces.

2 In the blender, mulch down the coconut, coconut water, chillies, mango, cummin seeds and turmeric, using a little water as necessary to create a pourable paste.

3 Blanch the vegetables for 3–4 minutes in plenty of water then strain, leaving enough blanching water to cover the vegetables. Bring back to the simmer.

4 Add the yoghurt, curry leaves and the paste from stage 2. Simmer for a short while until the vegetables are ready. Salt to taste.

5 Just prior to serving, heat and add the coconut oil. It should not be too thick. If it is very watery (controllable at stage 3), add some coconut milk powder to thicken it.

Tomato
Tamata, thakali

Belonging to the nightshade family, as do aubergine and potato, the tomato is a juicy fruit, normally round, though some species grow oval or pear shaped. When ripe it is mostly scarlet, though orange and green varieties are available. For decades flavour has been sacrificed by the larger sellers. Now, however, there are more interesting tasty types available such as plum and cherry tomatoes. Canned tomatoes (normally plum tomatoes) are an excellent product, which can be substituted for, or combined with the real thing. High in water content, and good for vitamin C, raw tomato yields 14 calories per 100 g (3½ oz).

Turnip
Shalgam

Turnip is a member of the *Brassica* (cabbage) family native to Europe. It is a spherical or carrot-shaped, white root (tuber), sometimes with a pinkish-purple tinge. It is high in water content, and low in sugar, hence it has less tasty flesh than parsnip, and yields 11 calories per 100 g (3½ oz).

Yam
Jamikand, senai, suran

There are two very different yam species. The yam (sometimes erroneously called the sweet potato) is the potato or aerial yam, and is similar to the red-skinned sweet potato. The yam is slightly more brown in colour than the sweet potato, it is more of a kidney shape, and the flesh is white and more bitter. In all other respects the two are similar, though unrelated.

The greater yam (illustrated) has a coarse, crinkled-brown, tough, sometimes hairy skin, and though sizes start quite small, some varieties are much larger than the sweet potato, reaching up to 50 cm (19 inches) in length. The greater yam is a tuber, indisputably native to China, and it had reached Africa by AD 900, probably having been carried down the spice route. It did not reach the West Indies until the 1500s, and was taken there, in reverse so to speak, by the Portuguese to feed their slaves in transit (see Cassava).

Yams are now readily available in the West. The skin is peeled and discarded and the white flesh is cooked as for potato. Yams are high in starch, but low in sugar, fibre and protein. Boiled or baked yams yield 120 calories per 100 g (3½ oz).

Banana Flower Kootoo

Kootoo hails from south India. It is a vegetable dish, here using banana flower, with sesame, chilli, tamarind and coconut to create a hot and sour curry. Occasionally one can buy banana flowers from Thai and Asian stores. Try this curry at least once for a true authentic taste of south India.

SERVES 4

2 whole banana flowers
6 tablespoons sesame oil
4–6 cloves garlic, finely chopped
2.5 cm (1 in) cube ginger, chopped
225 g (8 oz) red onion, finely chopped
2–4 fresh red chillies, finely chopped
8–10 curry leaves, fresh or dried
200 ml (7 fl oz) coconut milk
2 tablespoons tamarind purée (see page 45)
salt to taste

MASALA

2 teaspoons sesame seeds
1 teaspoon coriander, ground
1 teaspoon black pepper, ground
1 teaspoon black mustard seeds
½ teaspoon black cummin seeds

1 Pull off the first leaf from the banana flower, revealing the many long thin soft baby flowers. Pluck all these, discard the leaf, and continue like this until all the flowers are picked. Then chop most of them coarsely, keeping one or two for garnishing.
2 Heat the oil in a karahi or wok, stir-fry the masala ingredients for 1 minute, then the garlic for 1 minute. Add the ginger and stir-fry for a minute, then add the onion and continue for about 5 minutes.

Banana Flower Kootoo; in the coconuts are onion sambol, top, katta sambol, centre, and fresh minced green chilli

3 Add the chillies and curry leaves, and after a minute or so, the coconut milk and tamarind purée.
4 Add the banana flowers. Simmer for about 10 minutes, only adding water if it reduces too much. Salt to taste. Garnish with a few fresh banana flowers and red onion slices and serve with various colourful chutneys.

Thoran
Coconut and Cabbage Curry

Thoran probably originated in Kerela. It also is found in neighbouring states, called porial, thoora and palya in Mysore. Ingredients nearly always include fresh coconut and shredded cabbage.

SERVES 4

4 tablespoons polished split urid dhal
1 fresh coconut (use all its water and half the flesh)
20 raw cashew nuts
50 g (2 oz) coconut milk powder
250 g (9 oz) white cabbage, shredded
250g (9 oz) spinach, shredded
6 tablespoons mustard oil
2 tablespoons mustard seeds
salt to taste

MASALA

3–4 dried red chillies
2.5 cm (1 inch) piece fresh turmeric
OR ½ teaspoon turmeric powder

1 Soak the urid for up to 2 hours in ample water. Drain well.
2 Mulch the masala ingredients with the fresh coconut water and flesh and the cashews. Add the coconut milk powder and enough water to make it into a pourable paste.
3 Blanch the shredded cabbage and spinach until just tender. Drain.

4 Heat the oil in a karahi or wok and stir-fry the mustard seeds and urid dhal for 2–3 minutes.
5 Add the paste and stir-fry until simmering, adding just enough water to make it easily mobile.
6 Then add the cabbage and spinach. As soon as it is hot, salt to taste and serve at once.

Porial Kadama
Festival Vegetables

At New Year India's southernmost state, Tamil Nadu, holds a festival called Pongal at which this dish is always served with Pongal rice (see page 193).

SERVES 4

1 fennel bulb
1 kohlrabi bulb
1 celeriac bulb
15 cm (6 inch) piece white radish
225 g (8 oz) red sweet potato
2 tablespoons mustard blend oil
110 g (4 oz) onions, chopped
1 tablespoon split and polished urid lentils, roasted
120 ml (4 fl oz) coconut milk
1 large firm mango, skinned, stoned and chopped
a few fresh pineapple chunks
2–4 fresh red chillies, chopped
1 tablespoon fresh coriander, chopped
salt to taste

MASALA

1 teaspoon black mustard seeds
1 teaspoon cummin seeds
1 teaspoon sesame seeds
½ teaspoon turmeric
10–15 curry leaves, fresh or fried
1 teaspoon coriander seeds
½ teaspoon black cummin seeds

1 Peel the fennel, kohlrabi, celeriac and radish, discarding unwanted matter. Shred them through the food processor attachment or hand grater.

2 Blanch, steam or microwave the potato until soft. Cut into small cubes.

3 Heat the oil in a karahi or wok. Stir-fry the masala ingredients for 20 seconds, then the onion for 5 minutes.

4 Add the coconut milk and when simmering add all the vegetables, and simmer until tender.

5 Add the mango, pineapple, chillies and coriander. Stir-fry until cooked to your liking, adding a little water if needed, to keep things mobile. Salt to taste and serve at once.

Chilli Malai Bhutta

Spicy Sweetcorn in Cream

Here is a rare sweetcorn recipe, tempered with chilli and cream. Fresh sweetcorn is best.

SERVES 4

4 large fresh sweetcorn cobs
4 tablespoons ghee
225 g (8 oz) onion, finely chopped
150 ml (5 fl oz) single cream
60 g (2 oz) natural yoghurt
2 teaspoons white sugar
2–4 green chillies, chopped
2 tablespoons whole fresh coriander leaves
salt to taste
freshly milled black pepper to taste

MASALA

2 teaspoons sesame seeds
1 teaspoon white poppy seeds
½ teaspoon fennel seeds
¼ teaspoon wild onion seeds
pinch asafoetida

1 Pick all the leaves and hairs off the sweetcorn cobs and rinse them.

2 Place cobs in ample boiling water and simmer for 15–20 minutes. Drain.

3 When cool enough to handle, hold the first cob base down on a chopping board and carefully cut down the cob so that as much as possible of each grain of corn comes away. Separate any grains that stick together.

4 Repeat with the remaining cobs.

5 Heat the ghee and stir-fry the masala ingredients for about 30 seconds. Add the onion and continue to stir-fry for 3–4 minutes.

6 Remove from the heat and when fairly cool, add the cream, yoghurt, sugar, chillies and coriander, stirring in well.

7 Bring back to a simmer and when simmering add the sweetcorn grains. Stir well and when heated through, salt and pepper to taste. Serve hot.

Undui

Five-vegetable Stew

Undui is from the western Indian state of Gujarati. Traditionally the five vegetables are beans, aubergine, red pumpkin, sweet potato and a fifth vegetable, often served with besan kofta balls in it (see page 86).

SERVES 4

110 g (4 oz) green beans
110 g (4 oz) aubergine
110 g (4 oz) red pumpkin
110 g (4 oz) sweet potato
110 g (4 oz) broad beans
1 cup vegetable oil
ajowain seeds
4 cloves garlic, finely chopped
225 g (8 oz) onion
1 green chilli, chopped
1 tablespoon curry masala paste
  (see page 40)

6 tablespoons gram flour
⅓ teaspoon asafoetida
milk as required
200 g (7 oz) yoghurt
salt to taste
juice of 1 or 2 limes

1 Prepare and cook the green beans, aubergine, red pumpkin, sweet potato, and broad beans, then take them out separately and cut them into bite-sized pieces.

2 Heat the oil in a karahi or wok and stir-fry the seeds for 30 seconds. Add the garlic and cook for 30 seconds, then add the chilli, curry masala paste and onion, and cook until golden brown.

3 Mix the gram flour and asafoetida, with just sufficient milk to create a thickish paste.

4 Add the paste to the stir-fry, and briskly whisk it together adding enough milk to keep things mobile until it stops thickening.

5 Add the yoghurt and the vegetables. Continue to add milk as needed to keep things suitably mobile. Cook until simmering. Serve with bread and chutneys.

Note: you can add kofta balls at stage 5.

Caldine

Goan Mixed Vegetable Caldine

Caldine is a Goan stew. The word is derived from the Portuguese word caldeira – 'a boiling pan' and caldo – 'soup', although it has now evolved into a more solid dish, involving many ingredients.

SERVES 4

675 g (1½ lb) prepared cooked vegetables
  of your choice
3 tablespoons vegetable oil
4 cloves garlic, chopped

2.5 cm (1 inch) cube ginger, chopped
225 g (8 oz) onion, chopped
200 ml (7fl oz) coconut milk
12 cherry tomatoes, halved
2–4 green cayenne chillies, chopped
2 tablespoons cooked red lentils
2 tablespoons red wine vinegar
1 tablespoon fresh coriander leaves,
    chopped
salt to taste

MASALA
1 teaspoon cummin seeds
1 teaspoon coriander seeds
½ teaspoon turmeric

GARNISH
red chillies, shredded
fresh coconut flakes (or desiccated)

1 Chop the vegetables into bite-sized pieces.
2 Heat the oil in a large karahi or wok and stir-fry the masala, garlic, ginger and onion for 15 minutes on low heat until golden brown.
3 Cool enough to mulch down in the blender with enough water to make a thick pourable paste.
4 Heat the coconut milk in the karahi or wok. Add the tomatoes, chillies, lentils and the paste. When simmering, add the vegetables and stir-fry for a few minutes until they are very hot right through.
5 Add the vinegar and the fresh leaves. Give it a final simmer, salt to taste, garnish and serve at once.

Ottakuddi Porial
Shredded Bamboo Shoot

In India's Nilgiris (meaning 'blue mountains'), live tribal inhabitants called the Badagas. They grow bamboo shoots, an ingredient not usually found in India, but which thrive in the Nilgiri monsoon. Serve with Gass Dhotti, below, Avarai Uthaka (see page 118) and Pothittu – pancake with sweet sauce (see page 191).

SERVES 4
400 g (14 oz) fresh or canned whole
    bamboo shoots
4 tablespoons butter ghee
4 or 5 whole dried red chillies
20 or so fresh or dried curry leaves
2 teaspoons black mustard seeds
salt to taste

1 Clean the fresh bamboo shoots and shred them.
2 Heat the ghee, add red chillies, curry leaves and mustard seeds. As soon as the seeds start crackling add the bamboo shoots.
3 Once hot, salt to taste and serve.

Gass Dhotti
Potato Parathas

MAKES 8 LARGE PARATHAS
250 g (9 oz) mashed potatoes
150 g (5½ oz) plain flour
2 teaspoons cummin seeds
4–6 spring onions, leaves and bulbs finely
    chopped
2 red chillies, finely chopped (optional)
1 teaspoon aromatic salt (see page 39)
100 g (3½ oz) ghee

1 Mix the potato, flour, seeds, spring onions, chillies (if using) and salt to make a soft dough.
2 Make 8 or 12 small round balls from the dough, then roll these out to form round flat discs.
3 Heat 1 tablespoon of ghee on the tava or flat frying pan. Fry one disc handling it carefully so as not to break it, and turning it once to achieve a golden colour. Serve hot with the dishes mentioned above, although it goes well with anything.

Patra
Colcasia Leaf Roll

The colcasia is a plant with edible roots and leaves, described and pictured on page 107 (see Taro). Gujarat has this unique recipe, using gram flour. It is fiddly to make and the leaves are hard to come by, but they do appear at the Asian store from time to time. It is available canned (perhaps easier to find at the Asian store), called simply patra, and the work then is done for you.

SERVES 4
THE PASTE
85 g (3 oz) gram flour
2 teaspoons garlic purée
2 tablespoons lemon juice
1 teaspoon mustard seeds
½ teaspoon cummin seeds
¼ teaspoon asafoetida
2–4 fresh green chillies, finely chopped
salt to taste

THE LEAVES
8 colcasia leaves, about 20 cm (8 inches)
   each long after stalks are removed
vegetable oil for shallow frying

1 Make up the paste by mixing the ingredients with enough water to form a thick batter.
2 Wash the colcasia leaves then blanch them in boiling water for about 2 minutes to soften. Drain and cool.
3 Spread out the leaves on a work surface overlapping each leaf by about 7.5 cm (3 inches).
4 Spread the batter across the leaves as shown in diagram 1.
5 Fold over the tips of the leaves and the sides, pressing them on to the batter to create a rectangle about 25 x 10 cm (10 x 6 inches) – see diagram 2.

Patra with Kudai (bottom)

6 Smear a little more paste over the top surface, then roll up the rectangle like a Swiss roll. Use a dollop of paste to seal the end – see diagram 3.
7 Place the rolls seal side down in a steamer and steam for about a ½ hour.
8 Allow to cool overnight in the fridge if you wish, then cut into slices about 1.25 cm (½ inch) thick.
9 Just prior to serving, shallow fry each slice for a couple of minutes on each side. Serve hot as a snack or as an accompaniment with a main meal.

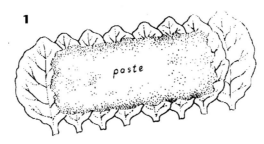

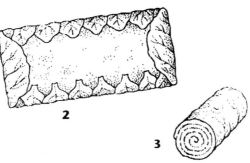

Note: to use from the can, open both ends of the can and press the cooked patra roll gently out. Cut it into slices and follow recipe at stage 9.

Gaju Kalya Foogath
Banana Curry

Foogath is a simple Goan dish, whose name derived from the Portuguese word refogar, meaning 'to stew in seasoning', using in this instance cashew nuts and plantains.

SERVES 4
4 plantains
2 or 3 dried chillies, whole
4 tablespoons Chinese rice vinegar
2 tablespoons vegetable oil
2 teaspoons yellow mustard seeds
4 cloves garlic, sliced
200 g (7 oz) onion, sliced
4 green chillies, chopped
½ red capsicum pepper, sliced
4 tablespoons coconut milk powder
salt to taste
chilli powder to taste

1 Peel and chop the plantains. Put them with the dried chillies and the rice vinegar into a covered glass bowl and microwave them to tenderness. Set aside.
2 Heat the oil in a karahi or wok and stir-fry the seeds for 30 seconds. Add the garlic and continue stir-frying for 30 more seconds. Add the onion, green chillies and red pepper, and stir-fry for about 5 more minutes, or longer if you wish until the onions are golden.
3 Add the plantain, chilli vinegar mixture and the coconut milk powder and stir-fry until tender.
4 Heat up to the sizzling stage, adding just enough water to keep things mobile. Add salt and chilli powder to taste, gently toss, and serve immediately.

Kaveri Rasa Kayi
Gourds in Coconut Gravy

The Kaveri is a big river in India's south-east. Typical ingredients of this dish include gourds flavoured with tamarind, coconut, fresh curry leaves, fenugreek seeds, and asafoetida.

SERVES 4

675 g (1½ lb) gourds of any kind, weighed
    after stage 1
2–4 green chillies, chopped
4 tablespoons vegetable oil
225 g (8 oz) onion, chopped
2 tablespoons tamarind purée (see page 45)
200 ml (7 fl oz) coconut milk
aromatic salt to taste (see page 39)

MASALA

1 teaspoon peppercorns, coarsely crushed
10–12 fresh or dried curry leaves
1 teaspoon fenugreek seeds, roasted and
    crushed
⅓ teaspoon asafoetida

1 Clean, peel and cut the gourds and cook to almost tender.
2 Slit the green chillies. Heat the oil in a karahi or wok, then add the masala ingredients and the green chillies. Stir-fry for about a minute.
3 Add the onion and stir-fry for a further 3 minutes.
4 Add the tamarind purée and coconut milk and the gourds and bring to the simmer. The gravy should be thick, but add a little water if needed.
5 Salt to taste and serve at once.

Avarai Uthaka
Bean Curry

This dish from the Nilgiri Badaga tribe whom we met on page 115 uses various kinds of bean. This is traditionally served with what the Badagas delightfully call koo (plain Basmati rice) and Pothittu (pancake with sweet sauce – see page 191).

SERVES 4

225 g (8 oz) fresh green Kenyan beans
4 tablespoons butter ghee
110 g (4 oz) canned broad beans
110 g (4 oz) canned lobia beans
100 g (3½ oz) onion
6 canned tomatoes and their juice
salt to taste

MASALA

3 teaspoons chilli powder
2 teaspoons ground coriander
1 teaspoon turmeric
⅓ teaspoon asafoetida

1 Top, tail and string the Kenyan beans as necessary. Cook them to tenderness.
2 Heat the ghee in a karahi or wok. Add the masala ingredients and stir-fry for a minute. Add the onions and stir-fry for a further minute.
3 Add the tomatoes and the beans. Salt to taste and serve when hot.

Kamal Kakri
Lotus Root Curry

The lotus is a greatly respected plant in India. The beautiful flower floats above its plant on lovely clear lake water. Nowhere is this more so than in Kashmir, Pakistan's and India's northernmost state, which nestles high in the Himalayan mountains. Roots, stem, seeds, and leaves are all eaten. Even the huge leaves are used as plates in the way that banana leaves are used in the south. It has been so for millennia: stone carvings of the lotus made by the Indus river Harapan valley civilisation dating back to 2500 BC give ample evidence of its popularity. Fresh lotus stems are found at Asian stores when in season. They taste similar to Jerusalem artichokes, and these can be substituted. They are also available canned, although they are not as subtle in this form.

SERVES 4

450 g (1 lb) lotus roots
4 tablespoons vegetable oil
2 teaspoons cummin seeds
3–4 cloves garlic, finely chopped
3 teaspoons ginger, finely chopped
110 g (4 oz) onion, finely chopped
2 tomatoes, chopped
4 tablespoons fresh coriander leaves,
    chopped
salt to taste

MASALA

1 teaspoon turmeric
1 teaspoon chilli powder
2 teaspoons garam masala (see page 38)

1 Wash, scrape and trim the lotus roots. Cut into slices or small cubes then boil in water until tender. Times vary according to the density of the particular root. If using the canned version, cube, wash and keep aside.
2 Heat the oil in a karahi or wok and add the seeds. When they crackle, add the masala ingredients, garlic and ginger, and stir-fry for 1 minute. Add the onion and stir-fry until golden (about 5 minutes).
3 Add the tomatoes, lotus and coriander leaves. Simmer until tender, then salt to taste and serve.

Kari
Exotic Vegetable Curry

Kari in Tamil means 'pepper', and writings from c. AD 300 show that meat cooked with pepper was called thallikari or just kari. Later this evolved into a spicy vegetable stew which is found in southern India to this day under the same name.

SERVES 4

450 g (1 lb) mixture of exotic vegetables, weighed after stage 1

1 teaspoon turmeric

1 fresh coconut

2 tablespoons mustard oil

1 teaspoon mustard seeds

1 teaspoon black urid lentils, polished

1 teaspoon dry red chillies, chopped

salt to taste

GARNISH

onion tarka (see page 43)

1 Prepare the vegetables, discarding unwanted matter and cutting into suitable pieces.

2 In a large saucepan bring ample water to the boil. Add the turmeric and vegetables and simmer for 5 minutes. Drain, discarding the water.

3 Open the coconut retaining the water. Shred or grate the flesh.

4 Heat the oil in a karahi, stir-fry the mustard seeds, lentils and chillies for 30 seconds. Add the coconut flesh and water and the vegetables and stir-fry until cooked to your liking. Salt to taste. Serve hot garnished with the tarka.

NON VEGETABLE ITEMS

Nuts

A nut is a fruit encased in a hard shell. Nuts are one of nature's best ways of storing, and have been used for food since long before mankind became civilised. They are high in potassium, fats, protein, and dietary fibre. Four main types are used in Indian cookery:

Almonds
(ground, flaked, whole)
Badam

Almonds are one of the most commonly used nuts in north Indian and Pakistani curries. They are used whole, unpeeled or peeled (blanched), and raw or fried in certain rich curries. They make a great garnish as do almond flakes, which can be raw or toasted. Ground almonds are used to thicken and flavour certain curry sauces.

Cashew nuts
Kaju

Whereas almonds are used in certain north Indian and Pakistani curries, cashews perform the same role in the south. They are used peeled (blanched) and raw or fried in certain curries. Like almonds, they make a great garnish and, being soft, they make a good paste when ground down with water and can be used in this way to thicken certain curry sauces.

Peanuts
Kalaka, moonfali

Peanuts are actually a legume or pulse, and are used less in Indian cooking than almonds and cashews. They can be used as a substitute for cashews. Redskin and pale-skin peanuts are available, as well as blanched polished peanuts.

Pistachio nuts
Pista

Certain Indian recipes require pistachio nuts. Always use fresh (not salted), shelled pistachio nuts, easily identified by their green colour.

Other nuts

Whether or not they are 'authentic' in Indian cooking, other nuts are excellent ingredients for the non-meat eater, and may be freely substituted for those suggested in any of the recipes in this book. Some examples are: pine nuts, sunflower kernels, macadamia nuts, walnuts, pecan nuts, hazelnuts, Brazil nuts, charoli nut, chirongi nut (the latter two are available at Asian stores).

Nuts can be roasted (as for garam masala) and fried, or simply eaten raw. Store as spices, in the dark in an airtight jar, but do not keep for over a year because they can go rancid, particularly the very oily types. Watch out for holes: nuts can often become home to weevils and grubs.

Looki Kalia
Red Pumpkin Curry

The Kalia style of curry cooking is peculiar to Bengal and Bangladesh. Red colours are mandatory, from the chilli and tomato. Spicing includes the white poppy seed.

SERVES 4

675 g (1½ lb) pumpkin and other gourds weighed after stage 1

110 g (4 oz) carrots, sliced

2 cloves garlic

2.5 cm (1 inch) piece ginger

225 g (8 oz) onion, coarsely chopped

1 tablespoon white poppy seeds

30 g (1 oz) almond flakes, blanched

4 tablespoons butter ghee

200 ml (7 fl oz) coconut milk

1 or 2 fresh red chillies, sliced

3 or 4 green chillies, whole

1 teaspoon tomato purée

1 teaspoon tomato ketchup

2 teaspoons garam masala (see page 38)

1 teaspoon fresh coriander leaves, finely chopped

salt to taste

MASALA

1 teaspoon panch phoran (see page 39)

5-cm (2-inch) piece cassia bark

2 or 3 bay leaves

250 g (9 oz) shallots

250 g (9 oz) shallots

½ teaspoon chilli powder

1 Cut open the pumpkin and/or gourds. Scoop out the stringy centre and seeds and discard. Cut away the flesh, then cut it into bite-sized pieces, and cook to tender.

2 Cut the carrot into strips and cook separately to tender.

Looki Kalia (Bengali red curry) in Caribbean coconut with pumpkin behind

3 In the blender, mulch down the garlic, ginger, onion, poppy seeds and blanched almonds, using just enough water to achieve a pourable paste.

4 Heat the ghee in your karahi or wok. Add the masala ingredients and stir-fry for 30 seconds. Add the paste and stir continuously for about 5 more minutes, using some of the coconut milk to keep things mobile.

5 Add the remaining coconut milk, the chillies, tomato purée, ketchup and carrots, and when simmering, the cooked pumpkin/gourds, the garam masala, leaves and salt to taste.

Karhi, Kadhi or Kudhi
Yoghurt Curry

This dish, with its various spellings, has been a Gujarati favourite for nearly 1,000 years. We know that, because a recipe for yoghurt beaten with gram flour and spiced with turmeric and asafoetida appears in early writings.

This is an interesting dish, sour and slightly sweet, and typical of Gujarati tastes. Here I am using paneer and whey (a by-product of paneer-making) as an optional flavourer, but they are by no means mandatory.

SERVES 4

250 g (9 oz) paneer, cut into small cubes (optional)

600 ml (1 pint) whey or water (optional)

50 g (2 oz) gram flour

2 fresh green chillies, finely chopped

450 g (1 lb) yoghurt

10–12 fresh or dried curry leaves

1 teaspoon sugar

1 tablespoon fresh coriander, finely chopped

aromatic salt to taste (see page 39)

onion tarka (see page 43)

MASALA

1 teaspoon cummin seeds

1 teaspoon turmeric

½ teaspoon asafoetida

GARNISH

garlic and/or onion tarka (see page 43)

1 Make the paneer (see page 46), retaining the measured quantity of whey. Allow 1 hour for this.

2 In a bowl, mix together the gram flour, the masala ingredients, the chillies and a little whey or water to make a pourable paste.

3 Heat the oil and stir-fry the paste. It will quickly start to thicken, so be prepared to drizzle in further whey, as though making a roux. Keep stirring until it won't thicken further.

4 Put the yoghurt into a 2.75 litre (5 pint) saucepan. Stir in the remaining whey or water, using a fork or whisk.

5 Bring to the simmer (but not the boil), regularly whisking, then reduce to a rolling simmer.

6 Whisk in the paste. Continue the rolling simmer for about 15 minutes, whisking from time to time. Add water if it becomes too thick.

7 Add the paneer, curry leaves, sugar, fresh coriander and salt to taste. Garnish with tarka and serve at once with kitchri or plain rice.

Note: karhi can be served without paneer, as a gravy. Alternatively you can add koftas or vadai dumplings, or vegetables such as cooked gourds or fried okra during stage 7.

Eggs, Pancakes and Nuts

This chapter is a bit of a mixed bag or a lucky dip. It contains various miscellaneous dishes featuring eggs, or pancake mixtures, bread European style, or nuts.

Eggs are popular all over the subcontinent. Mostly they are hen's eggs, though it should be pointed out that hens in India are much smaller then their huge Western sisters, and they lay less frequently, their egg being an average of 45 g (equivalent to a size 7 in the UK, the smallest size). Duck eggs are also enjoyed in places like Goa and Cochin, and quails' eggs are popular in the north of India. My recipe selection includes the Parsee speciality, curried scrambled egg, two boiled egg curries, three omelettes and sabzi nargissi korma, a kind of vegetable Scotch egg.

The next group of recipes in this chapter includes south Indian items made from rice flour, such as string hopper, uthapam, coconut pancake, and the celebrated masala dosa – rice pancake with curry stuffing. I have included recipes for pau bhaji, a Bombay favourite in which rolls or baps are stuffed with a curry filling, and vegetable kebab stuffed into French bread under the name of a torpedo.

Finally, while nuts can be added to just about any recipe in this book, I have given recipes for cashew nut curry, panch amrit (a rich curry featuring five nuts), and sabzi dilruba (nuts with quails' eggs).

Ekuri Aloo, scrambled egg with potato, makes a great snack, as here, served on a chupatti. Note the fresh turmeric at the top of the picture

Currants/Raisins/Sultanas
Kish mish, munacca

In ancient days the drying of fruit (which literally means the removal of its water content) was done by the sun. This method is still practised in the Third World today although it is done commercially using convection ovens. Once dried, the natural sugar content of the fruit intensifies and preserves the fruit indefinitely. Many fruits can be dried, and perhaps the most common are grapes. Currants are dried from small black grape varieties (named after the ancient Greek town of Corinth), where currants were produced in the centuries before Christ. Raisins are also from a dried black grape, but are generally larger and juicier than currants, and a paler brown. Sultanas are from larger white grapes, and are larger and juicier still, their colour ranging from golden to brown. All are seedless.

Eggs
Anda

True vegetarians do not eat eggs as they are the ova laid by the hen before the young are formed.

Eggs are protected by an inedible calcified shell which comprises about 12 per cent of the egg's total weight. The shell can be blue in the case of water birds, and some are speckled. Chicken egg shells are white or brown. There is no difference in their contents, but brown seems to be preferred by the consumer. Inside the egg is a transparent fluid, the albumen, which contains some protein, and goes solid and white when cooked, and the chrome-yellow yolk, which nourishes the embryo. The yolk contains protein, fat, potassium and sodium. Occasionally an egg contains two yolks (twins).

There are three quality grades and seven sizes of egg in the EU countries. Grade A is fresh, Grade B is less fresh and Grade C has been refrigerated for some weeks, and is used almost exclusively in food manufacturing. Size 1 weighs 70 g (2½ oz) or over, size 4 at 55–60 g (2 oz) is the most commonly sold size. Goose and turkey eggs are twice the size of the largest chicken eggs and taste richer, as do duck eggs, which are about 10 per cent larger. Quail eggs weigh about 15–20 g (less than 1 oz). Illustrated here at two-thirds size are quail, bantam, and poussin (young chicken) eggs, then four sizes of chicken egg (sizes 7, 5, 4, and 1). Chicken eggs yield 76 calories per 100 g (3½ oz).

Honey
Madhu

Honey was the world's first sweetener, predating sugar cane and palm sugar, and it had been cultivated long before the ancient Egyptians placed pots of it in their pyramids. Everyone knows about the astonishing activities of the honey bee – constructing its nest and its waxy honeycombs, buzzing into summer flowers to collect nectar – and the fabulous product of this process. Some strict vegetarians do not eat honey because it is an animal product. Honey is clear, dark-coloured and runny but it beomes harder and paler with age; if it is heat-processed, it stays runny throughout its shelf life. Small amounts of honey can be used in savoury curry recipes to great effect. Honey has a high sugar content (fructrose and glucose) and is high in calories, yielding 281 calories per 100g (3½ oz).

Soya Bean
Semsoy

Although the soya bean is probably the most important ingredient in Chinese cuisine it plays little or no part in village India. However, it does have attributes of which the non-meat eater should be aware: unremarkable and rather tasteless small, round beans can (as proven by Chinese cooking) be made into something amazing.

In its natural state the soya bean is small and pale cream in colour. When fermented it turns black, brown or yellow and is then soft enough to make into thick, salty flavoured pastes and thin, salty, runny sauces of varying strengths. The ancients learned to compress the soya bean into cheese-like blocks (see Bean Curd, page 127) which could be crumbled or cut and cooked. They also learned how to make cooking oil from it and a milk-like drink. They even used the unprocessed bean as a vegetable, both whole and sprouting. The soya bean can also be made into dried mince or meat chunks. When reconstituted, it is almost indistinguishable from the real thing, apart from taste.

Chicken Size 1   Chicken Size 4   Chicken Size 5   Chicken Size 7   Poussin   Bantam   Quail

Ekuri

Curried Scrambled Egg

Spiced scrambled eggs are the speciality of the Parsees, whom we met on page 81. Adding potato, as in the photograph on the previous pages, makes this dish into the more substantial Ekuri Aloo.

SERVES 4

2 tablespoons butter
1 teaspoon black mustard seeds
½ teaspoon white cummin seeds
½ teaspoon turmeric
2–4 cloves garlic, finely chopped
2 or 3 spring onions, bulbs and leaves, chopped
1 tablespoon fresh coriander leaves, chopped
1 fresh red chilli (optional), chopped
4–6 large eggs
4–6 tablespoons chopped boiled potato (optional)
salt to taste
garam masala to taste (see page 38)

1 Heat the butter in a non-stick saucepan. Stir the seeds for 10 seconds. Add the turmeric and garlic and stir-fry for a further 30 seconds. Add the spring onion, coriander and chilli (if using) and stir-fry for 2–3 minutes.
2 Break the eggs into a small bowl and whisk with a fork to mix the yolk and white. Add to the saucepan and whisk to amalgamate everything as the egg starts to set.
3 Add the optional potato and continue to stir until the egg sets fully (but doesn't go too dry).
4 Sprinkle with salt and garam masala and serve on a hot chupattis.

Ande Masala

Egg Curry

Hardboiled eggs make an excellent subject for currying.

SERVES 4

6–8 eggs (depending on size and appetite)
3 tablespoons vegetable oil
280 g (10 oz) Spanish onions, finely chopped
400 g (14 oz) canned tomatoes and their juice
2 tablespoons fresh coriander leaf, chopped
aromatic salt to taste (see page 39)

MASALA

1 teaspoon coriander, ground
1 teaspoon curry masala dry mix (see page 40)
1 teaspoon garam masala (see page 38)
½ teaspoon dry fenugreek leaves
½ teaspoon chilli powder
½ teaspoon turmeric

1 Mix the masala ingredients with water to make a paste.
2 Heat the oil in the karahi or wok and stir-fry the paste for 3 minutes, adding water as needed as the paste thickens.
3 Add the onion and stir-fry until golden (see page 43 for the technique).
4 Add the tomatoes and the coriander. Simmer for a further 5–10 minutes, then add just enough tomato juice to get the thickness of sauce that you require. Optionally mulch the sauce down in the pan with a hand blender.
5 During stages 3 and 4, boil the eggs for 15 minutes in simmering water. Remove the shells and rinse.
6 Quarter the hardboiled eggs, add them to the sauce and simmer until hot. Salt to taste and serve immediately.

Andai Bandai

Quail Egg Curry

SERVES 4

12–16 quails' eggs
2 tablespoons butter ghee
2 cloves garlic, sliced
2.5 cm (1 inch) piece ginger, shredded
110 g (4 oz) onion, thinly sliced
200 ml (7 fl oz) fragrant stock (see page 39)
1 or 2 fresh green chillies, shredded
1 tablespoon fresh coriander leaves, chopped
1 tablespoon fresh mint leaves, chopped
8 cherry tomatoes, halved
aromatic salt to taste (see page 39)

MASALA 1

1 teaspoon cummin seeds
1 teaspoon mustard seeds
½ teaspoon aniseed

MASALA 2

2 teaspoons curry masala dry mix (see page 40)
1 teaspoon garam masala (see page 38)
1 teaspoon dried mint
1 teaspoon dried fenugreek leaves
1 teaspoon chilli powder

1 Heat the oil in a wok or karahi, stir-fry masala 1 for 30 seconds, then add the garlic and ginger and stir-fry for another minute, then add the onion and stir-fry for about 5 minutes.
2 Add masala 2 and stir-fry for 3–4 more minutes. Add the stock or water and stir to the simmer.
3 During stages 1 and 2, put the eggs into boiling water and simmer for exactly 4 minutes to hardboil them. Shell, and rinse them.
4 Add the chillies, fresh coriander and mint leaves, hardboiled eggs and the tomatoes.
5 When the curry simmers again, add salt to taste. Serve at once.

Masala Poro

Spicy Omelette

One of my favourites is masala omelette. The masala in question is one or more of the items listed below. Of those, my absolute favourite is simply chilli.

SERVES 1

2 or 3 eggs, depending on appetite

¼ teaspoon salt

1 tablespoon vegetable oil

twist of fresh black pepper

CHOICE OF MASALA

green chillies, chopped

onion

tomato

fresh coriander

1 In a bowl, briskly beat the eggs and salt together with a fork or whisk.

2 Heat the oil on medium heat in a flat frying pan.

3 Pour in the beaten eggs. Deftly and swiftly twist the pan so that the egg rolls right round it.

4 Mix in your choice of masala (a maximum of 2 teaspoons).

5 Fry until just firm, shaping it into a torpedo shape in the pan.

6 Serve at once, with a twist of fresh black pepper.

Aromatic Omelette

This omelette contains aromatic items such as ginger, mushroom and fennel, and is more substantial than the preceding one, which makes it more suitable, perhaps, for a lunchtime or evening meal, served with a salad (see pages 58–9) and chutneys (see pages 183–4).

SERVES 1

3 large eggs

⅓ teaspoon aromatic salt (see page 39)

2 tablespoons oil

1 clove garlic, sliced

1 cm (½ inch) piece fresh ginger, sliced thinly into strips

3 or 4 spring onion, bulbs and leaves, chopped

2–4 mushrooms, any type, chopped

¼ fennel bulb, shredded

1 canned tomato, chopped

1 fresh red chilli, shredded

2 or 3 walnuts, chopped

2 or 3 fresh mint leaves, chopped

twist of fresh black pepper

MASALA

¼ teaspoon fennel seeds

1 green cardamom, crushed

¼ teaspoon black cummin seeds

¼ teaspoon garam masala (see page 38)

1 In a bowl, briskly beat the eggs and the salt together with a fork or whisk.

2 Heat the oil on medium heat in a flat frying pan. Stir-fry the masala for 30 seconds, add the garlic and ginger and stir-fry for 30 more seconds. Next add the spring onions and continue to stir-fry for about 2 minutes.

3 Pour in the beaten eggs. Deftly and swiftly twist the pan so that the egg rolls right round it.

4 Mix in the mushroom, fennel, tomato, chilli, walnuts, and mint.

5 Fry until just firm, keeping it flat in the pan. When firm, optionally turn it in the pan.

6 Serve at once, with a twist of fresh black pepper.

Kai Yad Sai

Thai Savoury Spicy Omelette

For this, the third of our omelette triumvirate, we have a Thai emphasis.

SERVES 1

3 large eggs

½ teaspoon ground white pepper

½ teaspoon light soy sauce

2 tablespoons soya oil

2 cloves garlic, finely chopped

1 cm (½ inch) piece fresh ginger or galangale, sliced thinly into strips

1 teaspoon lemon grass, very finely chopped

1 teaspoon Thai red curry paste

3 or 4 spring onion, bulbs and leaves, chopped

2 fresh red chillies, shredded

3 or 4 fresh basil leaves, chopped

1 In a bowl, briskly beat the eggs, pepper and the soy sauce together with a fork or whisk.

2 Heat the oil on medium heat in a flat frying pan. Stir-fry the garlic, ginger and lemon grass for 30 seconds. Add the curry paste and continue to stir-fry for about 1 minute.

3 Pour in the beaten eggs. Deftly and swiftly twist the pan so that the egg rolls right round it.

4 Mix in the spring onions, chillies and the basil leaves, and fry until the omelette is just firm, keeping it flat in the pan. When firm, optionally turn it in the pan.

5 Serve at once.

Sugar Cane

A member of the grass family, sugar cane is native to India. The cane that now grows worldwide can be found in the Third World on the streets, being pressed by vendors into a sweet, refreshing drink. Commercially the juice is reduced to a syrup by boiling, and then dried into crystals. It is then relatively simple to refine it further to make brown or white granulated sugar. Sugar beet (see Beetroot, page 61) can be processed in the same way. The sugar thus created is called sucrose. Natural sugar in fruit is called fructose. Pictured here are chunks of sugar cane with the outer casing removed.

Tofu or bean curd

Bean curd, better known by its Cantonese name, *doufu* or *tofu*, has the texture of cheese. It can be either soft or firm, depending on how it is processed. Normally it is white, but a red version is also available. Tofu is made by soaking and puréeing white soya beans. The purée is then boiled in water which is strained to make soya milk. This is brought back to the simmer and a curdling agent, such as lemon juice, is added. It is then restrained and the solid matter is compressed in moulds, and after some time a firm block of tofu results. The process was first invented around two thousand years ago by scientists of an emperor of the Han dynasty (206 BC–AD 221). Tofu is readily

available in packets from delicatessens and health-food shops. It is virtually flavourless and very high in protein. It is used for its texture and can be diced, sliced, minced or mashed then boiled, baked, stir-fried or deep-fried. Paneer, the Indian version of cheese, has similar characteristics to tofu, though it is made from milk (see page 46). Quorn is a relatively new man-made tofu substitute made from a mushroom-like fungi.

Paan Leaves

Called *paan* (or pan) in Hindi (and *vethilai* in Tamil) the leaf of the betel nut tree is not only a fundamental ingredient of paan, it has given its name to the paan industry. The leaf is darkish green and heart-shaped, with an average size of 13–15 cm (5–6 inches) in length (see photograph on page 188). The leaf itself is rather bitter in taste, and it is quite tough, although not scaly. It serves as a wrapping for a number of ingredients, which are then consumed as a breath freshener, digestive aid and tooth cleaner.

Betel Nut

A major ingredient of paan, the areka or betel nut grows on a very tall palm which is slimmer than the coconut tree. The nuts grow all over the subcontinent in clusters of several dozens. Each nut has an outer casing, rather like the horse chestnut or nutmeg, which is discarded to reveal the nut inside. It resembles a nutmeg in colour, shape and size. When dried it is cut with a purpose-made cutter, a two-handled guillotine, a cross between a secateur and a nut cracker, revealing mottled buff and brown colours inside. (The nuts and their cutter can be seen on page 189.) Called *supari* in Hindi, *supadi* in Nepalese and *pakku* in Tamil, it is cut into chunks, finely sliced or shredded and may be consumed on its own or in combination with other ingredients. It is said to be an aphrodisiac and a digestive. It is also used ceremonially. It is rather bitter and has an acquired taste. For more information about paan, see page 190.

String Hopper

A kind of very fine Sri Lankan nest noodle made from rice flour. Sri Lankan rice comes in various colours, as we see on pages 166–7. This means that string hoppers are available in pink too. Hoppers are made from rice flour paste that is extruded through a brass or wooden hopper press, then dried in the sun. (Dried hoppers are top left in the picture.) Traditionally they are eaten at breakfast time with sweetened coconut milk, and at other times with savoury dishes.

SERVES 4
8–12 small dried string hoppers

1 To cook, simply immerse the string hoppers in boiling water.
2 Take the pan off the heat, and remove them and serve hot. If you like, you can place a poached or fried egg on to the hopper.

Prasadam Avial
Plantain and Drumstick Curry

A traditional Kerelan dish using fried plantains, drumsticks, chilli, yoghurt and coconut. At holy Hindu feast times, the temples make special offerings known as prasadam to the local worshippers.

SERVES 4
¼ teaspoon turmeric
8 green cayenne chillies, chopped
2 tablespoons fresh coriander, very finely chopped
150 g (5½ oz) yoghurt
flesh of 1 coconut and its water
2 ripe plantains

String hopper with Prasadam Avial (in the brass bowl)

4 drumsticks
4 tablespoons coconut or sunflower oil
garlic chive leaves

GARNISH
desiccated coconut

1 Grind the turmeric, chillies, coriander, yoghurt and coconut flesh and water to a pourable paste, using water as needed.
2 Peel the plantains and chop them into bite-sized pieces. Cook them at a simmer for about 10–15 minutes or until tender. Drain and set aside.
3 Cut the drumsticks into 5 cm (2 inch) pieces and cook them by boiling for 30 minutes or until tender.
4 Heat the oil in a wok or karahi. Add the plantain pieces and stir-fry for a few minutes until the plantains are golden brown in colour. Add the paste and stir-fry for a couple of minutes, adding water to keep things mobile.
5 Add the garlic chive leaves and sufficient water to make a consommé-like consistency and bring to the simmer. Add the drumsticks and simmer for at least 5 minutes more.
6 Salt to taste and serve garnished with desiccated coconut.

Uthappam

Uthappam or oothappam are pancakes made of rice and urid dhal which is soaked and ground, then allowed to ferment. The rice should be samba (south Indian) rice, a small oval-grained variety, available at the Asian store. Traditionally the batter contains dried red chilli, ginger and onion. Recent developments include pizza-style toppings of garlic, tomato, onion and green chilli.

SERVES 4
110 g (4 oz) dried round (samba) rice
60 g (2 oz) split urid dhal
4 dried red chillies
2.5 cm (1 in) cube ginger, chopped
110 g (4 oz) shallots, finely chopped
½ teaspoon sugar
½ teaspoon salt
6 tablespoons sunflower or soya oil

OPTIONAL TOPPING
1 tablespoon garlic tarka (see page 43)
2 tablespoons onion tarka (see page 43)
1 tomato, chopped
2–4 green chillies, finely chopped

1 Soak the rice and urid dhal for at least 12 hours. Drain, then mix them and grind together in the blender using warm water to achieve an easily pourable pancake batter.
2 Put the batter in a warm place to allow it to ferment. For this to happen, the temperature should be between 37° and 54°C (100° and 130°F), and the place should be draught-free. Leave the batter for at least six hours, after which time it should be bubbling and have that yeasty smell which goes with fermentation.
3 Mix in the dried chilli, ginger, shallots, sugar and salt.
4 Mix together the garlic and onion tarkas, tomato and green chillies.
5 In a very hot tava or flat frying pan or griddle pan, add ¼ of the oil. Pour in ¼ of the batter. Quickly swirl it around the pan. Spread ¼ of the topping over the pancake. Cook until the pancake sets, then turn it over and briefly cook the other side. Turn it out.
6 Repeat with the other three pancakes.

Dosa

The Dosa is probably south India's best-known pancake. It is believed that they were the first of the family of Indian pancakes to be invented, and the honours go to the coastal town of Udipi a few miles north of Mangalore in the southern state of Karnataka. By the sixth century AD, they were being made as temple food for thousands of worshippers. They are made from a batter cooked very thin and crisp in Karnataka and thick and small in Tamil Nadu. Dosa are eaten like chupattis, or they are traditionally stuffed with a filling (as in the recipe below), when they are known as masala dosa. Today there are numerous dosa fillings – indeed one restaurant in Cochin calls itself 'The 36 Dosa House' – so feel free to invent your own. See the making of dosa at London's Malabar Junction on pages 8–11.

SERVES 4

200 g (7 oz) dried round (samba) rice

100 g (3½ oz) split urid dhal

½ teaspoon ground fenugreek seed

salt

6 tablespoons sunflower or soya oil

1 Soak the rice and urid dhal for at least 12 hours. Drain, then mix them and grind together in the blender using warm water to achieve an easily pourable pancake batter.

2 Put the batter into a warm place and allow it to ferment. For this to happen, the temperature should be between 37° and 54°C (100° and 130°F) and the place should be draught-free. Leave the batter for at least 6 hours, after which time it should be bubbling and have that yeasty smell which goes with fermentation.

3 Mix in the fenugreek and salt.

4 Heat ¼ of the oil in a large flat frying pan or spread it on a flat griddle heater.

5 Pour in ¼ of the batter. Spread it around the pan so that it becomes a thin disc. Paint oil onto it with a brush.

6 Ease the dosa off the hotplate.

7 Repeat with the other three dosa.

Dosa Masala
Pancake Stuffing

MAKES STUFFING FOR 4 DOSA

4 dosa

350 g (12 oz) boiled potatoes, cut into small cubes

2 tablespoons sesame oil

2 teaspoons mustard seeds

1 tablespoon chana dhal, uncooked

1 tablespoon black urid lentils, uncooked

1 teaspoon turmeric

4 cloves garlic, chopped

110 g (4 oz) onions, chopped

2 tablespoons cashew nuts (optional)

50 g (2 oz) peas

4 tablespoons desiccated coconut (fresh or dry)

1–4 fresh red chillies, chopped

10–12 curry leaves

salt to taste

1 Heat the oil in a karahi or wok. Stir-fry the mustard seeds and the chana and urid lentils for about 1 minute.

2 Add the turmeric, garlic, onion and nuts and stir-fry for 2–3 more minutes. Add a splash of water to keep things mobile.

3 Stir in the peas, potatoes, coconut, chillies and curry leaves. When sizzling, salt to taste.

4 Spread ¼ of the masala filling across the centre of a dosa. Fold the dosa over the filling.

5 Repeat with the other three dosa. Serve with coconut chutney, sambar and rasam.

FRUIT

Nowadays we are blessed with the biggest array of exotic fruit we have ever seen. In the UK we receive daily supplies from the Americas, Kenya and South Africa, Israel, Australasia, the subcontinent, Thailand, China, and Japan. We are privileged to be able to get hold of one or other variety of mango almost any day of the year, while the people of mango-producing countries like India, which cannot afford imports, are dependent on their brief annual crop. We take this for granted, but it is a logistic miracle that fruit picked 10,000 miles away can be on our tables, fresh and tasty, just twenty-four hours after picking. Here in the **Fruit Ingredients File** both familiar and less common fruits are discussed. Indeed, new species arrive in Britain regularly, and to help with the identification of what may be unfamiliar new and exotic items, some are illustrated here. I hope that you will get round to trying them all soon.

Ambarella

Native to the Polynesian island of Tahiti, and now cultivated in Thailand and the Far East, ambarella is an oval fruit, related to the mango. It is between 5 and 10 cm (2–4 inches) long, with five indentations along its length, and it ripens through green to yellow-green, usually with brown spots. It is high in sugar and has an average of 59 calories per 100g (3½ oz).

Apple
Maharaji, seb

Probably the world's most popular fruit, records of apple cultivation go back to Egyptian, Greek and Roman times. In Britain they were known to exist in the Stone Age. There are now over 7,000 varieties, some botanists say treble that. Apples are an excellent source of dietary fibre and vitamin C and they yield an average of 36 calories per 100 g (3½ oz).

Apple Banana
Chapal, chota kela

These baby bananas are a variety of the larger banana (see right). They are bred for their tiny size and for sweetness of flavour, but in all other respects they have the same characteristics as their bigger brothers.

Apricot
Khubani, zardaloo

Native to China, and a member of the rose family, this pitted fruit came eastward along the silk route until it reached the Mediterranean at the time of Christ. It was certainly in England by the 1600s and in America a hundred years later. The fruit is yellow in colour, with a red blush on its sun-facing side. Its flesh is yellow and juicy. Apricots are a good source of vitamin A and they yield, on average, 50 calories per 100 g (3½ oz).

Banana
Kela

Bananas are native to south-east Asia. They were introduced by the Arabs to Africa, whose name 'banana' we use today. In the 1700s the British took bananas to the West Indies where they are a major source of revenue, although in recent years they have been threatened by their cheaper Latin American counterpart.

Bananas grow in a remarkable way on low leafy plants. The tree is technically a huge herb, inasmuch as its trunk is not woody – it is a consolidated wrapping of leaves. The tree grows to 3–6 m (10–20 feet) tall and the very large, oblong leaves spread out from the top of the stem. The leaves are in one piece when they first open, but the wind soon tears them. (These are used for a variety of non-edible purposes, for example, to serve food on in rural areas.) Soon the plant develops a stem on which a purple cone-shaped bud emerges. It too comprises interwoven leaves. As the bud grows downward, the leaves open up one by one, to reveal twenty or more tiny creamy white fingers, each with a yellow ruff at the tip. Called hands, these soon begin to turn upwards and they become a cluster of tiny green bananas. This process is repeated many times until there are up to ten hands with up to 200 bananas growing on the plant. Eventually, the whole stem is cut down and the bananas, if fully ripened are yellow and ready for selling. Bananas for export are cut when green, and ripen on their journey. Cultivated bananas are not permitted to pollinate, so no seeds form, and the plant only produces one crop. After harvesting the bananas, the plant dies and is eventually cut away allowing a new plant to grow up from the roots for next season. In less controlled conditions, seeds develop at the core of the flower bud.

There are more than a hundred varieties of banana. Illustrated here are baby rice bananas from Thailand (1) (compare them with the apple bananas, left), pink bananas from Indonesia (2), 'Big Mike' from Jamaica (3) and pink bananas from Thailand (4).

Banana skin is easily peeled, the pulp is soft and sweet, and contains numerous very small edible black seeds. Flavours are similar, but depend on the banana's stage of ripeness. Plantains are bred for cooking (see page 103). Bananas are a good source of vitamins B6 and C, with potassium and carbohydrate too. They yield 60 calories per 100 g (3½ oz).

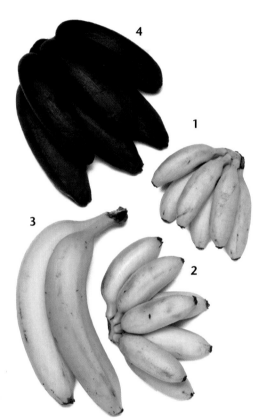

Banana Flower
Kele-ka-phul

The biology of the banana flower is discussed above. In Thailand, Bangladesh, Sri Lanka and south India, the flower is eaten in curry and other savoury dishes.

Pao Bhaji
Vegetable Curry Bap

This is street food from the real India where it is called pao bhaji – a vegetable curry filling, served hot or cold, in a scooped out bread roll or bap. A super snack at any time. Use leftovers and any of the fillings mentioned throughout this book, for example, rissoles from pages 47 and 63, and stuffing fillings, pages 63, 65, 74 and 99, and rice items from page 169. I have not given exact quantities, because there are many variables. But you will enjoy mixing and matching your own filling combinations.

SERVES 4
4 crisp fresh white or brown bread rolls, or
    baps

FILLING 1
chopped potato
curry paste
broccoli
peas
mustard seeds
spring onion

FILLING 2
Same as above with canned baked beans
    added

FILLING 3
cooked rice
curry paste
spring onions

Pancake Curry Roll

This is inspired by the dosa. It is a wheatflour pancake, simply stuffed with a savoury filling. Eat it with chutneys, salad and maybe a dhal dish.

MAKES 4 PANCAKES
50 g (2 oz) plain white flour
25 g (1 oz) melted butter
1 egg, beaten
150 ml (5 fl oz) milk, warmed

FILLING
Use any of the fillings on pages 63, 65, 74
    and 79

GARNISH
lime wedges

1 Mix the filling ingredients together, mash until smooth. Heat up and keep warm.
2 To make the pancakes, sift the flour into a bowl and mix in the butter, egg, and warm milk. Beat well and leave to stand for about 10 minutes.
3 The batter should be of pouring consistency. In a very hot tava, omelette or griddle pan, heat a little butter. Pour in enough batter to make a thin pancake when 'swirled' around the pan. Cook until set, then turn over and briefly cook the other side. Turn it out.
4 Repeat to make the remaining pancakes.
5 Spread ¼ of the filling across the centre line of one pancake.
6 Roll the pancake into a cylinder.
7 Repeat with the other three and serve with a lime wedge.

Sabzi Nargissi Kofta

This is none other than the celebrated Scotch Egg. But rather than using milk, here we cover the hardboiled egg with a crumbed vegetable coating before frying it.

MAKES 4, 8 OR 12 KOFTAS
4 large or 8 medium eggs, or 12 quails'
    eggs
pea roll mixture (see page 63)
1 egg, beaten
75 g (3 oz) semolina
75 g (3 oz) breadcrumbs
vegetable oil for frying

1 Hardboil the eggs, taking 15 minutes for large, 12 minutes for medium and 4 minutes for quails' eggs. When cool, shell, rinse and set aside. Remember to prick the blunt end of the eggs with a pin before boiling to prevent the eggs from cracking.
2 Make up the pea roll mixture below.
3 Wrap sufficient mixture around each egg, then coat each one with raw egg and roll in the semolina and breadcrumbs.
4 Shallow or deep-fry in oil until each is golden and evenly cooked. Serve hot with dhal and rice.

Note: pancakes of any type can be cooked in advance, stored between layers of foil and refrigerated for a day or frozen. Thaw, remove foil, and reheat in an oven or microwave.

Pao Bhaji with three fillings

Blackberry

Kair

The blackberry is one of some four thousand members of the rose family. It is native to America, and is comprised of clusters of numerous, tiny, fleshy, deep-purple spheres, each containing a seed, which grow around the stem. Cloudberry is an orange-coloured variety of blackberry, dewberry is grey-blue. Blackberries are a good source of vitamins A and C, and are also good for minerals. They yield 29 calories per 100 g (3½ oz).

Blueberry

Kair

The blueberry is native to America, and a member of the heather family (the cranberry is of this family, and also an American import). Blueberries are attractive tiny deep blue-purple spheres, coated with a dusty bloom. The mulberry and the smaller bilberry are close relatives. Blueberries are a good source of vitamin C and they yield 56 calories per 100 g (3½ oz).

Breadfruit

Barca

A member of the *Moraceae* family to which the fig and the mulberry also belong. The breadfruit is indigenous to the Indonesian and Malaysian islands. Its tree, much used for local timber, grows up to 18 m (59 feet) high, and was 'discovered' by Captain Cook, in his *Endeavour*. But it was in 1789 as the *Bounty* was en route to the West Indies with

breadfruit cuttings, when its crew mutinied. As breadfruit matures, it grows to some 30 cm (12 inches) in length and its myriad small, stud-like spines turn yellow as the fruit ripens.

Illustrated here are an immature green fruit and a more mature yellow one. The fruit has a distinctively unpleasant odour, which recedes during ripening, and disappears altogether during cooking. The jackfruit, native to India and Sri Lanka, is a larger, longer relative (in certain cases, over 1 metre/3¼ feet in length and 40 kg/18 lb in weight) with slightly sweeter flesh. Breadfruit and jackfruit seeds are eaten in the southern subcontinent and are sun-dried, then fried, roasted or curried. Another relative is the marang which is darker in colour than the jackfruit with an even sweeter flesh. None of these is related to the durian (see page 147). The breadfruit is a good source of vitamins, B1, B3, and C, and is also good for dietary fibre and some minerals. It yields up to 150 calories per 100 g (3½ oz).

Sabzi Dilruba

Vegetables in a Creamy Sauce

This recipe mixes crumbled paneer, eggs, nuts and vegetables. Such a combination has Iranian or Persian roots, and the recipe is a speciality of one of Edinburgh's finest vegetarian restaurants, the Kalpna.

SERVES 4

675 g (1½ lb) vegetables: 1 large marrow (about 450 g/1 lb); 110 g (4 oz) peas; 110 g (4 oz) runner beans
2 tablespoons vegetable oil
8 tablespoons curry masala gravy (see page 38)
2 tomatoes, quartered
1 recipe paneer, crumbled (see page 46)
3 tablespoons peanuts
6–8 whole quails' eggs, hardboiled for 4 minutes
OR 2 hens' eggs, hardboiled and chopped
50 ml (2 fl oz) single cream

MASALA

½ teaspoon turmeric
1 teaspoon ground cummin
1 teaspoon ground coriander
¼ teaspoon fenugreek seeds
¼ teaspoon asafoetida

1 Peel the marrow and cut into cubes. To blanch it, place in a strainer over a pan of boiling water, with the lid on the strainer, so the marrow is not immersed, then steam for 10 minutes.
2 Heat the oil. Stir-fry the masala ingredients for 1 minute, then add the curry gravy and fry for a further 5 minutes.
3 Add the peas, beans, and tomatoes and simmer for 3 minutes. Add the crumbled paneer, peanuts, whole or chopped eggs, marrow and cream. Add a little water if you require it, and some salt to taste. Serve when simmering.

Satrangi Korma
Cashew Nut Curry

Nuts can be added to just about any curry recipe. But this south Indian recipe features just cashews. It is quite rich and the portions need not be large. Serve it as an accompaniment dish.

250 g (9 oz) raw cashew nuts
4 tablespoons sesame oil
250 ml (9 fl oz) curry masala gravy
  (see page 38)
2 canned tomatoes, chopped
1 tablespoon fresh coriander, chopped
salt to taste

PASTE
2 cloves garlic
2.5 cm (1 inch) cube ginger
1 fresh coconut, flesh and water

MASALA
1 teaspoon mustard seeds
1 teaspoon sesame seeds
1 teaspoon white poppy seeds
½ teaspoon aniseed
⅓ teaspoon fenugreek seeds
10–12 curry leaves, fresh or dry

1 Put the paste ingredients into a blender or food processor and mulch until smooth and pourable, using water as needed.

2 Heat the oil in a karahi or wok. Stir-fry the cashew nuts until they turn golden. Watch carefully – they burn easily. Remove from the oil (which should be retained).

3 Using the same oil, stir-fry the masala ingredients for 30 seconds. Add the paste and stir-fry for a further 5 minutes.

4 Add the curry gravy, tomatoes and coriander and when simmering, mix in the cashews. Salt to taste, serve at once.

Panch Amrit
Five Nut Curry

This recipe has been in my collection for a long time. It was given to me by a talented young chef, Sanjiv Seth, who was responsible for staging Britain's first ever curry festival at Veeraswamy restaurant in 1983. The recipe uses five (panch) nuts, and amrit means 'holy potion' given to those who pray to the gods.

SERVES 4
4 tablespoons butter ghee
2 teaspoons mustard seeds
1 clove garlic, finely chopped
2.5 cm (1 inch) cube fresh ginger, finely
  chopped
225 g (8 oz) onion, chopped
50 g (2 oz) coconut milk powder
50 g (2 oz) ground almonds
2 green chillies, chopped
200 ml (7 fl oz) coconut water
400 ml (14 fl oz) water
110 g (4 oz) fresh coconut flesh, chopped
85 g (3 oz) cashew nuts
85 g (3 oz) almonds
85 g (3 oz) peanuts
85 g (3 oz) pine nuts
85 g (3 oz) charoli nuts (see page 119)
50 g (2 oz) sultanas
1 tablespoon sugar
salt to taste

MASALA
1 teaspoon turmeric
1 teaspoon coriander, ground
1 teaspoon cummin, ground

GARNISH
1 tablespoon fresh coriander, chopped

1 Heat the ghee in a karahi or wok. Add the mustard seeds and stir-fry for 20 seconds. Add the masala, garlic and ginger and stir-fry for a further 30 seconds. Add the onion and stir-fry for about 5 minutes.

2 Add the coconut milk powder, ground almonds and chillies, with sufficient water to keep things mobile for about 10–12 minutes.

3 Add the fresh coconut, nuts and sultanas. Cook for a further few minutes.

4 Add the sugar, salt to taste, and garnish with chopped coriander.

Vegetable and Dhal Curries

Lentils are one of India's most important ingredients. There are so many lentil recipes over there that making a choice for this chapter was never going to be easy. In the end I settled for some familiar dishes, such as tarka dhal, enjoyed all over India, sambar (a lentil and vegetable curry from the deep south of India), and aloo chole (potato and chick pea from the far north). Less familiar dishes are green moong with pink shallots from Kashmir and maahn from the Punjab. Shukta cholar is from Bengal and Bangladesh; sabzi haleem from Hyderabad uses crushed wheat; lobia diwanee is a black-eyed bean dish beloved by the Maharajas; while rajma sag rawash is spinach with rhubarb, hailing from Afghanistan. Piri piri dhal is ultra-hot lentil-stuffed chillies from Goa; kootu kazhani is a mixed vegetable hot and sour curry from Madras; kuthalam moong korma is a Tamil Nadu white lentil dish. Three from south India are: pachadi combining mango, gourd and yoghurt; payary moong upkari, featuring beans and green moong dhal, and dhal aloo sukha with dry-fried lentil and potato. Uppuma is a south Indian semolina savoury dish and Mysore bonda is a favourite snack from the exciting city of Mysore.

When you try the dishes in this chapter, make a point of comparing one from the north with one from the south just to experience the difference in spicing. Each of these dishes can be served on its own or with plain rice for a delicious meal.

Tarka Chana Dhal on a bed of plain rice

Cooking Pulses

1 Always pick through pulses by spreading them out on a table a few at a time and examining them. Small stones, even large pieces of grit are not uncommonly found. This is because the villagers still dry their pulses on the ground, or on flat roofs.

2 For the same reason a good cold water rinse is essential.

3 Soak the legumes (timings vary from pulse to pulse) to leech out the toxin lectin, and to soften them, thus shortening their cooking time.

4 Cooking can be done in a saucepan or in the microwave. As they absorb water, the pulses will expand to 1½–2 times their dried size. Use a saucepan large enough to allow for this.

Tarka Dhal
Spicy Lentils

The distinctive feature of this dhal dish is the slightly, but intentionally burnt caramelised taste of the fried garlic.

SERVES 4 (as an accompaniment)
225 g (8 oz) red split and polished lentils
450 ml (¾ pint) fragrant stock (see page 39) or water
2 tablespoons ghee
2 teaspoons cummin seeds
4–6 cloves garlic, thinly sliced
6 tablespoons onion tarka (see page 43)
salt to taste

1 Pick through the lentils to remove any grit or impurities. Rinse them in several changes of cold water, then soak for up to 20 minutes. Drain and rinse.

2 Boil stock or water and add the lentils. Cook for 30 minutes, stirring from time to time. The lentils will absorb the water to produce a creamy purée. Assist this texture by mashing with the back of the spoon.

3 Meanwhile, heat the ghee and fry the cummin seeds for 20 seconds. Add the garlic and stir-fry for about 1 more minute.

4 Add most of the onion tarka. When sizzling, add most of the stir-fry to the lentils. Salt as needed. Garnish with the remaining tarka.

Note: this dish is better cooked early – it will keep warm for ages, or it can be reheated. Make a larger quantity for freezing.

Tarka Chana Dhal
Spicy Lentils with Chick Peas

SERVES 4 (as an accompaniment)
As above plus:
100 g (3½ oz) chick peas

1 Pick through the chick peas to remove any grit or impurities. Soak them overnight to allow them to swell and soften. Strain and rinse well. Boil up at least 1.2 litres (2 pints) water. Add the chick peas and simmer for 45 minutes.

2 Add the chick peas to the above recipe at stage 4.

Note: a quicker alternative is to use a can of chick peas with their liquid (optional).

Sambar
South Indian Spicy Lentils

Sambar, also called huli and pulusu, is a traditional south Indian lentil dish, the mandatory ingredients of which are oily lentils, dried red chillies and tamarind. It is usually quite runny and contains vegetables such as gourds, okra, aubergine and drumsticks.

SERVES 4
3 tablespoons oily (toovar) lentils
1 or 2 drumsticks, cut into 5 cm (2 inch) pieces
50 g (2 oz) aubergine, diced into bite-sized pieces
1 teaspoon tamarind purée (see page 45)
2 tablespoons mustard blend oil
2 or 3 dried red chillies, whole
1 medium onion, sliced thinly
50 g (2 oz) gourd, any kind, diced into bite-sized pieces
4 okra
1 tablespoon coconut milk powder
1 tablespoon peas
salt to taste

SAMBAR MASALA
1 tablespoon gram lentils, ground
1 tablespoon black lentils, ground
1 tablespoon oily lentils, ground
1 tablespoon turmeric

MASALA
1½ teaspoons mustard seeds
1 teaspoon black peppercorns
½ teaspoon coriander seeds
¼ teaspoon fenugreek seeds
¼ teaspoon asafoetida
10–12 curry leaves

GARNISH
a few fresh curry leaves, whole

1 Bring 750 ml (1½ pints) water to the boil in a 3-litre (5¼-pint) saucepan. Add the lentils, drumsticks, aubergine and tamarind purée and simmer for 20 minutes.

2 During stage 1, add enough water to the sambar masala to make a pourable paste.

3 Heat half the oil in a wok or karahi. Add the sambar masala paste and stir-fry for about 2 minutes, then add this to the simmering ingredients.

4 Heat the remaining oil. Add the masala and stir-fry for 30 seconds. Add the dried chillies and the onion, and continue stir-frying for a further couple of minutes, then add this to the simmering ingredients.

5 By the end of 20 minutes at stage 1, with the items from stage 2 to 4 added, the sambar should be quite runny and soup-like, with everything nearly tender. Add the gourd pieces, okra, coconut powder and peas, and salt to taste.

6 Simmer for about 10 minutes more until everything is tender, garnish and serve.

Aloo Chole
Potato and Chickpea Curry

Here is a typical taste of north India.

SERVES 4
250 g (9 oz) whole chick peas
2 tablespoons butter ghee
1 large onion, chopped
4 green chillies
1 dessertspoon tomato purée
1 dessertspoon tomato ketchup
6–8 small potatoes, peeled and boiled
4 firm tomatoes
salt to taste
2 tablespoons fresh coriander leaves, chopped

MASALA
1 teaspoon cummin, ground
1 teaspoon chilli powder
1 teaspoon mango powder
½ teaspoon coriander, ground
½ teaspoon turmeric
¼ teaspoon black pepper, ground
2 cloves, ground
2 bay leaves, ground
½ teaspoon pomegranate seeds, ground

GARNISH
fresh coriander leaves

1 Soak the chick peas overnight to allow them to swell and soften.

2 Drain and rinse well. In a 3.5-litre (6-pint) saucepan, boil at least 2 litres (3½ pints) water. Add the chick peas and simmer for 45 minutes.

3 Simmer until tender (about 40 minutes). Drain off the water and set aside the chick peas.

4 Mix the masala with enough water to make a pourable paste.

5 Heat the ghee in a karahi or wok. Add the masala and stir-fry for about a minute. Add the onion and the chillies,

and continue to stir-fry for a further 3 or 4 minutes.

6 Add the tomato purée and ketchup, the potatoes and tomatoes, and, when well mixed in, add the chick peas, and stir carefully until everything is hot. Salt to taste, garnish and serve hot or cold.

Note: a quicker alternative is to use a can of chick peas with their liquid (optional). If served cold, it is not necessary to heat the canned chick peas at stage 6.

Moong Piaza
Green Lentils with Pink Shallots

250 g (9 oz) whole green lentils

3 tablespoons vegetable oil

1 tablespoon dried whole brown lentils

1 tablespoon poppy seeds

150 g (5½ oz) pink shallot, chopped

4–6 fresh green chillies

4–6 spring onions, bulbs and leaves, chopped

4–6 bite-sized cubes of cooked potato

2 teaspoons garam masala (see page 38)

1 Check through the green lentils for grit, then rinse in warm water three or four times. Set aside drained for about 10 minutes.

2 Measure water to approximately three times the volume of the lentils, and bring it to the boil in a saucepan. Put in the lentils. Simmer for about 30 minutes, stirring from time to time.

3 During stage 2, heat the oil in a karahi or wok. Stir-fry the dried brown lentils for about 30 seconds. Add the poppy seeds and continue stir-frying for 30 seconds more. Things should be popping by now, so calm them down by adding the pink shallots, chillies and spring onions, mixing them in well.

4 When sizzling, add a little water, the potato and garam masala and continue to stir-fry for a further 5 minutes.

5 Add the cooked green lentils and stir well. Cook for a further 5 minutes. The water will be absorbed into the lentils towards the end of the timing, so keep a good eye on it, adding more water if needed. The water should be well absorbed but not so the dish is too dry (add a little water at any stage during cooking if necessary). Salt to taste, stir, and serve at once.

Moong Piaza with pink shallots and pickled green chillies

Maahn
Black Lentils with Red Kidney Beans

A wonderful-tasting, highly nutritious dish, variations of which are found in the northern Punjab and in Kashmir. The keys to the gorgeous tastes are butter ghee, ginger, garam masala and, if you can obtain it, Kashmiri chilli powder. This is deep red and has a flavour like roasted bell pepper, with medium chilli heat. In its absence, use high-quality paprika with a little regular chilli powder.

SERVES 4

85 g (3 oz) red kidney beans

225 g (8 oz) whole black lentils

40 g (1½ oz) fresh ginger, finely chopped

1 tablespoon ghee or vegetable oil

200 g (7 oz) onion, thinly sliced

aromatic salt to taste (see page 39)

MASALA

½–2 teaspoons Kashmiri chilli powder

OR paprika/chilli powder mixture

¾ teaspoon coriander seeds, roasted and ground

1 teaspoon cummin seeds, roasted and ground

2 teaspoons garam masala (see page 38)

1 Soak the red kidney beans overnight for a minimum of 12 hours. Rinse well, then boil them for about 45 minutes. Drain and set aside.

2 Check through the whole black lentils for grit, then rinse in warm water three or four times. Drain and set aside for about 10 minutes.

3 Measure water to approximately three times the volume of the lentils, and bring it to the boil in a separate saucepan. Put in the lentils and half the ginger. Boil for 10 minutes, then simmer for a further 20–25 minutes, stirring from time to time.

4 During stage 3, mix the masala with enough water to make a pourable paste.

5 Heat the ghee, stir-fry the masala for a minute or so. Add the onion and the remaining ginger and continue to stir-fry for a further 5 minutes.

6 Add this to the lentils after their 20–25 minutes of cooking and stir well. Cook on for a further 15 minutes. The water will be absorbed into the lentils towards the end of the timing, so keep a good eye on it, adding more water if needed.

7 To test when ready mash a few lentils with the back of a spoon against the side of the pan. If they are soft, they're ready.

8 Add the kidney beans. The water should be well absorbed but not so that the dish is too dry (add a little water at any stage during cooking if necessary). Salt to taste, stir, and serve at once.

Note: a quicker alternative is to use a can of kidney beans. Discard their liquid and rinse them, and add them at stage 8. If left to stand overnight the dish will absorb water and become quite dry, so add a little more while reheating.

Shukta Cholar

Gourds with Bengal Gram Lentils

Gourd mixed with lentils is a popular combination in Bengal and Bangladesh. Any kind of gourd and any kind of lentil works well. Here I've used gram lentils (called cholar in Bengali). A typical local touch is the addition of sultanas to give it a hint of sweetness, although personally I can live without this, hence it's 'optional'. The sharp taste, however, is not dispensable, so leave in the lemon juice and lime pickle.

SERVES 4

125 g (4½ oz) gram lentils, split and
  polished
450 g (1 lb) any type of gourd or marrow,
  courgettes (weighed after stage 4)
6 tablespoons mustard blend oil
3 or 4 cloves garlic, sliced
4–6 spring onions, leaves and bulbs,
  chopped
2 or 3 fresh red chillies, sliced
1 or 2 tablespoons sultanas (optional)
1 tablespoon lime pickle flesh, finely
  chopped
10–12 fresh or dried curry leaves
2 tablespoons butter ghee
1 tablespoon fresh coriander leaves,
  chopped
salt to taste

MASALA

½ teaspoon turmeric
1 teaspoon celery seeds
1 teaspoon mustard seeds
½ teaspoon coriander
½ teaspoon garam masala (see page 38)
½ teaspoon ground cinnamon

1 Pick through the lentils to remove any grit or impurities. Rinse them several times, then drain and immerse in ample water for between 4 and 12 hours.

2 Drain and rinse the lentils, then measure an amount of water, twice their volumes into a 2.25-litre (4-pint) saucepan. Bring it to the boil.

3 Add the lentils and simmer for about 30 minutes, stirring from time to time and adding a little more water if needed. The water should be absorbed totally into the lentils, which should be quite soft, almost puréed.

4 Wash the gourds. Discard the peel if it is a coarse type (but retain if using courgettes or karela). Discard pith and seeds. Chop into delicate bite-sized pieces.

5 Timing this stage carefully, steam or microwave the pieces to tender so that they can be added hot to the stir-fry, at stage 8.

6 Heat the oil in a karahi or wok. Stir-fry the masala for 15 seconds. Add the garlic and stir for about 1 minute more. Add the spring onions, lower the heat, and stir-fry for a couple of minutes more.

7 Add the chillies, sultanas (if using), pickle and curry leaves and a little water, stir-frying for 2 or 3 minutes. Keep 2 tablespoons of this mix aside for garnish.

8 Add the drained lentils, the ghee and the vegetables, and stir-fry until they are hot right through.

9 Salt to taste, adding the fresh leaves.

10 Serve garnished with the 2 tablespoons of mixture saved earlier.

Lobia Diwanee

Special Occasion Black-eyed Bean Curry

A diwanee is a vast hall where the people assembled at the court of the Indian kings for an audience or a judgement. From time to time, the monarch's arrival and departure was accompanied by a noisy trumpeting procession of great pomp and circumstance. It would be followed by a banquet for the courtiers at which dishes of equal splendour were served. This celebratory dish contains many items regarded as essential luxuries by the latter-day maharajahs – sweetcorn, avocado, mango, and pomegranate, for example.

SERVES 4

110 g (4 oz) carrots
15 cm (6 inch) piece white radish
6 tablespoons vegetable oil
2–4 cloves garlic, sliced
6–8 spinach leaves
200 g (7 oz) canned sweetcorn, with its
  liquid
50 g (2 oz) fresh pomegranate
flesh of 1 firm avocado pear, cubed
flesh of 1 firm mango
200 g (7 oz) canned black-eyed beans
1 tablespoon fresh coriander leaves
salt to taste

MASALA

1 teaspoon ground cumin
1 teaspoon sesame seeds
½ teaspoon wild onion seeds
½ teaspoon aniseed
½ teaspoon mustard seeds

1 Dice the carrot and radish into diamond shapes, and cook to tender.

2 Heat the oil in a karahi and stir-fry the masala for 1 minute. Add the garlic and continue to stir-fry for a further minute.

3 Stir in the carrot and radish, the spinach, sweetcorn (with liquid), pomegranate, avocado, and mango. When hot, add the beans. Stir-fry gently until hot, add the coriander and salt to taste

Sabzi Haleem
Diced Root Vegetables with Whole Wheat

In central India is the former state of Hyderabad, once India's largest state and the home to the one of the richest ruling families. In the 1930s, Hyderabad's maharajah was alleged to be the richest man in the world. At his former palace, now a museum, one can see the silver model train which was set up to run around the 100-seater dining table to deliver sweets to each guest at the end of the meal. Haleem is a Hyderabadi delicacy, using wheat and meat; in this version, I have adapted it for vegans.

SERVES 4

50 g (2 oz) whole wheat grains
350 g (12 oz) red sweet potato
1 bulb celeriac
2 or 3 Jerusalem artichokes
1 medium-sized parsnip
1 large carrot
4 tablespoons vegetable oil
2 cloves garlic, finely chopped
2.5 cm (1 inch) cube ginger, finely chopped
110 g (4 oz) onion, chopped
150 ml (¼ pint) fragrant stock (see page 39) or water
2 tablespoons garam masala (see page 38)
aromatic salt to taste (see page 39)

MASALA

2 teaspoons ground coriander
2 teaspoons ground cummin
2 teaspoons curry masala dry mix (see page 40)

1 Soak the wheat in ample water overnight. Prior to cooking, rinse several times and drain. Boil for about 20 minutes, then drain.
2 Peel the sweet potato and boil it, then mash as for ordinary potatoes.
3 Quarter the celeriac and peel it, dice into 6 mm (¼ inch) cubes. Do the same with the Jerusalem artichokes, parnsip and carrot.
4 Boil these together until tender but not overcooked, test after 10 minutes.
5 During stage 4, heat the oil in a karahi or wok. Stir-fry the garlic and ginger for 2 minutes, add the masala ingredients and continue for 2 more minutes, then add the onion and stir-fry for about 5 minutes.
6 Add the stock or water and the wheat and simmer for about 10 minutes, until the liquid is reduced by about half.
7 Add the roots and tubers. When simmering, add the mashed sweet potato and garam masala and mix together well. Add salt to taste.
8 The mixture will now be the texture of mashed potato and when hot it is ready to serve.

Rajma Sag Rawash
Spinach with Rhubarb

Rhubarb is a popular vegetable in Afghanistan.

SERVES 4

2 stalks rhubarb
3 tablespoons butter ghee
4 cloves garlic, chopped
200 g (7 oz) onion, chopped
400 g (14 oz) baby spinach leaves and tender stalks
150 g (5½ oz) yoghurt
200 g (7 oz) canned red kidney beans
20 hazelnuts
2 tablespoons fresh coriander leaves, chopped
aromatic salt to taste (see page 39)

CHAR MASALA
(all roasted and ground)
½ teaspoon green cardamom seeds
½ teaspoon cummin seeds
5 cm (2 in) piece cassia bark
½ teaspoon cloves

1 Wash the rhubarb and cut it into about 1.25 cm (½ inch) pieces. Cook it to tender.
2 Heat the ghee in a karahi or wok. Stir-fry the garlic and onion for 3 minutes. Add the masala and continue stir-frying for 2 more minutes.
3 Add the spinach and add it to the karahi. Stir-fry for about 2 or 3 more minutes, chopping the spinach in as it reduces.
4 Stir in the yoghurt, beans, nuts, fresh coriander and salt to taste. Add a little water if needed. Serve when hot with naan bread.

Piri Piri Goan
Stuffed Hot Chillies

This is a fun recipe if you are a hothead. But if you do not like heat, it will be no fun at all, so avoid it. As the photo shows, the main features of the dish are the habañero or Scotch bonnet chillies, which can look so pretty when halved and stuffed with contrasting-coloured spicy potato, served optionally on a bed of massoor masala. Handle the chillies with care – they are seriously hot. Serve the dish with plain raita and plain rice. I have given a single-portion recipe here, but it can easily be stepped up if you have fellow chilli-heads to share with.

SERVES 1 (AS AN ACCOMPANIMENT)
1 habañero or Scotch bonnet chilli
1 tablespoon cooked potato
pinch panch phoran (see page 39)
pinch dried red chilli, chopped
⅓ teaspoon curry masala paste (see page 40)

GARNISH
1 fried or roasted cashew nut (as shown in
  photo)

1 Cut off the top of the chilli and scoop out any pith or seeds.
2 Mix together the potato, panch phoran, dried chilli and curry masala paste. Fill the chilli with it and garnish with a cashew nut.
3 Optionally, place it under the grill to soften the chilli and serve with Massoor Masala (see next recipe).

Massoor Masala

225 g (8 oz) whole red lentils
4 tablespoons ghee
2 teaspoons cummin seeds
4–6 cloves garlic, thinly sliced
6 tablespoons onion tarka (see page 43)
1 teaspoon chilli powder (optional)
salt to taste

1 Pick through the lentils to remove any grit or impurities. Rinse them in several changes of cold water, then soak for up to 20 minutes. Drain and rinse.
2 Boil 1.2 litres (2 pints) water. Add the lentils and cook for 30 minutes, stirring from time to time. They should be tender by now, so drain, and set the lentils aside.
3 Heat the ghee in your wok or karahi. Stir-fry the seeds and garlic for a minute. Add the onion tarka and the chilli powder, and mix in the lentils, simmering until everything is hot.

Kootu Kazhani
Hot and Sour Curry

This dish is found in Madras homes, where it is slow-cooked in a mud pot over a wood fire. Kootoo is a traditional south Indian mixed vegetable hot and sour curry, containing chilli, tamarind, sesame and coconut. The word kazhani means rice-washed water, and it is created by soaking the rice for a few minutes in water. The starchy stock produced is regarded as highly nutritious, imparting flavour to the gravy. It is served with that rice, so you can do the same and use the water.

SERVES 4
600 ml (1 pint) water
300 g (10 oz) basmati rice
200g (7 oz) aubergine
1 ripe plantain
100 g (3½ oz) long or Kenyan beans
200 g (7 oz) okra
1 raw mango
4 tablespoons sesame oil
2 teaspoons sesame seeds
½ teaspoon fenugreek seeds
10–12 curry leaves
2 or 3 fresh red chillies
2 tablespoons tamarind purée (see page 45)
200 ml (7 fl oz) coconut milk
200 g (7 oz) canned chick peas and their
  liquid
salt to taste

1 Put the rice into the water. After 10 minutes stir it carefully to release the starch, then strain it, retaining both the water and the rice. Cook the latter following the plain rice recipe on page 168.
2 Wash and cut the aubergine into slices. Strain, retaining the water, Peel and cut the plantain into cubes and the beans into 2.5 cm (1 inch) pieces. Blanch together in the rice water until nearly tender. Drain off the water and set the vegetables aside.
3 Cut the okra into 2.5 cm (1 inch) pieces. Peel and seed the mango and cut it into small cubes.
4 Heat the oil in a karahi or wok and stir-fry the seeds for 30 seconds. Add the okra and stir-fry for about five minutes. Then add the curry leaves, chillies, tamarind purée, coconut milk and chick peas with their liquid.
5 Simmer till everything is hot. Salt to taste.

Piri Piri Goan on a bed of Massoor Masala

Cherry
Cheri

Another member of the rose family and closely related to the plum, the cherry is an ancient fruit, native to central Europe and to China at least since 2000 BC. Cherries were cultivated by the Greeks and the Romans who almost certainly brought them to Britain. The fruit grows as a small sphere. The soft edible skin varies from pale greenish-yellow, through red to purple. The flesh is generally yellow, and surrounds the single inedible pip. Always buy cherries with their stalks on. They will be fresher and less likely to be blighted. Cherries are a good source of vitamin C, and yield 70 calories per 100 g (3½ oz).

Citrus family
Kaarna Khatta

The entire citrus family originated in China, and there are many species and thousands of varieties in the family. Citrus fruits are well known for their acidic tart attributes. Sweet members of the family include the familiar orange, tangerine and grapefruit. The latter, which is slightly more sour, contains an enzyme which accelerates the breakdown of fat, hence it is popular for dieting. Specialist citrus varieties are the mandarin, a small sweet orange of Chinese origin, and satsumas, the Japanese version of the mandarin. Clementines, named after the monk who 'discovered' them, are another mandarin type, and blood oranges are named for the colour of their deep-red skin and flesh. Lesser-known sweet members of the citrus family include shaddock, a large (up to 20 cm/8 inches) round yellow or pinkish fruit, named after the East India Captain who took its seeds from the East to the West Indies. The ugli fruit is named for its uncharismatic looks, but its flavour is a cross between grapefruit and tangerine. Pomello is an Israeli cross between shaddock and grapefruit. Other crosses include malaquina (mandarin and orange), ortanique (tangerine and orange), citrangequat (derived from kumquat – see page 153 – with its remarkable green seeds).

Sour members include lemons (originated in the Bay of Bengal, and taken in the 1300s to the Arabian Mediterranean for cultivation for trade) and limes (originated slightly further east, probably in Thailand and the East Indies). Although there is a marked difference between the flavours of lime and lemon, feel free to use either or both. Kaffir or makrut are 'sweet' knobbly limes used particularly in Thai cooking. Shatkora, are a larger member of the family, used as a sweet/tart vegetable in Bengal.

Citrus fruits are an excellent source of vitamin C, with some dietary fibre. They yield an average of 22 calories per 100 g (3½ oz).

Custard Apple
Sharifa, sita phoo

Custard apple is the general term given to a number of fruits belonging to the same family. They include: cherimoya (illustrated here) also called sherbet fruit, with its taste of pineapple; sugar apple, possibly the sweetest and most custardy; bullock's heart with the most solid custard texture; atemoya, the largest of the genre; and the sweet sop/monkey apple which is very sweet.

Native to tropical America, especially the Andes and Peru, and now grown in Sri Lanka, south India and Thailand too, custard apples grow on small shrub-like trees averaging 6 m (20 feet) in height. This yields a heart-shaped, pale green fruit between 5 and 10 cm (2–4 inches), whose rind has a scaly surface. The fruit has a number of black seeds embedded in a soft, sweet whitish custard-like flesh or pulp. Only the pulp is edible. It is an excellent source of vitamin C, good for dietary fibre, and also has some magnesium, potassium, and carbohydrate. The custard apple yields 74 calories per 100 g (3½ oz).

Date
Khajura

The date is a member of the palm family. Of the 4,000 palm species, two bear edible fruit, making them the best known – coconut and date. The tree is tall and swaying, with large 'scales' (which are, in fact, the remains of previous years' leaf growth). Leaves grow long and thin, like green feathers, at the top of the tree. The flowers are yellow, and the fruits grow on stalks in clusters, each of which may carry thirty or more dates. Each date contains a single, long, oval, inedible pit. Surrounding it is juicy but firm flesh, which is brown or purple when ripe. Being high in sugar (as much as 70 per cent) and low in water content, dates dry easily. This is well known by Arab nomads, who have carried dried dates in their wandering caravans for thousands of years. They call dates the 'bread of the desert'. Indeed dates, though synonymous with the Middle East, now also grow prolifically in California, Spain, North Africa, India and Sri Lanka. Dates are high in fructose, low in vitamins, and yield 275 calories per 100 g (3½ oz).

Durian
Kathal

Durian fruit are native to Malaysia, and are of the *Bombacaceae* family and are not related to breadfruit (see page 134). Durian are now cultivated in Sri Lanka and Thailand. They are the fruit of a very tall tree, which grows up to 30 metres (10 feet) high. The huge durian fruit, and the similar baobab are protected by triangular, prehensile, grey-green, inedible, prickly spines. The fruit, which measures up to 35 cm (13.7 inches) in length and weighs up to 3 kg (6½ lb) has a repulsive, very sulphurous odour, rather like that of rotten eggs. But once the spines are removed the odour disappears, revealing a sweet, whitish, creamy pulp, with a hint of vanilla, which can be eaten as it is. Durian pulp is not only regarded as a true delicacy by some, but also as an aphrodisiac. Unripe fruit can be cut into cubes and cooked for use in curries and other savoury dishes. Durian fruit are a good source of vitamins C, B1 and B3, and are good for dietary fibre as well as some minerals. They yield up to 180 calories per 100 g (3½ oz).

Fig
Anjeer

Originated in the Mediterranean and Middle East, the fig, of which over 700 varieties exist, is a member off the mulberry family. In fact the pear-shaped, pear-sized fig is a 'false fruit'. Within its pear-shaped skin casing are contained thousands of 'real' fruit, which are in effect seeds with a pink, fleshy coating. When ripe these ooze out of the outer casing's opening. The fig is high in sugars and fibres, is a good source of potassium and yields 40 calories per 100 g (3½ oz).

Gooseberry
Amla

Native to Britain and northern Europe, the gooseberry is on record as having been used by the Arabs as far back as the 700s. The gooseberry is a familiar sphere with a top and tail, usually pale green, sometimes purple, with whiter stripes, about 3 to 3.5 cm (around 1.2 inches) in diameter. Many have tiny erect hairs, but both these and the skin are edible. The flesh is quite crisp and tart, sweet and fragrant. Cooking gooseberries are larger than those destined to be eaten raw. Gooseberries have a high water content but are low in nutrients and yield 30 calories per 100 g (3½ oz).

Grape
Angoor

The grape, of which there are some 450 species, is a small ovate fruit. The skin, whose colour ranges from deep purple (called black) through maroon to pale green (called white), is edible, though often it is discarded. The flesh is edible, as are the pips, though they too are usually discarded. Seedless varieties are cultivated for eating. However, most grapes are grown for wines. Grapes were indigenous to the Caucasus,

indeed archaeological evidence shows that Armenia had invented the art of wine making by 3500 BC. Egypt copied the technique, then the Greeks and Romans in turn. Fresh grapes are an excellent source of vitamins B5 and C, with some potassium. They are an excellent source of vitamins B5 and C, with some potassium, and yield 70 calories per 100 g (3½ oz).

Grapefruit
see Citrus Family

Guava
Amrood

Native to Brazil and her neighbours, and now cultivated in the East, this member of the huge myrtle family, is the only one to become a commercially popular edible fruit. The fruit is pear-shaped and grows between 10 and 12 cm (4–5 inches) in length. The yellow or green peel is discarded while the pips can be eaten. The flesh is white, pink or red, depending on variety, and has a fragrant, sweet but slightly acidic taste. A relative is feijoa or pineapple guava, which has a dark green skin and white flesh. Guava is a good source of vitamins A and C and yields 70 calories per 100 g (3½ oz).

Pachadi
Mango and Gourds in Beaten Curd

This is another of those delightfully refreshing dishes from south India. Also called kalan, it combines minimal ingredients, the stars of which are mango, gourd and yoghurt, for maximum taste.

SERVES 4
4–6 firm mangoes
450 g (1 lb) gourd flesh, any type
4 tablespoons mustard oil
1 tablespoon mustard seeds
2.5-cm (1-inch) cube fresh ginger, finely
    sliced
4 green chillies, chopped
150 ml (5½ fl oz) natural yoghurt
salt to taste

GARNISH
4 tablespoons brown lentils, roasted

1 Halve the mangoes, stone them and scoop out small balls of flesh with a melon baller. Use any pulp or odd shapes as well. Discard the skins.
2 Boil or bake the gourd for about 20 minutes. Cool it enough to enable you to cut it open and cut the flesh into cubes. Discard the seeds, pith and skin.
3 Heat the oil in a karahi or wok. Stir-fry the mustard seeds for 1 minute, add the ginger and chillies, continue stir-frying for a minute more.
4 Beat the yoghurt briskly with a fork or whisk. Add it to the karahi, stirring rapidly to prevent it from curdling. Straight away add the gourd and when it is simmering, add the mango. Add a little water if needed and salt to taste.
5 Garnish with the roasted lentils and serve when hot.

Payary Moong Upkari
Green Beans and Lentil Curry

This is a simple curry (upkari) accompaniment dish featuring beans (payari) and green lentils. It is quite dry, so it needs a gravy-based curry to accompany it.

SERVES 4
500 g (1 lb 2 oz) cooked French beans, cut
    into 5 cm (2 inch) pieces
150 g (5½ oz) cooked green lentils
85 g (3 oz) onions
4 tablespoons vegetable oil
½ teaspoon turmeric
1 teaspoon mustard seeds
10–12 curry leaves
2–4 green chillies, chopped
100 ml (3½ fl oz) coconut milk
salt to taste

GARNISH
fresh coriander leaves, chopped
dried red chillies, roasted and chopped

1 Heat the oil in a karahi or wok. Stir-fry the turmeric, mustard seeds, curry leaves, and chopped green chillies for 1 minute.
2 Add the beans and the lentils, with the coconut milk.
3 When simmering, salt to taste and serve hot, garnished with the coriander leaves and the dried red chillies.

Dhal Aloo Sukha
Dry Fried Lentil and Potato

500 g (1 lb 2 oz) boiled potatoes
4 tablespoons cooked tarka dhal
    (see page 138)
1 teaspoon mustard seeds
10–12 fresh or dried curry leaves
3 slit green chillies
1 teaspoon turmeric
½ teaspoon asafoetida powder
salt to taste

GARNISH
fresh coriander leaves, chopped

1 Heat the oil in a wok and stir-fry mustard seeds, curry leaves and chillies. Add the turmeric and asafoetida and continue to stir-fry for a further 30 seconds.
2 Add the potatoes and lentils and toss the mixture. Salt to taste, and serve hot, garnished with freshly chopped coriander leaves.

Uppuma
Semolina Savoury Pancake

The Uppuma is a south Indian semolina savoury disc the size of a pancake, but thicker. Its alternative name is upma or uppittu. It can be eaten at any meal or as a snack.

SERVES 4

250 g (9 oz) semolina
5 tablespoons vegetable oil
1 teaspoon mustard seeds
10 fresh curry leaves
2 dried red chillies, chopped
2 tablespoons washed black lentils
   (split and polished)
1 tablespoon washed gram lentils (split and
   polished)
pinch of asafoetida
2.5 cm (1 inch) ginger, chopped
110 g (4 oz) onion
2 green chillies, chopped
500 ml (18 fl oz) boiling water
2 tablespoons cooked and diced carrots
   (optional)
2 tablespoons cooked green peas (optional)
salt to taste

1 Heat the oil and fry the mustard seeds, curry leaves, dried chillies, lentils, and asafoetida for 1 minute.
2 Add a little water, and add the ginger, onion, and green chillies and briskly continue stir-frying.
3 Mix in the semolina, and when sizzling, add the boiling water, and mix well to smooth paste.
4 Cook on medium heat for about 10 minutes or till soft, dry and lightly browned, adding more water if required.
5 Stir in the carrots and green peas (if using). Salt to taste and when the uppuma is dry but soft, serve with chutney.

Mysore Bonda
Lentil Flour Rissoles

Bonda literally means 'balls'. This speciality is a favourite snack in the exciting city of Mysore, only in this case the bondas are lemon-sized and shaped. Serve them with a sambar and chutneys. They can be frozen after cooking.

MAKES 6–8 BONDA

450 g (1 lb) black lentils (split and polished)
30 g (1 oz) desiccated coconut
4 green chillies, finely chopped
pinch of asafoetida
pinch of bicarbonate of soda
10 curry leaves
2 tablespoons mustard blend oil
½ teaspoon salt
oil for deep-frying

1 Pick through the lentils to remove any grit or impurities. Rinse in several changes of cold water, then soak for up to 8 hours. Drain and rinse.
2 In a blender, grind the dhal, using just enough water to achieve a smooth paste.
3 Add the coconut, green chillies, asafoetida, bicarbonate of soda, curry leaves, mustard blend oil and salt. Mix thoroughly.
4 The mixture should be mouldable, neither too wet nor too dry. Mould mixture into 6–8 lemon shapes.
5 Heat the oil to 190°/375°F for deep-frying.
6 Place the bonda in the oil, one by one, so as not to lower the oil temperature too quickly. Deep-fry for about 8–10 minutes or until cooked and deep golden in colour.
7 Remove from the pan, shaking off excess oil, and place on kitchen paper.
8 Serve hot with chutneys and sambar.

Kuthalam Moong Korma

This recipe is from the Courtallam region of Tamil Nadu. The locals say the white gravy reminds them of the frothy waters of the Courtallam Falls.

SERVES 4

2 coconut
4 cloves garlic, chopped
5 cm (2 inch) cube ginger
110g (4 oz) onion
25g green chilli
2 teaspoons garam masala (see page 38)
3 teaspoons coriander seeds, roasted and
   ground
4 tablespoon vegetable oil
10 to 12 curry leaves
110g (4 oz) cooked beans, diced
110g (4 oz) cooked carrot, diced
110g (4 oz) cooked cauliflower florets
110g (4 oz) cooked potatoes, diced
110g (4 oz) green peas, frozen and thawed
2 tablespoons chopped coriander leaves
salt to taste

GARNISH
fried curry leaves
green chillies
sliced tomatoes

1 In a blender, mulch down the coconut, garlic, ginger, onion, green chilli, garam masala and coriander, using enough milk to achieve a pourable paste.

2 Heat the oil in a karahi or wok. Add the paste and stir-fry adding milk as necessary to keep things mobile.
3 After 5 minutes, add further milk to achieve a thin sauce. When it is simmering, add the curry leaves and cooked vegetables. Bring to the simmer. It should be quite runny.
4 Garnish and serve.

Curries from outside India

Curry is by no means exclusively Indian and perhaps the most exciting journey we can take in this book is to the curry lands beyond India. To the south and east of India I have included dishes from Sri Lanka, Burma, Thailand, Malaysia and Indonesia. To the north I have included dishes from Bangladesh, Bhutan, Tibet, Nepal, Pakistan, Afghanistan and Iran. Further afield there is a visit to Japan for kare udon, Japanese curry noodles, and from the Caribbean there is a Grenada hot pot. The combined populations of all these countries, is close to 1 billion. Add to that India's 1 billion and we are looking at well over a third of the world's population, whose diet includes variations on the theme of curry, as often as three times a day.

A journalist recently told me that curry-eating was a fad which will pass. I cited the above statistic (which does not include aficionados in the West) and she remained unimpressed. She also claimed that home cooking was a thing of the past, and that supermarket ready meals would soon take over. Now it's time to prove her wrong, using the recipes in this chapter to prepare for yourself a delicious home-cooked meal.

Three Pithu, with atcharu pickle (right) and coconut sambal plus potato rasam in a separate wooden bowl, served with wheat papadoms

Pithu
Rice Cakes (Sri Lanka)

Pithu or puttu is made from a mixture of flour, moulded into a cylindrical shape of about 5 cm (2 inch) in diameter, which is then steamed to become a firm 'cake'. In Sri Lanka they use a special bamboo pithu mould. Here we use metal 5 cm (2 inch) pastry cutters or ring moulds placed over a bamboo steamer. Pithu is a favourite breakfast food, eaten, as in the picture on pages 150–1, with a sambol, pickle and aloo rasam, or jaggery and plantains.

MAKES SEVERAL PITHU, depending on depth
200 g (7 oz) rice flour
200 g (7 oz) plain white flour
50 g (2 oz) coconut milk powder
1 teaspoon salt

GARNISH
desiccated coconut
fresh curry leaves

1 Mix together the flours, coconut milk powder and salt with warm water to achieve a moist mouldable breadcrumb texture.
2 Insert the mixture into the moulds (see above).
3 Using a purpose-made steamer, or a saucepan with a close-fitting bamboo or metal steamer tray, bring some water to the boil. Put the moulds on to the steamer tray, placed above the water with the lid on, and steam for about 10–15 minutes, depending on pithu size.
4 Press the pithu out, garnish and serve hot

Aloo Rasam
Potato Consommé

Simply add some potato to the rasam recipe on page 57.

Jak Mallum
Jackfruit or Breadfruit with Pawpaw in Coconut (Sri Lanka)

Mallum or mallung is a Sinhalese or south Sri Lankan curry combining any vegetables to hand and coconut.

SERVES 4
1 fresh coconut
500 g (1 lb 2 oz) jackfruit or breadfruit, weighed after stage 3
mashed flesh of 1 small pawpaw (optional)
3 tablespoons mustard or coconut oil
4 cloves garlic, sliced
225 g (8 oz) red onion, thinly sliced
2–6 fresh green chillies, chopped
salt to taste
20–25 strands saffron

MASALA
1 tablespoon black mustard seeds
6–10 fresh or dried curry leaves

1 Prepare the coconut keeping the water aside and finely grating the flesh of one half only.
2 Put the flesh of the other half into the blender and mulch with the water to a thick paste.
3 Remove the flesh from the jackfruit or breadfruit, discarding skin, seeds, and pith. Cut into bite-sized pieces.
4 Cook to tender. Drain and set aside.
5 Meanwhile, heat the oil in a wok or karahi. Stir-fry the masala for 30 seconds. Add the garlic and onion and the chillies and stir-fry for about 5 minutes.
6 Add in the coconut paste and continue to stir-fry for a further couple of minutes. Add water to achieve a relatively runny creamy sauce. Add the pawpaw (if using) and saffron and simmer for a couple of minutes.
7 Add the jackfruit or breadfruit and when simmering, salt and serve.

Temperadu Bendakka
Tempered or Devilled Okra Curry (Sri Lanka)

Temperadu or devilled style, which means – hot, hot, hot!

SERVES 4
500 g (1 lb 2 oz) okra, weighed after stage 3
4 tablespoons sesame or sunflower oil
2–6 cloves garlic, thinly sliced
110 g (4 oz) onion, finely chopped
4 red cayenne chillies, sliced
4 canned tomatoes, mashed
salt to taste

MASALA
1 teaspoon ground cummin
1 teaspoon chilli powder
4–6 dried red chillies, chopped
1 teaspoon ground coriander
⅓ teaspoon turmeric
pinch asafoetida

1 Mix the masala with enough water to make a thickish paste.
2 Heat the oil in a wok or karahi. Stir-fry the garlic for about 30 seconds. Add the onion and the masala paste and continue to stir-fry for 5 minutes. Add the tomatoes.
3 During this time (and no earlier, to prevent them from going sappy) wash and dry the okra and cut their stalks. You can slice them into discs, but I prefer to keep them whole.
4 Add them at once to the karahi and briskly stir-fry for 5 minutes. They will be sealed by then, at which time you can add a little water to create a gravy. Salt to taste and as soon as the curry is hot, serve.

Kiwi fruit

So called because this Chinese native, one of three species of edible fruits called Chinese gooseberry, was first grown commercially in New Zealand in 1910. It has pretty green flesh with tiny black pips surrounding a cream-coloured core, and makes an attractive garnish. It is an excellent source of vitamin C and dietary fibre and yields 40 calories per 100 g (3½ oz).

Kumquat

This tiny citrus fruit, also spelt cumquat, is native to Malaysia, Japan and China. Eaten whole, with skin, it has a tangy, acquired, aromatic flavour., and is delicious preserved for months in alcohol such as a liqueur or brandy. It is an excellent source of Vitamin C and good for dietary fibre, and yields 48 calories per 100g (3½ oz).

Loquat

Also called Japanese medlar (which hints at its Oriental ancestry), loquat is a member of the rose family. It has orange-coloured, pear-shaped fruit about 3 to 9 cm (1¼–3½ inches) in length. The similar-coloured luscious flesh tastes like a cross between apple and apricot, and contains several large brown inedible pits. Loquats contain small amounts of sugar and fibre and yield 41 calories per 100g (3½ oz).

Love Apple
Kaith, jambu

A native of Thailand, and occasionally available in the West, the love apple or rose apple is pear-like in appearance. Its edible skin is bright green, often with a light crimson blush. Its white flesh is crispy and apple-like, and its numerous seeds are edible. The love apple contains sugar and fibre and yields 37 calories per 100g (3½ oz).

Lychee
Leechi

The lychee is a member of the *Sapindaceae* family. Only a few of the thousand members produce edible fruits, and of those only two are regularly exported to the West – the lychee and the rambutan (see page 190). The lychee, in its canned form, is a cliché from the Western Chinese restaurant; it is much more fascinating fresh. It grows to some 3 cm (1.2 inches) in diameter, and has a crimson-coloured, knobbly skin. Peeled away this reveals an opaque, pearl-coloured fruit, surrounding a brown seed. The skin and seed are inedible. The flesh is quite fragrant and juicy. It has a near relative called the lungan/longan or the more enticing name, 'dragon's eye', which has brown skin and an astonishing grey-green flesh. The lychee contains small quantities of minerals and fibre and yields 64 calories per 100 g (3½ oz).

Mango
Am

The mango originated in the East Indies. It has been cultivated in India for over 6,000 years, and is the most revered fruit there, earning itself the title 'Queen of Fruit', as well as substantial revenue as an export crop. Mango grows seasonally on a pretty tree, whose dark leaves spread out like a huge parasol. Today there are many varieties and many tropical growers. The fruit grows to an average of 30 cm (12 inches) and, depending on the variety, can be round, oval, kidney- and even heart-shaped. Skin colours range from green through yellow to pink, maroon and purple, again depending on type.

The two big names in the mango world are 'mulgoba', a round red variety and the kidney-shaped 'alphonso'. Flesh, surrounding the single pit, is always orange-coloured and very luscious. Flavours, even within the same type, vary from continent to continent, but the best mangoes are sweet, apricot, peach and spice all combined. Mango is an excellent source of vitamins A and C, and also good for sugar, fibre, potassium, and vitamin B. It yields 15 calories per 100 g (3½ oz).

Khaeng Ped-daeng Magaswirat
Red Curry Vegetables (Thailand)

Thai red curry uses red ingredients, in this case vegetables, and a delicate blend of lemon grass, lime leaf and basil, which when mixed with coconut will give you a subtle red colour and those astounding Thai fragrances.

SERVES 4

8 slices canned bamboo shoot
8 pieces baby sweetcorn, cooked
110 g (4 oz) fresh beansprouts
1 red pepper, sliced
2–6 red chillies, sliced
2–6 green chillies, sliced
8 pieces cooked carrot, sliced
2 sweet potatoes, cooked, peeled, and sliced
110 g (4 oz) pumpkin cooked, peeled, and sliced
3 tablespoons sunflower or soya oil
4 cloves garlic, finely chopped
5 m (2 inch) piece galingale or ginger
3 or 4 teaspoons bottled red curry paste
400 ml (14 fl oz) can of creamy coconut milk
1 stalk lemon grass, finely chopped
4 fresh lime leaves, shredded, or 8 dried and whole
1 teaspoon fish sauce (optional)
OR salt to taste
3 tablespoons chopped basil leaves

GARNISH
chives
fresh coriander leaves

1 Prepare the vegetables first and set aside.

Khaeng Ped-daeng Magaswirat – with sweet potato, carrot, red pepper and Chinese mixed veg

2 Heat the oil in a wok. Stir-fry the garlic for 30 seconds. Add the galingale or ginger, and continue stir-frying for 30 seconds more. Add the red curry paste and stir-fry for about 1 more minute.
2 Add the coconut milk, lemon grass, and lime leaves and simmer for about 5 minutes, stirring occasionally to allow the coconut to thicken. It may look as though it is curdling, but it cannot do this so don't worry.
3 Add the vegetables and simmer until everything is hot, stirring frequently. If it needs a little water, add it sparingly to keep things mobile.
4 Add the fish sauce (if using) or salt and the leaves and continue to cook for about 3 more minutes.
5 Garnish and serve with plain rice.

Note: Red curry paste is made with a ground mixture of shrimp paste, fish sauce, oil, fresh basil, coriander root, galangale or ginger, garlic, chilli powder and fresh red chillies. Paprika and fresh red bell pepper can be substituted for the chilli powder and chillies in milder versions. True vegetarians can miss out the shrimp paste and fish sauce.

Peeteepeepowk Onon
Bean Sprouts in Golden Coconut Milk (Burma)

If you love fresh bean sprouts as much as I do, you will enjoy this Burmese recipe which simply and lightly cooks bean sprouts (which must be very fresh, of course) with garlic and ginger in a coconut sauce, made golden with the use of turmeric.

SERVES 4

450 g (1 lb) fresh bean sprouts
6–10 spring onions, bulbs and leaves

2 tablespoons vegetable oil
2–4 cloves garlic, finely chopped
5-cm (2-inch) cube fresh ginger, finely chopped
½ teaspoon turmeric
200 ml (7 fl oz) creamy coconut milk
salt to taste

GARNISH
fresh coriander leaves
spring onion leaves

1 Wash and drain the bean sprouts.
2 Chop the spring onions into thin slices, reserving a sprinkling of leaves for garnishing.
3 Heat the oil in a wok or karahi , and stir-fry the garlic for 1 minute, add the ginger and continue for another minute, then add the spring onions and stir-fry for a further 2–3 minutes. Add the turmeric and stir-fry for 1 more minute.
4 Add the coconut milk to the pan.
5 When simmering, add the bean sprouts and stir-fry until hot. The mixture should not be dry so add a little water if needed. Salt to taste, garnish, and serve immediately.

Peeteepeepowk Net Shwe
Bean Sprouts with Deep-fried Golden Tofu (Burma)

Tofu can be added to virtually any recipe.

SERVES 4

As above plus:
225 g (8 oz) tofu

1 Cut the tofu into cubes and deep-fry it at 190°C/375°F for about 4 minutes.
2 Add the hot fried tofu (or paneer, see page 46) to the above recipe at stage 5.

Mangosteen
Amla

Mangosteen is regarded by aficionados as the most delicious of all fruits, and, like the mango in India, it is known as the 'Queen of Fruit' in its Malaysian and Indonesian homelands. Mangosteen trees grow up to 20 m (over 65 feet) tall, with thick foliage. The fruit is encased in a thick purplish-brown inedible skin or rind. It is round and about 5–8 cm (2–3 inches) in diameter and the flesh comprises several pods the colour, shape and texture of garlic, but very sweet and luscious. Note, however, that if the flesh is going brown, it will have lost its taste. Dried mangosteen is used in India as a souring agent. Mangosteen should not be confused with mango, neither should it be confused with kokum, a plum-like, dark, purple-black souring agent. The mangosteen, like the mango, is an excellent source of vitamins A and C, as well as containing fibre, potassium, and vitamin B. It yields 15 calories per 100 g (3½ oz).

Melon
Kharbooja, tarbooj

Melon belongs to the huge squash family which has some 850 species, including cucumber, marrow, pumpkin, squash and gherkin. Native to central Asia, specifically Iran, the melon is high in water content, and loved for its juicy flesh. The Greeks cultivated it, indeed they named it, *cucimus melo* meaning 'big apple'. The Romans also cultivated melon, and Pope Paul IV loved it so much, he allegedly died of a melon excess in 1471.

Popular melon varieties include: cantaloupe, named after the town of Cantalupa near Rome; net or nutmeg melon, so called because of the brown tendril-like formations on the green skin; galia (named after an Israeli melon-grower's daughter) has a distinctive tendril pattern on the skin and green flesh; honeydew has a pale buff skin and flesh ranging from light green to orange; honey melon is oval with yellow skin and cream-coloured flesh.

Melon is an excellent source of vitamin C, and is also good for potassium and dietary fibre. Watermelons are larger and generally have crimson flesh and dark green skin, with or without white longitudinal stripes.All melons are good sources of vitamins C and B and yield an average of 24 calories per 100 g (3½ oz).

Nectarine

Originating in China the nectarine was given its name by the Greeks, *nekter* meaning 'the drink of the gods'. Nectarine is a relative of the peach, with no direct relationship to the plum. It has a vibrant red and yellow skin with firmer flesh than the peach, surrounding its pit. It is a good source of vitamins C and B3, potassium and dietary fibre, and yields 47 calories per 100 g (3½ oz).

Kurilo
Nepalese Asparagus

Asparagus is rarely found in traditional curry recipes, but I was given this one many years ago by Chef Rhaman, now retired, who at the time was responsible for chef training at the Welcome Sheraton Group of hotels. The recipe is one of my favourite ways of enjoying asparagus. Try to get the tastier green variety in preference to the white.

SERVES 4
24 green asparagus stalks
2 tablespoons sunflower or light oil
1 clove garlic, finely chopped
1 tablespoon green masala paste
  (see page 45)
150 ml (5 fl oz) double cream
85 ml (3 fl oz) soured cream

GARNISH
garam masala (see page 38)
fresh red chillies, chopped
salt to taste
fresh coriander leaves

1 Cut the asparagus into 5 cm (2 inch) lengths, keeping the tips intact, and discarding the stalk where it becomes tough.
2 Do not boil asparagus – it becomes mushy and loses flavour. Steam for 15 minutes, or even better, microwave for about 3 minutes.
3 Meanwhile, heat the oil in a karahi or wok. Stir-fry the garlic for 30 seconds. Add the green masala paste and stir-fry until simmering, then add the creams.
4 To serve, place the asparagus into a serving dish and pour the sauce over it. This minimises the risk of breaking the fragile tips. Garnish with a sprinkling of garam masala, fresh red chillies, salt, and fresh coriander leaves.

Thakkali Chugander
Sri Lankan Beetroot

Sri Lanka is thought of as a hot, luscious beautiful tropical island. Its name aptly means 'resplendent isle'. But it is not searingly hot everywhere. The country is also renowned for its tea, and tea needs a cooler damper climate to flourish. It finds these conditions in the hills of Nuwara Eliya, as do root vegetables like beetroot. It was the British who brought these items to Sri Lanka, so it is rare to find beetroot recipes in the curry lands.

SERVES 4

450 g (1 lb) boiled beetroot

110 g (4 oz) beetroot leaves, or red spinach leaves

2 tablespoons sesame oil

1 teaspoon aniseed

½ teaspoon celery seeds

6 canned tomatoes, mashed

1 tablespoon garam masala (see page 38)

salt to taste

1 Peel and dice the beetroot into 2 cm (¾ inch) cubes or slices.

2 Wash the leaves, remove any tough stalks, then shred the leaves coarsely.

3 Heat the oil in a wok or karahi. Add seeds and stir-fry for 30 seconds. Add the tomatoes and the beetroot and stir-fry until hot. Add a sprinkling of water and then the leaves. Continue to stir-fry for 2–3 minutes as they reduce into the mixture.

4 Add the garam masala and salt to taste. Serve hot.

Badenjan o Bokhara Koresh
Aubergine and Plums with Beetroot in a Sweet and Sour Gravy (Iran)

The notion of combining sweet fruit, in this case red plums (bokhara) and sugar with savoury and sour ingredients is typically Persian. The specialised ingredients here can be obtained from many Asian or Middle Eastern stores.

SERVES 4

450 g (1 lb) aubergine

250 g (9 oz) red plums, stoned

3 tablespoons butter ghee

4 cloves garlic, chopped

225 g (8 oz) onion

1 tablespoon brown sugar

175 ml (6 fl oz) fragrant stock (see page 39) or water

1 tablespoon fresh pomegranate seeds

2 teaspoons sumac powder

1 teaspoon dried barberries

2 tablespoons gormeh sabzi (dried herb mixture)

150 g (5½ oz) beetroot, cooked and shredded

aromatic salt to taste (see page 39)

oil for deep-frying

GARNISH

fresh mint leaves, chopped

1 Slice the aubergine and place in chilled salty water for 1 hour in the fridge to take away its bitter taste. Drain, rinse and dry the aubergine.

2 Heat the oil in a deep fryer to 190°C/375°F. Deep-fry the aubergine slices, then remove and set aside on kitchen paper to drain any excess oil for about 5 minutes.

3 Heat the ghee in a karahi, stir-fry the garlic for 30 seconds, then add the onion and the sugar and continue stir-frying for about 5 minutes.

4 Add the stock or water, plums, pomegranate seeds, sumac, barberries and gormeh sabzi. Simmer for about 5 minutes.

5 Then add the beetroot and aubergine, and simmer for a final 5 minutes, or until the aubergine is really tender, stirring frequently. Salt to taste, garnish, and serve hot with pullao rice and/or naan bread.

Kuah La Da
Peppery Curry (Malaysia)

This favourite recipe gives typical Malaysian tastes.

SERVES 4

1 large aubergine

4 courgettes

2 large green cabbage leaves

3 tablespoons vegetable oil

1 tablespoon tamarind purée (see page 45)

salt to taste

sugar to taste (optional)

MASALA PASTE

225 g (8 oz) onion, chopped

2.5 cm (1 inch) cube fresh ginger or galingale

6 candlenuts or macadamia nuts OR 12 cashew nuts

2 dried red chillies

1 teaspoon turmeric

1 teaspoon ground black pepper

1 Put the masala paste ingredients into a food processor or blender and grind until smooth, using minimal water as needed.

2 Wash all the vegetables. Cut the top off the aubergine and dice it into pieces

about 2.5 cm (1 inch) square. Top and tail the courgettes and slice them. Place both these in ample salty cold water to prevent discolouring. Coarsely cut up the cabbage leaves, removing any inedible stalks.

3 Heat the oil in a wok or karahi. Stir-fry the spice paste for about 4 minutes. Add the tamarind purée and about 600 ml (1 pint) water. Bring to the boil and add the vegetables.

4 Simmer for about 5 minutes, then add salt and sugar (if using) to taste. Serve with a rice dish or plain noodles.

Kothu Roti
Chopped Bread Curry (Sri Lanka)

The basis of this dish is chopped up chupatti which is stir-fried with anything to hand, i.e. leftovers. The spicing is called black masala, because, as the picture shows, the resultant curry is very dark in colour. In fact, only the garnish gives it contrasting colour.

SERVES 1

2 chupatti, cut into bite-sized pieces
6–8 pieces fried paneer (see page 46)
1 hardboiled egg, chopped
4 tablespoons butter ghee
4 cloves garlic, finely chopped
2 tablespoons onion tarka (see page 43)
150 ml (5 fl oz) coconut milk

BLACK MASALA

2.5 cm (1 in) piece cassia bark
6 cloves
2 brown cardamoms
2 teaspoons coriander seed
1 teaspoon black peppercorns

Kothu Roti on chupatti with banana, banana flower, green chilli, curry leaf, coriander and white onion

1 teaspoon cummin seeds
1 teaspoon fennel seeds
½ teaspoon fenugreek seeds

GARNISH

fresh coriander leaves
chilli
lime wedges

1 Dry roast the black masala for slightly longer than for garam masala, so that it goes darker, but does not burn. Cool and grind.

2 Heat the ghee in a flat frying pan. Stir-fry the garlic for 30 seconds, then add the onion tarka and bring to the sizzle. Add the ground black masala, and when sizzling, add just enough of the coconut milk to keep things mobile. Bit by bit over about 5 minutes, add the remaining coconut milk, keeping things at the simmer.

3 Add the chupattis, paneer, and egg, and stir until it is hot and a uniform dark colour, then serve, garnished with coriander leaves, chilli and lime wedges.

Sajur Tchampur
Indonesian Vegetable Curry

SERVES 4

675 g (1½ lb) total weight chosen from the following, after preparing them: Chinese leaves, baby sweetcorn, bean sprouts, mangetout, gourds
2 tablespoons soya oil
4 cloves garlic, sliced
5 cm (2 inch) cube galingale or ginger, sliced
110 g (4 oz) pink shallots, sliced
1 inch (2.5 cm) cube fresh turmeric
OR ½ teaspoon turmeric powder
2 tablespoons skinned chopped peanuts
2–4 whole red chillies
3 tablespoons desiccated coconut
3 tablespoons sesame oil

1 teaspoon shrimp paste (optional; true vegetarians should omit)
250 ml (9 fl oz) fragrant stock (see page 39) or water
2 stalks lemon grass
4 bay leaves
100 ml (3½ fl oz) canned coconut milk
3 tablespoons fresh basil leaves, chopped
sweet soy sauce to taste

MASALA

1 teaspoon Sichuan peppercorns, crushed
1 teaspoon fennel seeds
1–2 star anise

GARNISH

1–2 red chillies, chopped
macadamia or cashew nuts, chopped

1 Roast and grind the masala ingredients.

2 Grind the soya oil, garlic, galingale or ginger, shallots, turmeric, peanuts, chillies, and coconut, using water to achieve a pourable paste.

3 Heat the sesame oil in a karahi or wok over a high heat, then stir-fry the ground masala for 20 seconds. Add the shrimp paste (if using) and stir-fry for a further 30 seconds. Add the ground paste. Stir-fry for 10 minutes, adding water as needed to keep things mobile.

4 Meanwhile, in a saucepan, bring the stock or water, lemon grass, and bay leaves to the simmer, and simmer for 2 minutes.

5 Add the vegetables. Simmer until the vegetables are crisp.

6 Add the fried paste, coconut milk and basil leaves and stir until simmering again. Add soy sauce to taste.

7 Transfer to a serving bowl, garnish with chopped red chillies and nuts, and serve with a rice dish such as nasi goreng or plain noodles.

Bonjon e Burance
Aubergine in Yoghurt (Afghanistan)

A typical Afghan combination of lightly spiced yoghurt and aubergine. (Use canned aubergine for a rapid result.)

SERVES 4
225 g (8 oz) leeks, weighed after stage 1
400 g (14 oz) canned aubergine, and juice
3 tablespoons butter ghee
150 ml (5 fl oz) yoghurt
aromatic salt to taste (see page 39)

MASALA
1 teaspoon ground coriander
1 teaspoon ground cummin
½ teaspoon ground cassia or cinnamon

GARNISH
chilli powder
garam masala (see page 38)

1 Wash the leeks and remove unwanted leaves and the roots, then thinly slice into disks, and push out the layers into rings.
2 Heat the oil in a karahi , stir-fry the masala ingredients for 1 minute, then add the leek and continue stir-frying for about 5 minutes.
3 Add the aubergine and its juice and cook for 2–3 minutes
4 Reduce the heat and add the yoghurt, stirring briskly. Salt to taste.
5 Serve hot garnished with chilli powder and garam masala.

Khumbi Imli Bhutani: mushroom (shiitake, oyster, chanterelle and pied de mouton), yucca-cassava, caramelised onion, Chinese mixed veg and tamarind

Arbi Katki
Taro and Mango (Pakistan)

Arbi, also called colcasia, taro or dasheen is a root which grows prolifically in the northern subcontinent. This recipe comes from the Sindh area of Pakistan.

SERVES 4
450 g (1 lb) taro root, weighed after stage 1
1 large, firm sour mango
6 tablespoons sesame or sunflower oil
110 g (4 oz) onion, finely chopped
aromatic salt to taste (see page 39)

MASALA
2 teaspoons cummin seeds
2–4 dried red chillies
1 teaspoon black mustard seeds
1 teaspoon mango powder
½ teaspoon ground green cardamom

GARNISH
2–3 tablespoons fresh coriander leaves, finely chopped

1 Peel the taro and cut the flesh into 3.75 cm (1½ inch) cubes. Immerse them in ample boiling water and cook for 20 minutes or until nearly tender. Drain and set aside.
2 During stage 1, cut open the mango and cut away the flesh from the skin and stone. If it is very soft, scoop it out; if firm, use a knife and dice it into 6 mm (¼ inch) pieces.
3 Heat the oil in a karahi. Stir-fry the masala for 1 minute, then add the onion and continue for about 5 more minutes.
4 Add the nearly tender taro cubes and the mango and stir-fry for about 10 minutes or until the taro is tender. If at any time it starts sticking, add a splash of water. Keep on stir-frying for another 5 minutes or so. Salt to taste.
5 Serve hot, garnished with the fresh coriander leaves.

Khumbi Imli Bhutani
Mushroom in Tamarind sauce (Bhutan)

Bhutan is landlocked in the Himalayan foothills, between Tibet and India, east of Nepal. It has a king, and a Buddhist population of 1.5 million. Rainfall is high and temperatures range from bitterly cold in the north to hot in the southern forests. Somewhere in between mushrooms grow, and this dish typifies Bhutanese tastes with its use of Indian spices and tamarind, and Chinese soy sauce.

SERVES: 4
450 g (1 lb) mushrooms, mixed types
2 tablespoons vegetable oil
2–4 cloves garlic, finely chopped
110 g (4 oz) onion, finely chopped
2.5 cm (1 inch) cube fresh ginger, finely chopped
2 dried red Kashmiri chillies, shredded
2 fresh red chillies, chopped
1 tablespoon brown sugar
2 tablespoons tamarind purée (see page 45)
600 ml (1 pint) fragrant stock (see page 39)
2 baby corn cobs
3 or 4 cubes canned yucca-cassava root, chopped (optional)
aromatic salt to taste (see page 39)

1 Clean the mushrooms as necessary.
2 Heat the oil in a wok or karahi and stir-fry the garlic for 30 seconds. Add the onion, ginger, chillies and sugar and stir-fry for 3-4 minutes.
3 Add the tamarind purée and stock.
4 When it is simmering add the mushrooms and baby corn and salt to taste. Serve as soon as they are hot.

Hare Kari

Nepalese green curry

This Gurkha recipe uses canned peas plus bright green peas, cooked minimally so that they retain their colour, enhanced by curly kale and Brussels sprouts. The latter can be omitted or substituted with cooked sweet chestnuts.

SERVES 4

8 Brussels sprouts

4 large curly green kale leaves

200 g (7 oz) canned peas and their juice

250 g (9 oz) frozen peas, thawed, or fresh

2 tablespoons vegetable oil

4 cloves garlic, chopped

1 tablespoon curry masala paste
   (see page 40)

2 tablespoons brinjal pickle, ground to a
   purée

10 tablespoons onion tarka, chopped
   (see page 43)

1 tablespoon garam masala (see page 38)

salt to taste

1 Peel off the outer leaves of the Brussels sprouts, and cut away any tough ends. Cook until tender in ample boiling water. Drain and set aside.
2 Trim the kale leaves into reasonably sized pieces, and blanch to soften them, then set aside.
3 Heat the oil and stir-fry the garlic for 30 seconds. Add the curry paste and pickle and stir-fry for another minute.
4 Add the liquid from the canned peas, and when simmering, add the tarka and garam masala, stirring continuously until the mixture reduces to a thick paste.
5 Add both lots of peas, the sprouts and the kale, and stir everything together. Salt to taste, and once it is hot, serve.

Hare Kari with peas, Brussels sprouts and curly kale

Jinstel Pachae-Shya Shokhok Gobtshe

Celery, Pak Choi and Potato Curry (Tibet)

Tibetan curries contain Indian spices and Chinese soy sauce. Since a branch of the the silk route ran just north of Tibet linking China to the India, ingredients from both cultures found their way into Tibet. Tibetan food can now be found in Nepal and the Balti area of Pakistan. This typical recipe is a celery (jinstel), pak choi (pachae-shya), and potato (shokhok) curry (gobtshe).

SERVES 4

6 sticks celery, chopped

200 g (7 oz) pak choi, chopped

300 g (10 oz) cooked potato, cubed

2–3 tablespoons ghee

3–6 cloves garlic, finely chopped

225 g (8 oz) onion, finely chopped

1 tablespoon black molasses sugar

200 ml (7 fl oz) fragrant stock (see page 39)
   or water

1 tablespoon fresh coriander leaves, very
   finely chopped

dark soy sauce to taste

MASALA

1½ teaspoons turmeric

1 teaspoon fennel seeds

2–3 star anise

5 cm (2 inch) piece cassia bark

4–6 cloves

1 Heat the ghee or oil in your karahi on high heat. Stir-fry the masala for 30 seconds, then add the garlic and continue stir-frying for 30 seconds.
2 Add the onion and reducing the heat, stir-fry for about 10 minutes, allowing it to became translucent and begin to brown. Add the sugar towards the end of the process to help the caramelisation.
4 Add a little stock or water, the celery and pak choi. Simmer and stir-fry on a lower heat for about 10 minutes, adding the remaining stock. (Note: it reduces quicker if you add the stock bit by bit.)
5 Add the potato, coriander leaves and soy sauce to taste.

Chinese Vegetable Curry

There is a type of curry one may not expect to find in a book such as this. It is the Chinese curry. Nowhere does it ever appear in China, yet it apparently thrives at Chinese restaurants in the UK. There is nothing 'authentic' about it. It is very distinctive, being made from curry powder and cornflour, and it can be used as a sauce which goes with any cooked Chinese ingredient. Here I am using a typical rapid vegetable stir-fry.

SERVES 4

CURRY SAUCE

2 heaped tablespoons cornflour

1 teaspoon curry masala dry mix
   (see page 40)

500 ml (18 fl oz) milk

2 tablespoons soya oil

STIR-FRY

3 tablespoons soya oil

4 cloves garlic, sliced

5 cm (2 inch) cube ginger, sliced

4–6 spring onions, leaves and bulbs,
   chopped

1 red pepper, cut into diamond shapes

4–6 baby sweetcorn cobs, sliced

several slices bamboo shoot, shredded

85 g (3 oz) bean sprouts

some pineapple chunks (optional)

110 g (4 oz) leaves pak choi

3 or 4 oyster mushrooms, sliced

salt or soy sauce to taste

1 For the curry sauce, mix the flour and curry masala in a jug, with enough milk until it is well mixed and easily pourable. Have the remaining milk and a whisk standing by.

2 Heat the oil in a saucepan and pour in the above mixture, briskly whisking from the start. It will immediately start to thicken. Pour in the milk continuously, but not too fast, whisking all the time, and attempting to stay just ahead of its thickening, to avoid lumps. Take the pan off the heat if things are going too fast, but don't stop whisking. Soon it will thicken no further, and it will gently bubble in the pan. Set it aside.

3 Heat the second batch of oil in a wok or karahi. Add the garlic and ginger and stir-fry for 30 seconds. Add the spring onions and stir-fry for a further minute.

4 Add the pepper, sweetcorn, and bamboo shoots, bean sprouts, and pineapple (if using). When these have sizzled for a couple of minutes, add the pak choi and mushrooms. Mix everything in well as the pak choi reduces. You may need a tiny quantity of water to help things blend.

5 Add the curry sauce, and continue to stir-fry briskly until everything is hot.

6 Add salt or soy sauce to taste, garnish with a chilli tassel and serve.

Kare Udon
Japanese Curry Noodles

Kare ko, pronounced kar-ay koe, a curry powder, is a relatively new ingredient in Japan, introduced there by British traders in the nineteenth century. The Japanese use it or curry paste to flavour their noodle broths, and this dish, nice though it is, bears no resemblance to Indian curry flavours. Use fresh vegetables if available, but if it's one of those days you haven't had the time to go shopping, or planned what to cook, you can resort to your kitchen stores and use canned vegetables and frozen beans and stock. It will be ready in almost no time.

SERVES 4

250 g (9 oz) dried Japanese udon or ramen
  noodles
OR 450 g (1 lb) fresh egg noodles
500 ml (18 fl oz) vegetable stock
50 ml (2 fl oz) mirin rice wine
2 teaspoons curry masala paste
  (see page 40)
Japanese shoyu sauce to taste (or light soy
  sauce)
110 g (4 oz) fresh Kenyan beans, chopped
85 g (3 oz) canned straw mushrooms
110 g (4 oz) fresh bean sprouts

GARNISH

spring onion leaves, shredded
ginger, shredded
chilli powder
black sesame seeds

1 Cook the noodles in ample boiling water, for the few minutes it takes for them to become as *al dente* as you wish. Then drain them and set them aside, keeping them warm if possible, for use later.

2 Heat up the stock. Add the mirin, curry paste and the shoyu sauce for

salting to taste. Put the beans, straw mushrooms with their juices, and bean sprouts into the broth to heat them up.

3 Put the hot noodles into four serving bowls. Ladle the broth on top, ensuring the vegetables are evenly distributed.

4 Garnish and serve.

Grenada Hot Pot
Grenada Curry (Caribbean)

Far from Asia, there is a part of the world renowned for its own special style of curry – the Caribbean. Grenada's lush humid vegetation makes it the only Caribbean island where top grade nutmeg and mace grow prolifically. This curry uses nutmeg, mace and two other local assets, grenadine, a syrup made from pomegranate, and dark brown crème de cocoa.

SERVES 4

4 tablespoons vegetable oil
6 cloves garlic, chopped
300 g (10 oz) onion and sliced
300 ml (½ pint) fragrant stock (see page 39)
  or water
200 g (7 oz) cassava root, peeled, cooked,
  and cubed
200 g (7 oz) sweet potato, peeled, cooked,
  and cubed
3 or 4 bay leaves
1 or more fresh red cayenne chillies, sliced
1 or more extra hot Scotch bonnet chillies
  (optional)
2 tablespoons green bell pepper, chopped
1 teaspoon black peppercorns
1 teaspoon green peppercorns in brine
3 tablespoons sun-dried tomatoes in oil,
  chopped
1 tablespoon fresh coriander leaf, chopped
30 ml (1 fl oz) grenadine
30 ml (1 fl oz) dark crème de cocoa
salt to taste

WHOLE MASALA

6 whole green cardamoms

2 teaspoons fennel seed

10 whole cloves

5 cm (2 inch) piece cassia bark

4 whole star anise

2 or 3 pieces mace

GROUND MASALA

1 teaspoon coriander

½ teaspoon cummin

½ teaspoon paprika

½ teaspoon ginger

½ teaspoon turmeric

GARNISH

nutmeg

1 Heat the oil in a wok or karahi. Add the whole masala, and stir-fry for 30 seconds. Add the garlic and stir-fry for 30 more seconds. Add the ground masala and the onion and stir-fry for a further couple of minutes.

2 Add the stock with bay leaves, chillies, bell pepper and peppercorns.

3 Simmer for about 5 minutes then stir in everything else but the salt.

4 After a few more minutes test for tenderness. Salt to taste, mix in well, garnish with liberal amounts of fresh grated nutmeg, and serve at once with rice or bread.

Passion Fruit and Granadilla

Native to the tropical Americas, passion fruit is so called, it seems, because when it was 'discovered' by the Spanish conquistadors, they felt its flowers, or stigma, symbolised the torture of Christ. That it flowers during the period of passion or Lent added to their case that the native Americans must be converted to Christianity or despatched to their maker at once.

Passion fruit grows to a smooth sphere around 5–8 cm (2–3 inches) in diameter. It has a tough, inedible red or purple skin which starts out smooth but wrinkles as the fruit ages. The flesh is pink with edible grey seeds. The granadillo or grenadillo, also from the Americas, is a close relative of the passion fruit, and its name means 'baby pomegranate'. Its skin is yellow, its seeds are blacker than the passion fruit's and it has less flavour. Both fruits are used for their juice. They are an excellent source of dietary fibre and also good for vitamin C. They yield 75 calories per 100 g (3½ oz).

Pawpaw
Papita

The pawpaw or papaya is also called the tree melon, which gives the clue that it indeed grows on trees! The Spaniards 'discovered' it in the West Indies and central America, but it is now grown in most tropical countries, including India and Sri Lanka. The tree is small with soft wood, greyish bark and a short life. Both bark and unripe fruit yield a milky sap.

There are numerous varieties of pawpaw, the largest of which grows to about 12 cm (5 inches) in length. It is pear-shaped with greenish-yellow skin and soft, juicy orange-yellow flesh and dark brown seeds. To eat ripe pawpaw, scrape out and discard the seeds and then scrape out and eat the flesh, discarding the skin. Unripe pawpaw is pickled and used in curries. Puréed papaw is used as baby food. Pawpaw (like pineapple and kiwi fruit) has an enzyme called papain, derived from the sap of the tree and the rich, milky skin of the unripe fruit, which breaks down protein. In the subcontinent, where meat can be very tough, this is massaged into raw meat and left for some time, and tenderises the meat considerably. Pawpaw is a good source of vitamin C and yields 39 calories per 100 g (3½ oz).

Peach
Arhoo

Like the apricot, the peach is native to China, and a member of the rose family. Depending on the species, the fruit's colour varies from all yellow to yellow with a red blush on its sun-facing side. Its skin has a soft rather furry feel, while the flesh surrounding the pit is yellow and juicy. Peach is a good source of vitamins A and C, and yields an average of 38 calories per 100 g (3½ oz).

Accompaniments – Rice, Bread, and Relishes

Rice, India's main staple, dating back 9,000 years, is considered to be curry's natural partner. Wheat is India's other ancient staple. The three major types of unleavened bread (roti) – chupatti, puri, and paratha – are flat discs. They are made with ata, flour of a harder, more glutinous grain than that of the West, and finer ground, creating a more elastic dough. They can also be made with plain flour (maida), gram (besan), maize (makkhi), millet (bajra), barley (koda), and rice (chaval) flours. Spicing and stuffing create further variations still. Naan breads, also discs, are leavened, meaning they rise.

Raita, chutney, and pickle are all classes of relish, the word defined in the dictionary as 'appetising or spicy food added to a main dish to enhance its flavour'. Relishes do play a very important role in Indian cuisine, acting as a counter to the rich tastes of the curries, by refreshing the palate.

Raitas are always fresh, simple yoghurt-based mixtures. Chutney, deriving from the Hindi word, *chatnee*, can be split into two types, one that is freshly prepared and must be eaten the same day, the other that is cooked and preserved, often in a sugar syrup, such as the celebrated mango chutney. Pickles are always cooked in oil with little or no sugar, and are usually spicy and salty. They too are preserved.

Here are some super examples of rice, bread, and relishes.

Many types of rice are available. Here we see four types of cooked rice, and one uncooked (top centre). This is samba rice, the round-grained rice beloved in south India and Sri Lanka. Different colours of round-grained rice (bottom) are also found in those countries. Top left is 'black' Thai rice (which actually cooks to a beetroot-red colour). Contrast this with the true black long-grained American wild rice, here attractively combined with Thai Jasmine rice.

Cooking Rice

There are many ways to cook perfect fluffy-grained flavourful rice. My own methods have been honed over many years, and they certainly do work. What I recommend if you are new to rice cooking, is at first to remove all variables. That way you will be repeating the same thing each time, and not attempting to cope with different conditions. For example, I use the same good brand of basmati rice and rinse it for a minimal time. I use the same pan each time and the same hob. The time taken for water to boil depends on the former two items and is a huge variable. Use boiling water, not cold or lukewarm. Another important factor, is time. Do not imagine that rice must be served as soon as it is cooked. In reality, the longer you give the rice to absorb the water/steam, after cooking, the fluffier and more fragrant it will be. So it can be cooked well in advance of being served. After 30 minutes it can be served and is fluffy, but it can be kept in a warm place for up to 90 minutes, improving in fluffiness all the time. There are two different ways of cooking rice: by boiling and by absorption. The above notes apply to both.

Plain Rice by Boiling

SERVES 4
(Use the smaller quantity for smaller appetites, and the greater for larger appetites)
225–350 g (8–12 oz) basmati rice
1.25–1.75 litres (2–3 pints) water

1 Pick through the rice to remove grit and impurities.

2 Boil the water. It is not necessary to salt it.

3 Rinse the rice briskly with fresh cold water until most of the starch is washed off. Run boiling kettle water through the rice for its final rinse. Strain and add immediately to the boiling water. Put the lid on and start timing.

4 When the water returns to the boil, remove the lid, and stir to ensure that no grains are sticking to the bottom of the pan. Stir gently so as not to break the grains.

5 After 6 minutes, remove and taste a few grains. If the centre is no longer brittle, but has a good *al dente* bite to it, remove from the stove and drain. The rice should seem slightly undercooked.

6 Shake off excess water. Transfer the rice to a warmed serving dish. Place it into a warming drawer for at least half an hour to dry and separate. Stir gently once during this time to aerate and loosen the rice.

Plain Rice by Absorption

Cooking rice by a pre-measured ratio of rice to water is undoubtedly the best way to do it. Provided that you use basmati rice, the finished grains are longer, thinner and much more fragrant and flavourful than they are after boiling.

The method is easy, but many cookbooks make it sound far too complicated. Instructions invariably state that you must use tightly lidded pots and precise water quantities and heat levels, and never lift the lid during the boiling process, and so on. However, I lift the lid. I might stir the rice, and I've even cooked rice by absorption without a lid. Also, if I've erred on the side of too little water, I've added a bit during 'the boil'. It's all naughty, rule-breaking stuff but it still seems to work.

Cooking rice by absorption does need practice. You may need to try it a couple of times, but then you will do it with confidence. Here are some tips: Use top-quality basmati rice, and choose a pan, preferably with a lid, which can be used both on the stove and in the oven. Until you have had lots of practice, always use the same pan, so that you become familiar with it.

As a rough guide, use 225 g (8 oz) rice: 450 ml (16 fl oz) water for smaller appetites, and 350 g (12 oz) rice: 700 ml (24 fl oz) water for larger appetites. Keep an eye on the clock. The timing of the boil is important or you'll burn the rice at the bottom.

If you intend to let the rice cool down for serving later, or the next day, or to freeze it, do not put it in the warmer. It is better slightly undercooked for these purposes. My foolproof method using a quantity for 'average' appetites and with an easy ratio to remember of 1:2 appears on page 50 (step by step).

Colouring Rice

There is no doubt that colouring your rice adds greatly to its appearance. This can be done the traditional way, using the natural colourings turmeric and saffron, or the modern way, using dyes.

To get your grains evenly coloured using turmeric, it must be added to the boiling water. The less turmeric you use the paler the colour, which can range from orange to pale yellow.

Saffron must be added after any frying, or else its fragrance will be destroyed. 'Bury' the saffron strands in cooked rice and leave it unstirred for 30 minutes or more. Mix in well just before serving.

Multi-coloured Rice

To achieve the different coloured rice effect seen in restaurants you have to use tartrazine food colouring. The best colour is sunset yellow which requires just a tiny fraction of a teaspoon on top of the rice before it goes in the warmer. Do not stir. Allow the colouring 30 minutes to soak into the rice and then stir. You'll get a mixture of coloured grains from deep to pale yellow mixed in with white and very attractive it looks too.

Flavouring Plain Rice

The following recipes suggest spicings for plain rice, cooked in either of the above ways. The method is the same for each variation. It is as follows:

1 Heat the ghee or oil and stir-fry the relevant masala for 30 seconds.
2 Add the fried masala and other ingredients, including the plain rice, and stir until hot. Serve at once.

Quick Pullao Rice

Note: *the turmeric here can be omitted, or it can be boiled with the rice to give an overall colouring.*

SERVES 4
1 recipe plain rice
½ teaspoon turmeric (optional – see above)
1 tablespoon butter ghee
1 tablespoon coconut milk powder
1 tablespoon ground almonds
pinch food colouring powder, sunset yellow
   (optional)

MASALA
1 teaspoon fennel seeds
1 teaspoon black cummin seeds

Brown Rice

SERVES 4
Add 225 g (8 oz) onion tarka (see page 43)
   to 1 recipe plain boiled rice.
1 teaspoon allspice, freshly ground

Green Rice

SERVES 4
Simply add green food colouring to 1 recipe
   plain rice as described above.

Coconut Rice

SERVES 4
1 recipe plain rice
flesh of 1 coconut, chopped into small
   5 mm (¼ inch) pieces
2 tablespoons coconut oil

MASALA
1 tablespoon black urid lentils
1 teaspoon mustard seeds
1 teaspoon dry red chilli, chopped

Cinnamon Rice

SERVES 4
1 recipe plain rice
1 tablespoon butter ghee

MASALA
10 cm (4 inch) piece cassia bark
1 teaspoon ground cinnamon

Mustard Rice

SERVES 4
1 recipe plain rice
1 tablespoon mustard blend oil
110 g (4 oz) button mushrooms, chopped

SPICES
1 teaspoon mustard seeds
1 teaspoon black peppercorns
½ teaspoon fennel seeds
4 fresh green chillies, chopped

Lemon Rice

Note: *the turmeric in this case must be boiled with the rice water to give an overall colouring.*

SERVES 4
1 recipe plain rice
½ teaspoon turmeric
1 tablespoon mustard blend oil
2 tablespoons cashew nuts, fried
1 tablespoon coconut milk powder
2 lemons, freshly squeezed

MASALA
1 teaspoon mustard seeds
1 teaspoon sesame seeds
6 curry leaves, fresh or dry

Chilli Rice

SERVES 4
1 recipe plain rice
2 teaspoons sunflower oil

MASALA
1 teaspoon mustard seeds
6–8 dried red chillies
1 teaspoon chilli powder

Chilli Recheade
Stuffed Chilli

Recheade, pronounced 'rech-ard', is derived from the Portuguese word recheado – meaning variously 'stuffed', 'filled', 'full', or 'crammed'. This gives us the clue that here is a Goan speciality, and that being the case, chilli is bound to feature with star billing. And feature it does, in the form of a Hungarian yellow wax chilli stuffed with a tempting rice filling. To achieve maximum contrast, I have used American wild rice.

SERVES 4

4 large or 8 medium large chillies, any
   colour
300 g (10 oz) dry American wild rice

1 Boil the rice which, because it has husks, will take much longer than milled rice. Allow 20–30 minutes, depending on type. Keep testing and tasting until you are satisfied. Drain and keep hot.
2 Slit the chillies open lengthways down one side.
3 Microwave or blanche them to tender.
4 Carefully open the slit and, with scissors, snip out the pith and scoop out the seeds.
5 Equally carefully, insert the rice as shown in the picture. Use any spare rice as a bed on which to serve the chillies.

Nasi Goreng
Indonesian Fried Rice

Nasi means 'stir-fry' and goreng means 'rice' in Indonesian. Here is one of their national dishes.

SERVES 4

225–350 g (8– 12oz) basmati rice
½ teaspoon ground turmeric
2 tablespoons ghee
2 cloves garlic, crushed
5 cm (2 inch) cube galingale or ginger,
   chopped
several pieces cooked gourd
110 g (4 oz) mixed frozen vegetables,
   thawed
1 tablespoon fresh coriander, chopped
1 tablespoon fresh basil, chopped
3–4 tablespoons cooked peas

PASTE

3 cloves garlic
3–4 spring onions, bulbs and leaves,
   chopped
1 large soft lemon grass bulbs, chopped
½ teaspoon tamarind purée (see page 45)
½ teaspoon blachan shrimp paste (optional)
½ teaspoon ketjap manis
½ teaspoon brown sugar
1–2 teaspoons sambal manis

GARNISH

fresh basil, finely chopped
fresh coconut, grated
macadamia or cashew nuts, chopped

1 Pulse the paste ingredients in a food processor or blender, using enough water to make a purée.
2 Cook the rice using either the boiling or the absorption method, adding the turmeric before the rice goes into the water. It can be hot or cold but it must be as fluffy as possible.
3 Heat the ghee in a karahi or wok. Stir-fry the garlic for 30 seconds. Add the galingale or ginger and fry for a further 30 seconds. Add the paste and briskly stir-fry for 1–2 more minutes.
4 Add the gourds, vegetables, coriander, basil, peas, and rice. Stir carefully to mix thoroughly. Garnish with basil, coconut and chopped nuts and serve.

Chilli Recheade with American wild rice

Mushroom Pullao

Iran invented the polou thousands of years ago. It evolved into Turkish pilav, Greek pilafi, Spanish paella and Indian pullao. Rice and almost any main ingredient can be used in pullao. Everything cooks together in a large pan, the water being absorbed, and the other flavours amalgamating as the contents of the pan are stirred. The curry-house pullao is a simpler affair. There is not time to make huge pots of pullao the real way, and restaurateurs don't want to be left with unordered food. So the main ingredient (here it is mushroom) is merely stirred into cooked pullao rice, along with peppers and curry masala paste, just before serving.

SERVES 4

250 g (9 oz) fresh mushrooms, any type
2 tablespoons butter ghee
slivers red pepper and/or chilli
1 tablespoon curry masala paste
   (see page 40)
350 g (12 oz) pre-cooked pullao rice
   (see page 50)
salt to taste

1 Wash the mushrooms as required and chop them into bite-sized pieces.
2 Heat the ghee in a large wok or karahi, and stir-fry the peppers, chilli and paste for about 2 minutes. Add the mushrooms and stir-fry, adding a few splashes of water to keep things mobile.
3 Add the rice. Mix well, stirring gently so as not to break the rice grains.
4 Salt to taste when hot, or keep in a warmer until you are ready.

Mushroom Pullao, here using shiitake, oyster, chanterelle and pied de mouton mushroom varieties

Biriani Sabzi

Rice Cooked with Vegetables in the traditional Way

This dish also derives its name from Iran. The Persian word berenji is a type of rice. It was the Moghuls, themselves of Persian ancestry, who developed the dish into a classic. In it, a main ingredient (say vegetables) is par-cooked and strained, its stock reserved. Rice is washed, then fried with spices. A layer is spread inside a flat pot. A layer of vegetables follows, then more rice. This is repeated until the ingredients are used up, but rice must be on top. The stock is then poured in, the dish is sealed and slowly oven-cooked for an hour or more. The result is myriad tastes and flavours.

SERVES 4

4 medium-sized potatoes, peeled and
   quartered
4 sweet red potatoes
4 small carrots
1 parsnip peeled and quartered, lengthways
1 aubergine, chopped
1 red pepper, chopped
2 large onions, coarsely sliced
4 fresh plum tomatoes
4 tablespoons butter ghee
4 large cloves garlic, chopped
⅓ teaspoon salt
8 asparagus tips, chopped
110 g (4 oz) fresh beans, chopped
110 g (4 oz) canned sweetcorn
50 g (2 oz) fried almonds
2 tablespoons butter ghee
300 g (10 oz) basmati rice
600 ml (1 pint) fragrant stock (see page 39)
⅓ teaspoon salt
30 saffron stamens, infused in 50 ml (2 fl oz)
   warm milk
1 tablespoon onion tarka (see page 43)

MASALA

1 teaspoon cummin seeds, roasted
1 teaspoon coriander seeds, roasted
¼ teaspoon chilli powder
½ teaspoon turmeric
4–6 bay leaves
4–6 green cardamoms
2 brown cardamoms
4 to 6 cloves
5 cm (2 inch) piece cassia bark
1 teaspoon fennel seeds
2 star anise

1 Preheat the oven 180°C/350°F/Gas 4.
2 Place both types of potato, carrots, parsnip, aubergine, pepper, onions, and tomatoes on to a greased oven tray, and bake for about 30 minutes. Remove from the oven and set aside.
3 Rinse the rice until the water is more or less clear, then strain.
4 Heat the 4 tablespoons of ghee in a wok or karahi, and stir-fry the masala for 1 minute, then add the garlic and stir-fry for a couple of minutes more. Add the first batch of salt, the oven-baked vegetables, plus the asparagus, beans, sweetcorn and almonds.
5 In a separate wok or karahi, heat the second batch of ghee and add the rice and stir-fry it for the few seconds it takes to absorb the ghee. Add the stock, second batch of salt and the saffron milk and let it cook into the rice in the open pan, for just 3 minutes.
6 Place one-third of the rice in a layer in a warmed lidded casserole pot of 2.25–2.75 litre (4–5 pint) capacity. Add a layer of half the vegetables. Add one-third more rice, then the remaining vegetables, ending with a layer of rice. Pour on any remaining juices.
7 Place it in the still hot oven. Cook for 30 minutes, lid on, then turn off the heat, leaving the rice undisturbed for a minimum of 10 further minutes.
8 Fluff up before serving.

Sabzi Biriani-e-Dum Pukht

Rice and Vegetable Pie

Dum pukht is a cooking term meaning 'containing the steam'. The technique originated in ancient Persia where food was par-cooked in a pot. A close-fitting lid was sealed with pastry dough, then the sealed pot was surrounded with hot coals, buried in the sand for a few hours and left undisturbed to finish off for an hour or more. Here is a modern version of the recipe, using pastry as the lid, and of course the modern oven. This is a perfect vehicle for finishing off biriani. The magical moment comes when the pastry is cut and the fragrant steam escapes.

225 g (8 oz) ready-made puff pastry,
   thawed if frozen
1 batch vegetable biriani, recipe on
   page 173
1 tablespoon mint leaves, chopped
4 tablespoons coriander leaves, chopped

1 Follow the biriani sabzi recipe above, cooking the biriani for 20 minutes at stage 7.
2 Turn the oven up to 220°C/ 425°F/Gas 7.
3 During stages 1 and 2, grease a 1.2 litre (2 pint) pie dish. Roll out the pastry so that you have sufficient to line the dish with a layer of pastry, leaving enough for the all-important lid.
4 Line the dish. Place the hot biriani on top of the pastry lining, and top with the mint and coriander leaves. Put the pastry lid in place and seal well.
5 Put the dish into the preheated oven, and bake for 25–30 minutes.
6 Serve at once.

Khitchri

Rice with Lentils

Khitchri is a very ancient Indian dish. It combines rice with green lentils. The first written reference to it was by the Moroccan explorer Ibn Battuta, on his eight-year voyage to India. In 1342 he wrote, 'The munj (moong dhal) is boiled with rice and then buttered. This is what they call Kishri, and on this they breakfast every day.' My grandmother used to cook khitchri, and here is her truly authentic recipe dating from 1902. I still cook it for a perfectly substantial meal, served with chutneys and pickles.

SERVES 4
600 ml (1 pint) boiling water
6 tablespoons butter ghee
2 teaspoons shredded ginger
300 g (10 oz) basmati rice
150 g (5½ oz) whole green lentils, cooked

MASALA
1 teaspoon black peppercorns
10 cloves
3 or 4 cardamoms
6 bay leaves
6 small sticks cassia bark

GARNISH
3 or 4 tablespoons onion tarka
   (see page 43)

1 Measure the water and bring it to the boil.
2 Heat the ghee in a suitable lidded pot. Add the ginger, and the masala ingredients and stir-fry for a minute.
3 Add the rice gently stirring so as not to break any grains, ensuring the oil coats the rice, as it heats up.
4 Add the measured boiled water and stir in well. As soon as it starts bubbling put the lid on the pan and reduce the heat to under half.

5 After 3 minutes stir in the lentils, and resume the process, turning the heat off after a further minute.
6 After a further 3 minutes, inspect. Has the liquid on top been absorbed? If not, replace the lid and leave for 2 minutes. If and when it has, stir the rice well, ensuring that it is not sticking to the bottom. Now taste. It should not be brittle in the middle. If it is, add a little more water and return to high heat.
7 Keep in a warm place, then serve, garnished with the tarka, after a minimum of 30 minutes.

Basic Dough-making

Before we get down to the individual breads, it is important to study basic dough-making techniques. Once you have mastered the method, you will confidently produce perfect bread. The main secret lies in the first kneading, or mixing of the basic ingredients, flour and water. This requires patient and steady mixing either by hand or by machine, transforming the tacky mass of flour and water into a dough. It should be elastic without being sticky and should feel satisfying to handle. It should also be pliable, springy and soft.

Basic Unleavened Dough Method

1 Place the flour in a large ceramic or glass bowl.
2 Add warm water little by little and work it into the flour with your fingers. Soon it will become a lump.
3 Remove it from the bowl and knead it with your hands on a floured board until the lump is cohesive and well combined.
4 Return it to the bowl and leave it to rest for 10 minutes, then briefly knead it one more time. It is now ready.

Chupattis
Dry Unleavened Bread Discs

Nothing can be simpler than chupatti-making. A disc of dough is rolled thin to about 15 cm (6 inches) in diameter. It is dry-cooked in a tava, a flat griddle pan. It cooks fast, puffing up slightly and obtaining distinctive scorch marks. To eat it at its best, it should be served at once, though, as with all Indian breads, it can be reheated or even frozen. A chupatti which puffs up is known as a phulka.

MAKES 8
450 g (1 lb) wheat (ata) flour
warm water

1 Make the unleavened dough as described above.
2 Divide the dough into eight equal parts and shape each one into a ball.
3 On a floured board, roll each ball into a thin disc about 15 cm (6 inches) in diameter.
4 Heat a tava until very hot. Place one chupatti on to the tava, then after a minute or two turn and cook the other side.
5 Repeat with the other chupattis and serve immediately

Rotla
Gujarati Chupatti, Decorated with Fingerprints

There is a Gujarati speciality bread called rotla or bhakri. The dough is rolled out into a thick, chupatti-style disc, which is then decorated with a series of depressions made with the fingertips and baked. Traditionally this is made with millet flour (bajra) and is a lovely silver-grey colour. A variation on this is to use Mexican blue maize flour, which comes in various shades

from bright turquoise, through slate blue, to purple. A variation in shape is called batlou. Debra is another variation, where spinach and chilli are incorporated into the dough. Instructions for making batlou and debra follow.

Note: the dough for these items does not stick together like wheat flour, so they are quite tricky to roll out and cook. It is like working with sand! The cooked result is a fairly dry and cracked, fragile bread, but tasty, none the less. An option is to add some wheat flour to the millet or maize flour.

MAKES 4
450 g (1 lb) millet or maize flour
water

1 Mix the flour with water to make a dough. Divide the dough into 4 equal parts. Shape each lump into four balls. It is not as easy as using wheat flour, see note above.
2 On a floured work surface, roll the balls into discs of about 12.5 cm (5 inches) in diameter.
3 With the tip of your forefinger, make a series of small depressions all over the rotlas.
4 Heat a tava until very hot. Place one rotla on to the tava. Watching that it does not burn, after a minute or two turn and briefly cook the other side.
5 Repeat with the other rotlas and serve immediately.

Batlou
Gujarati Square Chupatti

To make 4 batlous, follow the Rotla recipe above. Simply make the batlou square instead of round, and omit the finger depressions.

Missi Roti

Spinach, Chilli and Onion Chupatti

Many Indian breads are adapted by kneading green vegetables into the dough. The Gujarati gram flour chupatti debra incorporates spinach and chilli. Talipeeth is more akin to a pan-fried paratha with turmeric, chilli and fresh chopped coriander leaves being incorporated into the dough. And from the Punjab is bathuway ka roti, a paratha with spinach. Missi roti is a wheat flour chupatti with a kneading of spinach, chilli, and onion.

MAKES 8
450g (1lb) wheat flour
warm water
4 tablespoons spinach leaves, chopped, blanched, drained and cooled
1 tablespoon fresh green chilli, chopped
1 tablespoon onion, finely chopped
½ teaspoon salt

1 Make the unleavened dough as described above, mixing in the remaining ingredients with the flour.
2 To prepare and cook, follow the chupatti recipe in full.

Pictured are some less common varieties of Indian bread. At the top are two roghni naans, with a tomato-based spicy topping. Below left are two missi roti, containing spinach, chilli and onion. Centre and right are three rotlas, distinguished by their fingerprint depressions, the grey one (centre) using millet (bajra), the pink one using Mexican 'blue' maize flour, and the last one from a bluer variety of the same flour. At the bottom are two gram flour breads: batlou is a Gujarati square chupatti, and the smaller round bread is a Bengali gram flour puri called radha bollibi

Puri

Deep-fried Bread Disc

Smaller balls of dough are rolled into thin discs of about 5 cm (2 inches) in diameter, which are then deep-fried. They should puff up. Again, eat at once, before they deflate.

MAKES 16
450 g (1 lb) wheat flour
2 tablespoons butter ghee
warm water
vegetable oil for deep-frying

1 Make the unleavened dough as described on page 175, adding the ghee during stage 2.
2 Divide into 4 then divide each one into 4 more – you will have 16 similar sized pieces.
3 Shape each piece into a ball then roll out to 10 cm (4 inch) discs.
4 Preheat the oil to 190°C/375°F and immerse one disc in the oil at a time. It should sink to the bottom and rise to the top immediately and puff up.
5 Remove after 30 seconds. Repeat with the other puris. Serve at once before they deflate.

Radha Bollobi

Bengali Gram Flour Puri

Bengalis, in the north-east of India, adore gram flour (besan), so much so, that one of its names is 'Bengal gram', the chana dhal flour with a gorgeous, blonde colour and unique flavour. Radha Bollobi is a Bengali speciality bread made with gram flour.

MAKES 16
225 g (8 oz) gram flour
1 teaspoon sugar
½ teaspoon aromatic salt (see page 39)

1 Following the recipe for unleavened bread on page 175, mix the gram flour with water to make a dough, adding the sugar and salt at an early stage.
2 Divide the dough into 4 equal lumps, and divide each lump into 4, to get 16 small equal-sized lumps.
3 Shape each lump into a ball, then on a gram-floured work surface roll each ball into a small thin disc of about 7.75 cm (3½ inches) in diameter.
4 Heat the oil in the deep-fryer to 190°C/375°F and immerse one disc in the oil. It will sink initially, then rise, puffing up a bit, but (unlike those made with wheat flour) not like a balloon. Turn it when it does this and remove after 30 seconds or so, when it should be golden. Shake off excess oil and place on kitchen paper.
5 Repeat with the remaining puris. Serve as hot and fresh as possible.

Paratha

Here, ghee is incorporated with a large amount of dough, thinly rolled out and folded over itself like puff pastry, to create a layered disc of about 20 cm (8 inches) in diameter. It is pan-fried to create a crispy, yet soft bread. An alternative way to achieve layering is to make a long rope from the dough which is coiled into a cone then rolled into a disc. This is called lachadar (rope or snake) paratha. Aloo paratha is stuffed with spicy potato.

MAKES 4
450 g (1 lb) wheat flour
110 g (4 oz) butter ghee
warm water
4 tablespoons ghee, to fry the parathas

1 Make the unleavened dough as described on page 175, adding the ghee at stage 2.

2 Divide into 4 balls and roll each as thinly as you can. Flour it, then fold over and over, like puff pastry. Roll out again into 4 discs of 20 cm (8 inches) in diameter.

3 Melt a tablespoon of ghee in a frying pan. Fry one paratha on one side and then on the other, until golden brown. Shake off excess oil and repeat for the others. Serve hot and crispy.

Stuffed Paratha

MAKES 4
1 batch paratha dough, as above
4 tablespoons ghee, to fry the parathas

FILLING
6 tablespoons mashed potato
2 tablespoons frozen peas, thawed
1 fresh chilli, chopped
1 tablespoon fresh coriander, chopped
½ teaspoon aromatic salt (see page 39)
½ teaspoon coriander, ground
2 teaspoons white cummin seeds, roasted

1 Mix the filling ingredients together and make the paratha dough exactly as in the previous recipe.

2 Divide the dough into 8 balls, and roll each ball into a thin disc of about 15 cm (6 inches) in diameter. You will need a pair of discs for each paratha.

3 Lightly spread 2 tablespoons of filling over one disc, leaving 2 cm (1 inch) clear around the edge. Brush the edge with ghee, place another disc on top and press the two together to seal.

4 Sprinkle with flour and roll lightly to a disc of about 20 cm (8 inches) in diameter. Fry in 1 tablespoon of ghee and serve.

5 Melt a tablespoon of ghee in a frying pan. Fry one paratha on one side and then the other, until golden brown. Shake off excess oil and repeat for the others. Serve hot and crispy.

Lachadar Parathas

MAKES 4
1 batch paratha dough, as above
4 tablespoons ghee, to fry the parathas
7 tablespoons melted ghee

1 Make the paratha dough exactly as above.

2 Divide into 4. Mix in the melted ghee and roll each portion into long snake-like strips at least 37.5 cm (15 inches) long.

3 Coil one snake into a shape like a three-dimensional ice-cream cone. Lightly press down on it with the palm of your hand to make a disc.

4 Roll out to a disc of about 18 cm (7 inches) in diameter.

5 Heat 1 tablespoon of ghee in a tava and gently fry the paratha until it is golden brown, turn and fry other side.

6 Repeat with the other parathas. Serve hot.

Bathuway Ka Roti
Spinach Paratha

This is a spicy Punjabi bread. The dough mixture is kneaded with spinach and spices. It is then rolled in layers and fried.

MAKES 4
Ingredients as lachadar paratha above, plus:
4 tablespoons spinach leaves, chopped, blanched, drained and cooled
1 tablespoon fresh coriander leaves, chopped
1 teaspoon cummin seeds, roasted
½ teaspoon dried fenugreek leaves
½ teaspoon salt

1 Follow stages 1 and 2 of the previous recipe, adding the above ingredients at stage 2. Then follow the rest of the recipe to its end.

Debra

To make 4 debras, follow the recipe for Rotla on page 175, adding exactly the same ingredients to the dough as given in the Bathuway Ka Roti recipe above.

Leavened Dough

Four thousand years ago, the Egyptians discovered how to ferment dough by adding yeast, causing it to aerate with tiny bubbles, and rise. The process is called leavening. The Egyptians also invented the side-opening clay oven, tonir, and thus baking began. In ancient Persia, it was called the tanoor, the bread, nane lavash. It was the forerunner to India's tandoor, although we do not know how or when it turned into an upright sphere with a narrow-necked opening at the top. Nane evolved into naan (pronounced narn), cooked by placing a disc inside the tandoor neck. Before we start making naan, we need the basic recipe for leavened dough, using fresh yeast as the raising agent.

450 g (1 lb) strong white flour
25 g (1 oz) fresh yeast
warm water

1 Dissolve the fresh yeast in a small bowl containing a little lukewarm water.
2 Place the flour in a large ceramic or glass bowl at room temperature.
3 Make a well in the centre and pour in the yeast and sufficient warm water to combine the mixture into a lump.
4 Turn the lump out on to a floured board and knead with the heel of your hand.
5 Return the dough to the bowl and leave in a warm, draught-free place to ferment and rise (this is called proving). This can take an hour or so, during which time the dough should double in size. It should be bubbly, stringy and elastic.
6 Turn out the dough and knock back to its original size by re-kneading it. Use fairly soon, or else it will prove again.

Naan Bread

The following are raising agents: fresh yeast, though rarely used at the restaurant, is the most effective, though it gives a slightly more sour taste; yeast powder is weaker, but acts faster; yoghurt does work, but it must be home-made (factory-made culture is too weak); self-raising flour with bicarbonate of soda is a common restaurant mixture. Milk is said to make the dough tastier, with or without water, and sugar can be added to make it sweeter. Kalonji (wild onion seeds) and/or sesame seeds are traditionally added to the dough. Ata (wholemeal wheat) flour makes an interesting alternative naan. Try any or all of these alternatives at least once to decide which version you prefer. When hanging in the tandoor, gravity makes naan go teardrop-shaped. At home we must 'cheat' by pre-shaping them, and cooking them under the grill. The whole process is shown in the step-by-step sequence on page 51. Naans, like their unleavened counterparts, can have a myriad ingredients kneaded into the dough. They can also be grilled with toppings. Here are some examples.

Plain Naan
Leavened Bread Disc

MAKES 4
1 batch leavened dough (see above)
2 teaspoons sesame seeds
½ teaspoon wild onion seeds
lukewarm water
1 tablespoon melted ghee

1 Make the leavened dough as described above, adding the seeds during the first kneading.

1 Follow the plain naan recipe on page 51 to the end of stage 2.
2 Divide the dough into four equal parts.
3 On a floured work surface, roll out each piece into a tear-drop shape at least 5 mm (¼ inch) thick.
4 Preheat the grill to three-quarters heat, cover the rack pan with foil, put the naan onto it, and set it in the midway position.
5 Watch it cook (it can easily burn). As soon as the first one develops brown patches, remove it from the grill.
6 Turn it over and brush the uncooked side with a little melted ghee. Return it to the grill and cook until it is sizzling, then remove.

Peshawari Naan
Sweet Leavened Bread Disc

Made sweet and rich by the addition of sultanas and almond flakes to the dough.

MAKES 4
1 batch leavened dough (see above)
2–3 tablespoons almonds, flaked
1–2 tablespoons sultanas
2 tablespoons ghee, melted

1 Follow the plain naan recipe above to the end of stage 2.
2 Roll each part out to a disc of about 7.5 cm (3 inches) in diameter, placing almonds and sultanas in the centre of each one. Pick up the outside of the disc and bring it together at the centre, over the fruit and nuts, and press firmly, making a 'patty'. Flour the patty and roll out to 20 cm (8 inches) in diameter.
3 Complete as for the plain naan recipe.

Paneer Naan

Cheese-filled Leavened Bread Disc

MAKES 4

1 batch leavened dough (see page 179)
1 tablespoon ghee
4 tablespoons crumbled paneer
  (see page 46)

1 Follow the peshawari naan recipe on page 179 replacing the almonds and sultanas with the paneer.

Badami Naan

Leavened Bread Disc with Almonds

MAKES 4

1 batch leavened dough (see page 179)
1 tablespoon ghee

4 tablespoons blanched almonds, chopped

1 Follow the peshawari naan recipe on page 179, omitting the sultanas.

Roghni Naan

Leavened Bread Disc with a Spicy Red Topping

This ancient Kashmiri favourite comprises a standard naan bread which is smeared with saffron water and ghee and topped with a spicy tomato and garlic sauce. When grilled it goes a lovely red colour. Who said pizza is a new thing?

MAKES 4

1 batch plain naan dough (see page 179)
1 tablespoon vegetable oil
1 teaspoon garlic purée
1 teaspoon curry masala paste (see page 40)
4 canned tomatoes, finely chopped
20–25 strands of saffron
4 tablespoons warm milk
melted vegetable ghee

SPICES

½ teaspoon white poppy seeds
½ teaspoon sesame seeds
¼ teaspoon wild onion seeds

GARNISH

sprigs of coriander or dill

1 Heat the oil in a karahi or wok, and stir-fry the garlic purée for 1 minute, then add the spices and continue for a further minute. Add the curry paste and the tomatoes and stir-fry for a further 10 minutes. Remove from the heat and set aside.
2 Put the saffron strands into the warm milk and over the next few minutes, mash the strands to maximise colouring.
3 Follow the plain naan recipe to the end of stage 5.
4 Turn over and brush the uncooked side with the saffron and milk, then with the melted ghee. Spread a quarter of the stir-fry mixture over it.

5 Return it to the grill and cook until it is sizzling. Remove and repeat with the other naans.
6 Garnish with some sprigs of coriander or dill and serve at once.

Khurmee Naan

Leavened Bread Disc Topped with Dates and Jaggery

Also from Kashmir, this naan bread variation is smeared with a sweet mixture of dates (khurma) and jaggery (or gur), a sweet molasses-type extract.

MAKES 4

1 batch plain naan dough (see page 179)
6–8 soft dates, stoned and finely chopped
1–2 tablespoons jaggery
  OR brown sugar syrup
4 tablespoons melted butter ghee

1 Gently heat the jaggery or syrup so that it just melts. Remove it from the heat and add the dates.
2 Follow the plain naan recipe to the end of stage 5.
3 Turn the naan over and brush the uncooked side with the melted ghee. Then spread a quarter of the date mixture over it.
4 Return it to the grill and cook until it is sizzling.
5 Repeat with the other naans and serve at once.

Relishes – Raita, Chutney and Pickle

No Indian meal is complete without a selection of four or more fresh and bottled items. It is fun to choose and make up your own selection. The following recipes give you a wide choice, which should help to inspire you. Since yoghurt is used in so many Indian dishes, as well as raita, I have started by giving my tried-and-tested home-made yoghurt recipe.

Dahi or Dohi
Home-made Yoghurt

Neither the Indian restaurateur nor the Indian home cook ever thinks about buying yoghurt. They make it. It's not difficult and it is a skill well worth mastering. Not only does home-made yoghurt cost a fraction of the factory version, it is also fresher and creamier too. To start a yoghurt you need fresh (not UHT) or powdered milk. You also need a live bacteriological culture called bulgaris (available from health food shops), to start the process. As this is present in yoghurt itself you can use factory yoghurt as a starter, although this is weaker than the proper culture and can result in a thinner yoghurt.

The key points are:
• boiling the milk, which ensures there are no competitive bacteria left alive to vie with the bulgaris in the yoghurt
• using fresh culture or yoghurt as the starter
• keeping the newly mixed yoghurt warm enough to ferment and multiply for the first few hours
• stopping fermentation by chilling to prevent it from becoming too sour.

MAKES ABOUT 425 G (15 OZ) YOGHURT
600 ml (1 pint) milk
1 tablespoon milk powder
1 tablespoon bulgaris culture or fresh
  yoghurt

1 Bring the milk to the boil, add the milk powder, then keep it simmering for 2–3 minutes. Use a 2.3-litre/4-pint pan, and it won't boil over.
2 Remove from the heat and allow to cool to just above blood temperature, about 20–30 minutes. It should be no cooler than 40°C/104°F and no hotter than 45°C/113°F. The age-old test in the Middle East, albeit rather unhygienic and perhaps a little masochistic, is to immerse the fingertips in the milk. Once you can keep them in it for 10 seconds it is ready.
3 In a mixing bowl combine the yoghurt culture or yoghurt with a few drops of the warmed milk. Mix well. Add more and more milk until it is at pouring consistency.
4 Pour this and the remaining milk into a non-metallic bowl. Cover with cling film then put it in a warm, draught-free place to ferment (the airing cupboard or a pre-warmed switched-off oven are ideal).
5 Leave it fermenting undisturbed for at least 6 hours and no more than 8. The longer it is left the sourer it becomes. Put it into the fridge to stop fermenting for at least 2 hours.

Note: fermentation will stop if the temperature exceeds 54°C/130°F or goes below 37°C/100°F.

Raita

Raitas are yoghurt mixed with a small quantity of savoury items. One or more raitas goes well with with snacks and main meals. They are normally very mild and the most effective antidote to very hot tastes in the mouth. (Water is less effective.)

Plain Raita or Dahi
Unflavoured Natural Yoghurt

SERVES 4
150 g (5½ oz) plain yoghurt

Serve chilled.

Spiced Raita Yoghurt Chutney

1 BATCH PLAIN RAITA PLUS:
salt or black salt to taste
½ teaspoon chilli powder and/or
½ teaspoon garam masala (see page 38)

Raita Variations

Almost anything savoury can be mixed into the plain or spiced raitas above. Here are some suggestions:

Beetroot Raita

Add bottled vinegared beetroot, chopped with a little liquid.

Carrot Raita

Add shredded carrot

Chilli Raita

Add 3 or 4 fresh green or red chillies, chopped

Chilli Jeera Raita

Add 1 teaspoon each chilli powder and cummin (ground), plus some roasted cummin seeds

Coconut Raita

Add 3 tablespoons fresh coconut, shredded
OR 2 tablespoons coconut milk powder

Cucumber Raita

Add cucumber cut into matchsticks

Green Mint Raita (Tandoori Raita)

Add:
1 teaspoon sugar
1 teaspoon bottled vinegared mint
¼ teaspoon mango powder
a little green food colouring (optional)

Kerelan Raita

Add the following, all fried and cooled:
1 teaspoon mustard seeds
1 tablespoon onion tarka (see page 43)
1 dried red chilli, chopped
1 teaspoon ginger, finely chopped

Clockwise from red chilli: mixed pickle purée, sweet mango chutney, chilli pickle, Dom's tomato chutney, fruit and nut mango chutney, coconut and maldive fish sambol, with Kerelan raita in the centre

Mixed Raita

Add cucumber, onion, tomato and fresh coriander, all chopped.

Fresh Chutneys

As I mentioned earlier in the book, fresh salads are not part of India's heritage apart, that is, from this chutney, called cachumber.

Cachumber Salad

SERVES 4

1 large red or white onion, thinly sliced
2 green chillis, thinly sliced
½ green pepper, thinly sliced
2 tomatoes, thinly sliced
½ fresh mango, thinly sliced
1 tablespoon coriander, freshly chopped
1 tablespoon vinegar
1 tablespoon olive or sunflower oil
1 teaspoon fennel seeds
salt to taste

1 Combine everything in a bowl, including salt to taste. Cover and chill for up to 24 hours.

Imli Gajar
Shredded Carrot with Tamarind

SERVES 4

3 or 4 large carrots
4–6 tablespoons tamarind purée (see page 45)
juice of 1 lemon, freshly squeezed
1–2 tablespoons jaggery or brown sugar
1 or 2 teaspoons chilli powder
salt to taste

1 Wash and scrape the carrots, then shred them, using a mandolin, grater or a food processor.
2 Mix the remaining ingredients together, adding enough water to make a runny mixture.
3 Combine mixture well with the carrots so that all the carrot is covered with the liquid. Add salt to taste.
4 Place in a serving bowl and refrigerate for at least 6 hours.
5 Serve when ready.

Podina

SERVES 2

2–3 spring onions, leaves and bulbs, very finely chopped
1 teaspoon bottled minced coriander
2 teaspoons bottled vinegared mint
4 tablespoons fresh mint leaves, finely chopped
juice of 1 lemon
salt to taste

1 Combine all the ingredients together with enough water to make it mobile. Chill and serve.

Dhania Narial
Fresh Coriander/Coconut Purée

SERVES 2 TO 4

1 large bunch coriander leaves (stalks removed)
1 small onion, coarsely chopped
2 tablespoons coconut, fresh or desiccated
1 tablespoon lemon juice
salt to taste

1 Process all the ingredients together in a blender, using just enough water to make a thick paste. Chill and serve. Use within a few days or freeze. This chutney can be used in cooking in place of fresh coriander.

Fresh Chilli Purée

MAKES ABOUT 700 G (1½ LB) CHUTNEY
450 g (1 lb) fresh green chillies, stalks
 removed
1 bunch coriander leaves, stalks removed
300 ml (½ pint) clear distilled malt vinegar

1 Combine all the ingredients in a
food processor and grind to a purée.
You may need a little more vinegar.
Stored in a screw-top jar, this will last
indefinitely.

Fresh Chilli Tassels

An attractive garnish, these are easily
made, using fresh chillies of any size or
colour. Leave the stalks on. Cut just
below the stalk, lengthways towards
and right through the tip. Make several
cuts. Immerse in a bowl of cold water
containing ice cubes for 30–60 minutes
and the tassels will form. Drain and use
at once.

Vinegared Chillies

Simply put fresh green or red chillies in
vinegar. Nothing more, nothing less.
Lasts for ever. Use only very fresh
chillies and place them, stalks and all,
into a lidded jar. Fill the jar to the brim
with distilled clear vinegar. Leave for a
few days, then use, or keep for as long
as you wish.

Minced Green or Red Chilli

225 g (8 oz) red or green chillies (but not
 mixed colours)
distilled clear vinegar

1 De-stalk the chillies. Put them in the
food processor and pulse, adding just
enough vinegar to achieve a coarse
purée. Store in a clean lidded jar and
top off with more vinegar. The purée
can be used at once or days or even
years later. Green chillies will, of course,
lose their bright green colour over time,
but not their taste.

Devil Chutney

*A hot speciality from the Nilgiri Hills.
Must be eaten fresh as it won't keep.*

MAKES 110 G (4 OZ) CHUTNEY
50 g (2 oz) whole red chillies, dry
25 g (1 oz) dates or plums, mashed
25 g (1 oz) onion
2 cm (¾ inch) piece ginger
2 cloves garlic
juice of 2 limes
1 teaspoon sugar
salt to taste

1 Mulch everything down in a blender
to obtain a coarse purée. If the lime
juice does not achieve a pourable
texture, help things along with a little
water.
2 Chill and serve.

Coconut Sambol

*A Sri Lankan meal would be incomplete
without this chutney.*

SERVES 4 (GENEROUSLY)
flesh of 1 fresh coconut, grated
OR 50 g (2 oz) desiccated coconut
10 dried red chillies
50 g (2 oz) onion, chopped
juice of 1 lime
2 green chillies
2 teaspoons salt

1 Mulch everything down in a blender
to achieve a coarse purée. If the lime
juice does not create a pourable texture,
help things along with a little water.
2 Chill and serve.

Katta Sambol

*Because this sambol contains an ingredient
called Maldive fish (a product comprising
chippings of dried fish blended with chilli,
available from certain Asian stores) it will
not suit the true vegetarian.*

SERVES 4 (GENEROUSLY)
60 g (2 oz) Maldive fish
remaining ingredients as above

1 Follow the recipe for coconut
sambol, adding the fish at stage 1.

Onion Sambol

*Dark in colour, sweet and sour in taste,
this is another Sri Lankan favourite.*

SERVES 4 (GENEROUSLY)
110 g (4 oz) onion tarka (see page 43)
50 ml (2 fl oz) lime juice
lots of white pepper
salt to taste

1. Mix the lime juice into the tarka and
season. Chill and serve.

Persimmon (Sharon Fruit)

The persimmon or kaki fruit is native to China and Japan, and is called the 'apple of the Orient'. The fruit is tomato-shaped and grows up to 4 cm (1.5 inches) in diameter. When ripe, the fruit is orange with purplish coarse leaves. Because they go off quickly, they are sold unripe when their flavour is rather bitter. If ripened at home the bitter taste gives way to a sweet, aromatic flavour, and apple-like texture. The Israeli version of this fruit is not only the sweetest available in the West, it is also seedless. Called sharon fruit, it was named after the daughter of the original grower. Persimmon is an excellent source of vitamins A and also has some vitamin C. It yields 77 calories per 100 g (3½ oz).

Phylasis fruit (Chinese Lantern)

Originating in Peru, this fruit has a unique feature when it first develops on the tree. It has a translucent white or buff papery covering which gives rise to its alternative name Chinese lantern, with varieties including cape gooseberry (grown in South Africa, hence the name) and the larger tomatillo. As the fruit begins to ripen, its covering opens into five leaves, resembling the panels of a parachute, under which is suspended a green, spherical berry, about 1–1.5 cm (less than ½ inch) in diameter. This

ripens to a deep orange colour. The whole fruit (including the seeds) is edible and has a sweet, fragrant taste. It is a good source of vitamin C and yields 40 calories per 100 g (3½ oz).

Pineapple

Ananas

The pineapple is believed to have originated in Latin America, and it appears in Mayan picture writings. However, it also appears in similar ancient Indian art, long before Columbus, and begs the question how could this fruit appear in both continents? It is one of the great culinary mysteries. When the post-Columbus Spanish 'discovered' pineapple, they gave it the name *pina*, meaning fir cone, whose structure the fruit resembles. It grows as a perennial, stemless plant, up to 1 m (39 inches) in height, with narrow, grey-green, serrated leaves, about 30–40 cm (12–15 inches) long. In botanical terms, the fruit is an inflorescence (a collection of flowers) which grows to around 15 cm (6 inches) in length out of the serrated leaves. The fruit itself is protected by inedible yellow 'scales' and has a topknot of small leaves. The scales must be discarded, along with the black 'eyes' in the flesh, the remains of the flowers. The central pithy core is also inedible, leaving luscious pale yellow flesh with a sweet, tart, acidic flavour. Miniatures are great for stuffing. Pineapple is a good source of vitamin C and yields 55 calories per 100 g (3½ oz).

Plum

Alucha, alu bhukara, jamus

A member of the rose family, originally from eastern Asia, and now found in temperate and tropical climates worldwide. The many varieties have luscious yellow flesh surrounding a pit, and skin ranging from green through red. Damson (must be cooked), greengage (very sweet and green in colour), mirabelle (a small golden variety) and sloe (sour and best cooked) are all near relatives. Plums dry well, in which form they are known as prunes. The plum is good for dietary fibre and yields 37 calories per 100 g (3½ oz).

Prickly Pear

Its prickly and botanical name, *cataceae* gives the clue that this is indeed the edible fruit of a cactus, emanating from America, where the fruit is much enjoyed for its juicy watermelon-like flavours and slight acidity. Also called horned melon, Barbary fig, Indian fig or tuna fig, it is now cultivated in Spain, Morocco, Italy and Israel. The oval fruit grows to about 7–10 cm (2.75–4 inches) in length and is available ripe from green to orange. Beware its prickles, although they should have been scraped off during cropping; if not they are painful to extract from your fingers. Discard the skin but eat the copious seeds and flesh. The prickly pear is a good source of vitamin C and yields 56 calories per 100 g (3½ oz).

COOKED CHUTNEYS AND PICKLES

Dominique's Sweet Plum Chutney

In my previous Bibles I have given recipes for mango chutney and for a gorgeous red fragrant sweet tomato chutney developed by Dominique. Here is a brand new chutney she has devised along the same lines.

MAKES 600 G (1 LB 4OZ) CHUTNEY

450 g (1 lb) Victoria plums, quartered and stoned

150 ml (5 fl oz) water

150 ml (5fl oz) cider vinegar

225 g (8 oz) granulated/caster sugar (must be white)

3 cloves garlic, finely chopped

MASALA

4 bay leaves, fresh or dried

1½ blades mace

1 teaspoon green or white cardamom

1 In a 1.4 litre (2¼ pint) heavy saucepan, bring the water, vinegar and masala to the simmer. Add the sugar, and stir gently while it dissolves.

2 Raise the heat and bring to a boil. Add the plums and garlic and lower the heat to achieve a gently rolling simmer for 30 minutes. It will appear watery at first, but will reduce. Stir occasionally at the beginning, and more regularly towards the end of the cooking time, making sure it doesn't stick to the bottom of the pan while the mixture reduces.

3 The finished chutney is jam-like and should have reduced by two-thirds.

4 Remove the pan from the heat and let it cool sufficiently to bottle in sterilised, warmed jars. Cover and label. It can be eaten at once, or it will keep indefinitely.

Sweet Red Chilli Chutney

Another cooked recipe. Definitely one for the chilli-heads.

MAKES ABOUT 700 G (1½ LB) CHUTNEY

450 g (1 lb) fresh red chillies, chopped

175 ml (6 fl oz) water

225 g (8 oz) sugar

2 cloves garlic, chopped

5 fl oz (150 ml) distilled white wine vinegar

MASALA

2–3 bay leaves

1 teaspoon black cummin seeds

½ teaspoon coriander seeds

1 Follow the plum chutney recipe above exactly, substituting the chillies for the plums.

Lemon (or Lime, Mango, or Aubergine) Pickle

MAKES ABOUT 900 G (2 LB) PICKLE

450 g (1 lb) lemons (or limes, or green mango, or aubergines), weighed after stage 1

10 large cloves garlic, chopped

450 ml (¾ pint) vegetable oil

2–8 fresh green chillies

900 ml (1½ pints) distilled white vinegar

1 tablespoon salt

1 tablespoon sugar

MASALA

1 teaspoon turmeric

1 teaspoon ground cummin

1 teaspoon chilli powder

1 teaspoon garam masala (see page 38)

2 teaspoons paprika

1 Choose your fruit/vegetable. In the case of lemons or limes, quarter them. Mangoes and aubergines need de-pitting and chopping.

2 Mulch the garlic and masala ingredients in the blender with just enough vinegar to make a paste.

3 Heat one-third of the oil in a wok. Stir-fry the paste for a couple of minutes. Add the fruit/vegetables and chillies and continue to stir-fry for about 10 minutes, stirring regularly.

4 Meanwhile put the vinegar, the salt and sugar into a large pan and bring to the simmer. Add the above, stir-fry and simmer and occasionally stir for about 30 minutes. During this time, add most of the remaining oil and cook gently until the vinegar boils out and the oil comes to the top. Put aside to cool slightly.

5 Sterilise and lightly warm some screw-top jars in the oven to ensure they are dry.

6 Heat the remaining oil. Fill the jars with the pickle, pouring some of the hot oil on top to seal it and put on lids. Can be eaten at once, but improves greatly with age, and if made correctly will last for ever.

Green Chilli Pickle

This large batch lasts a while and is worth the effort. It is adapted from a recipe by Curry Club member Trevor Pack.

450 g (1 lb) fresh green chillies
300 ml (½ pint) vegetable oil
6 cloves garlic, finely chopped
2.5 cm (1 inch) cube ginger, finely chopped
675 g (1½ lb) onion, finely chopped
1 tablespoon muscovado sugar
1 tablespoon salt
300 ml (½ pint) distilled clear vinegar

SPICES
4 tablespoons ground cummin
2 tablespoons turmeric
1 tablespoon curry masala paste
   (see page 40)

1 Make a paste of the spices by adding water.
2 Heat the oil in a large saucepan. Add the garlic, ginger and onion and stir-fry for 5 minutes.
3 Add the paste and stir-fry for a further 10 minutes.
4 Add the chillies, sugar, salt and vinegar and simmer for a further 15 minutes. Allow to cool a little.
5 To finish follow stages 5 and 6 of the previous recipe.

Mixed Pickle

When you have just a spoonful or two left in your pickle or chutney bottles, mix all the remnants together and rebottle. Depending on what you use, you'll get a different pickle every time. Incidentally, I find that mulching down the pickle with an electric hand blender gives a very interesting texture, and the pickle goes further that way too.

Atcharu Pickle

Sri Lankan Vinegared Vegetable Pickle

A picture of this pickle appears on pages 150–1. My method uses small pickled onions plus their vinegar, with additional vegetables and a masala.

MAKES ABOUT 1 KG (2.2 LB)
400 g (14 oz) bottled pickled onions and
   their vinegar
additional malt distilled vinegar
225 g (8 oz) carrot, sliced
225 g (8 oz) Kenyan beans, sliced
8 cloves garlic, peeled
4–8 green chillies, whole
1 teaspoon salt

MASALA
2 teaspoons crushed mustard seeds
1 teaspoon paprika
½ teaspoon chilli powder
½ teaspoon curry masala dry mix
   (see page 40)

1 Strain the pickled onions, retaining the vinegar.
2 Measure this vinegar with the additional vinegar to obtain a total amount of 150 ml (5 fl oz).
3 Heat the vinegar in a wok and add the masala. Stir until simmering. Add the carrots, beans, garlic, and whole chillies, and simmer for around 5 minutes.
4 Take off the heat. Mix in the pickled onions and salt. Put aside to cool slightly.
5 Sterilise and lightly warm some screw-top jars in the oven to ensure they are dry.
6 Fill the jars with the pickle, ensuring equal distribution of the liquid. It will need a vinegar top-up to fill. Put on the caps. Can be eaten at once, but improves greatly with age, and if made correctly will last for ever.

Fruit and desserts

To say the people of India and her neighbours have a sweet tooth is an understatement. Yet many of the puddings at the Indian restaurant leave much to be desired. In my previous books, I have given recipes for Indian puddings, and here are a few favourites, including jalebis, those syrup-drenched crispy spirals, moyra banana, with its complementary sauce, pancakes with creamy stuffing or a sweet coconut sauce, rice pudding, that age-old standby, and exotic fruit salad. I have also included several new recipes, among them rice noodles with grenadine, sweet fritters, walalappan – dark egg custard, sago and dhal (rice) pudding, and vermicelli pudding with saffron.

In the subcontinent, there is a phenomenon which has no parallel in the West. It is a massive industry, called simply 'paan'. It involves an army of 'paan wallahs' – traders – who prepare 'paan masalas' or mixtures, dispensing their wares in smart restaurants, at home door-to-door, or at street kiosks. The observant visitor to India will have noticed those street kiosks with their bright dark green paan leaves and dozens of silver pots containing all sorts of weird and wonderful ingredients. The kiosks are invariably busy. Morning, noon and night, at home, at restaurants and in the street, people are forever chewing paan.

Paan, an acquired taste, is best defined as a collection of edible ingredients, ranging from very bitter to very sweet. Some are dry seeds, and some are acidic and alkaline wet pastes. On page 127 we see the two ingredients which form the basis of paan – the leaf and the betel nut.

Some paan ingredients are found at the Indian restaurant in the West, particularly in the form of a coloured and fragrant mixture called supari, served as the conclusion to the curry meal.

Try all the desserts. And to finish off, why not try paan, a mixture of seeds, leaves, and bittersweet ingredients which helps to digest all that has gone before!

SOME PAAN INGREDIENTS

Spices

Certain aromatic spices can be chewed on their own at any time, for example aniseed, green cardamom, cloves and fennel seeds.

Seeds

Seeds from the squash or gourd family. Magaz is a melon seed and charmagaz is a combination of four (char) squash seeds – cucumber, marrow, water melon and pumpkin. All are oval cream-coloured discs with a tasty nutty flavour.

Nuts

Pine nuts (*chilgoza*) are also good in this context. As is the cuddapah almond or in Hindi, the *chirongi* or *charauli* which is small, round, pale brown and quite aromatic, almost minty in flavour.

Betel Nut and Tobacco

The bitter taste so beloved by many paan eaters comes from the betel nut itself, optionally enhanced by tobacco shreds.

Sweeteners

To counter the bitter tastes, sugar crystals or sugar balls are used. Factory made sugar-coated fennel seeds or the smaller sugar-coated aniseeds come in white or bright colours – red, pink, orange, yellow and green (using food colourings).

Supari Mix

25 g (1 oz) sugar-coated aniseed
25 g (1 oz) fennel seeds, roasted
1 tablespoon sunflower seeds
1 teaspoon betel nut, shredded

Mix all the ingredients together and store in an airtight jar, where it will keep well for months.

PRESENTATION

Paan eating is taken for granted in the subcontinent and it is often presented in beautiful and elaborate paan boxes (*paana bata*). Traditionally they are made of silver or brass (as illustrated on the previous pages), the leaves being placed in the box, while the owner's choice of ingredients – seeds, pastes, betel – are on a tray above. For the less extravagant there are portable kits, comprising, perhaps, a shallow silver leaf box with an accompanying embroidered pouch with enough pockets to hold a selection of favourite ingredients.

Patishapta Pitha
Pancakes with a Creamy Filling

As this dish is particularly rich, I suggest you make only 4 pancakes, though the batter mixture will make more. That's because if you're like me, the first one never works!

MAKES 4–6 PANCAKES
PANCAKES
50 g (2 oz) plain white flour
25 g (1 oz) melted butter
1 egg, beaten
150 ml (5 fl oz) milk, warmed
1 teaspoon white sugar
2 or 3 drops vanilla essence

FILLING
110 g (4 oz) soft cream cheese
50 g (2 oz) thick soured cream
1 teaspoon white sugar
½ teaspoon ground cardamom
¼ teaspoon freshly grated nutmeg

GARNISH
icing sugar
more nutmeg
lime wedges
warm maple syrup

1 First, make the 4 pancakes (see note on page 133). Sift the flour into a bowl and mix in the butter, egg, warm milk, sugar and vanilla. Beat well and leave to stand for about 10 minutes. It should be of pouring consistency.
2 In a very hot omelette or griddle pan, heat a little butter. Pour in enough batter to make a thin pancake when 'swirled' around the pan. Cook until set, then turn over and briefly cook the other side. Turn it out. Repeat with the remaining batter. Allow the pancakes to go cold (see note on page 133).
3 Mix the filling ingredients together, mash until smooth.

4 Spread one quarter of it across the centre line of one pancake and roll it into a cylinder. Repeat with the other three.

5 Warm the syrup.

6 To serve, dust the cold pancakes with icing sugar and nutmeg and serve with a lime wedge, and some warm maple syrup.

Pothittu
Pancakes with a Sweet Sauce

From the Nilgiri Hills of south India, comes this pancake, with a distinctive sauce of coconut and sesame seeds. It is enjoyed by the Badaga tribe as a pudding, and also as an accompaniment to a savoury dish, avarai uthaka (see page 118 for recipe).

MAKES 4–6
PANCAKES
ingredients as above

SWEET SAUCE
400 ml (14 fl oz) creamy coconut milk
50 g (2 oz) sesame seeds, crushed and
    roasted
50 g (2 oz) gur, jaggery, or sugar
⅓ teaspoon salt

1 Heat the coconut milk in a non-stick pan. Add the sugar and simmer for a short while to thicken. Add the sesame seeds and salt, and set aside keeping it warm.

2 Make the pancakes following stages 1 and 2 of the recipe above. Serve them hot with the sauce poured on top.

Quince

Quince is high in pectin and was once greatly in demand for jam-making. Depending on the variety, of which there are many, it can be either apple- or pear-shaped. Its yellowish flesh is too hard to eat raw, but goes soft, fragrant and pink when cooked. Japonica is a close relative with similar attributes. Qunice is high in sugars, potassium and fibre, and yields 25 calories per 100 g (3½ oz).

Rambutan

Member of the *Sapindaceae* family (see also Lychee), the rambutan is native to Malaysia and Indonesia. It grows to an oval shape, some 4 cm (1.5 inches) in length, and has an orange-, yellow- or crimson-coloured, knobbly skin, made distinctive from the lychee by numerous short green hairs. Indeed it is named for this characteristic, *rambat* in Malay meaning 'hair'. It is also known in Malaysia as the 'fruit of the gods'. Once the skin is peeled away, a translucent, cream-coloured flesh surrounding a brown seed is revealed. The skin and seeds are inedible; the flesh is fragrant and juicy, but less so than the lychee's. The rambutan has small quantities of minerals and fibre and yields 64 calories per 100 g (3½ oz).

Raspberry
Kair

Raspberry is a member of the rose family, and, like the blackberry, comprises many fruits (called compound). Normally red, raspberry is also available in black, brown, orange, pink, purple and yellow. Raspberries grew wild in prehistoric Britain, and have been cultivated since the 1600s. The loganberry (or tayberry) is a cross between the raspberry and blackberry; boysenberry is a purple version. Raspberry is an excellent source of dietary fibre and is also good for vitamin C and minerals. It yields 22 calories per 100 g (3½ oz).

Red Currant
Lal kair

Native to Britain and northern Europe, and related to the gooseberry, redcurrant is well known in its red form, but there are also black and white varieties, with similar characteristics. The small translucent spheres grow to around 11 mm in diameter. Skin, seeds and flesh are all edible.

Rhubarb

Originating in Tibet and the Himalayas, rhubarb was used medicinally centuries before Christ. It was doubtless the Arabs who brought it westward, and their name for it was *ribas*. It was introduced into Britain in the 1500s, but its use was confined to herbal remedies until Victorian times, when it became a major fruit. It grows in pink or red stalks or stems. Being a leaf stem, it is technically a vegetable, and it can be used in savoury dishes. The leaves should be discarded since their oxalic content makes them poisonous. Rhubarb contains vitamin C and dietary fibre and yields 6 calories per 100 g (3½ oz).

Moyra Banana

In the state of Goa there is a town called Moyra. It is not a place where tourists go, and it is largely unremarkable. But it was in this town that I found this deliciously simple recipe, which uses a particular kind of local banana. This is not exported, but I found it works well with ordinary bananas, and better still with miniature or apple bananas. The sauce can be made well in advance. It preserves like jam.

SERVES 4

1 tablespoon raisins
3 tablespoons golden sultanas
1 tablespoon mixed nuts, chopped
2 tablespoons butter ghee
4 tablespoons light brown sugar
2 tablespoons sherry or rum
4 large fresh bananas

1 Coarsely grind the raisins, sultanas and nuts in a food processor with a little water.
2 Heat the ghee with an equal quantity of water. Add the sugar and stir well. When simmering add the ground mixture. Simmer for a while so that it thickens a little.
3 Add the sherry or rum then take off the heat. Peel and chop the bananas. Pour the hot sauce over them and serve at once, with a dollop of soured cream, or vanilla ice cream.

Sweet Pongal Rice
Creamy Rice Pudding

At New Year south Indians hold a festival called Pongal. The great temple complex in Tamil Nadu's Madurai is essential visiting for all Hindus, especially at Pongal. Food is closely associated with Hindu religious festivals and the temples specialise in cooking for the masses, and dispensing it liberally to all comers. This Pongal rice is an example and it is served with porial kadama (see page 113). The rice can be cooked the long way, but the method I use here is a really quick one, using that excellent product, canned rice pudding. Add sweetened condensed milk and several hours' work is reduced to minutes. It can be served hot, but seems to more flavoursome served cold.

SERVES 4

400 g (14 oz) canned creamed rice
10–15 saffron stamens
4 tablespoons milk, warmed
100 ml (3½ fl oz) canned sweetened
  condensed milk
½ teaspoon ground green cardamom

GARNISH
freshly grated nutmeg

1 Mix the saffron and warmed milk and leave to stand for 5 minutes or so. Mash the saffron with the back of a spoon.
2 Mix the remaining ingredients, including the saffron and milk in a non-stick pan, and gently warm them up. Garnish with the nutmeg. Serve hot or cold.

Falooda
Rice Noodles with Grenadine

Falooda, of Persian origin, is a sweet milky pudding with sago or wheat noodles, and a favourite of the emperor Jehangir in the 1600s, who enjoyed it in a thin consistency as a drink. It can be served with fruit jam, or cold with crushed ice. Fruit syrup is commonly used. Here I am using a fabulous Caribbean ingredient – grenadine, the pomegranate syrup from the nutmeg isle, and rice-thread noodles which cook really quickly.

SERVES 4

600 ml (1 pint) milk
50 g (2 oz) dry rice-thread noodles
6 tablespoons sugar
4 tablespoons grenadine syrup

1 Bring the milk to the simmer. Crunch up the noodles and add them to the milk with the sugar. Simmer for 5 minutes. Mix in the grenadine, and serve hot.
2 Alternatively, allow it to cool, and serve it with crushed ice.

Moyra Banana

Thuppathittu
Sweet Fritter

This deep-fried sweet fritter from south India is rather like a sweet bhaji. It can be eaten on its own or as a topping to other sweet dishes in this chapter.

MAKES 8–10 THUPPATHITTU
BATTER
85 g (3 oz) plain white flour
½ teaspoon salt
50 g (2 oz) sugar
1 teaspoon baking powder

50 g (2 oz) chopped cashew nuts
25 g (1 oz) raisins
vegetable oil for deep-frying

GARNISH
icing sugar
lime wedges

1 Mix the batter ingredients together, adding sufficient water to achieve a thickish paste which will drop sluggishly off the spoon. Leave to stand for at least 10 minutes, during which time the mixture will fully absorb the moisture.
2 Meanwhile, heat the deep-frying oil to 190°C/375°F. This temperature is below smoking point and will cause a drop of batter to splutter a bit, then float more or less at once.
3 Inspect the mixture. There must be no 'powder' left, and it must be well mixed. Mix in the nuts and raisins. Scoop out an eighth of the mixture and place it carefully in the oil. Place all eight portions in, but allow about 15 seconds between adding each one so the oil will maintain its temperature.
4 Fry for about 10 minutes each, turning once, until they are light golden in colour. Remove from the oil in the order they went in and drain well.

5 Serve dusted with sugar and with lime wedges. Or they can be allowed to cool, and then frozen. Reheat in deep hot oil for about 2 minutes, but don't let them get too brown. Serve hot.

Jalebi
Syrup-drenched Crispy Spirals

On pages 12-13 we see jalebi, those curly golden spirals of batter immersed in sticky syrup, being made by a professional in Southall. This can, with a little practice, be done at home, and it's worth mastering if you enjoy sweet sticky things. They can be served hot or cold.

MAKES 8–10 JALEBI
225 g (8 oz) plain flour
15 g (½ oz) fresh yeast
warm water
½ teaspoon saffron
300ml (½ pint) warm water
225 g (8 oz) white sugar
½ teaspoon rosewater
vegetable oil for deep-frying

1 Dissolve the fresh yeast in a small bowl containing a little lukewarm water.
2 Place the flour in a large ceramic or glass bowl at room temperature.
3 Make a well in the centre and pour in the yeast and sufficient warm water to combine the mixture to make a thickish batter. Add the saffron and put the batter in a warm place for a couple of hours to ferment.
4 Make the syrup by boiling the 300 ml (½ pint) water then adding the sugar. Boil for about 10 minutes, stirring often. Take off the heat when you get quite a thick syrup. Add the rosewater. Set the syrup aside to cool.
5 Stir the batter well. Add a little warm water if needed but keep it quite thick.

6 Preheat the deep-fryer to 190°C/375°F. Now here's the tricky bit. You've got to get the batter into the deep-fryer oil in a controllable thin spiral. Fill a large plastic bag with the batter. Grasp it firmly then lift one corner away from the batter and cut a tiny hole in the bag with a pair of scissors. The hole should be smaller than pencil size.
7 Squirt the batter into the hot oil in squiggles and figure-of-eight shapes. The correct size for each jalebi is about 7–10 cm (3–4 inches) in diameter, but don't worry if yours are bigger or smaller. To stop pouring, lift the bag's corner up and away.
8 Do not over-cook them, and turn them over once. When golden on both sides, remove from the oil, drain well and plunge straight into the cold syrup in a nearby bowl or dish.
9 Soak them in the syrup for a maximum of 5 minutes, then remove and allow them to cool, or serve warm.

Walalappan
Dark Egg Custard

Sri Lanka's most popular pudding, served at parties and weddings, looks like wet ginger cake or a firm, dark 'crème caramel'.

SERVES 4
200 ml (7 fl oz) coconut milk
500 g (1 lb 2 oz) jaggery
75 g (3 oz) cashew nuts, roasted and
    chopped
3 eggs, lightly beaten

MASALA
1¼ teaspoon each:
ground cinnamon
cardamom
cloves
nutmeg

1 Bring the coconut milk to the simmer. Add the jaggery, and once this is dissolved, add the cashews and whisk in the egg and the masala.

2 Bring the water to the simmer in a steamer pan.

3 Pour the mixture into four open oven bowls, cover with greased paper and steam for 40–45 minutes.

4 Serve hot or cold

Edible Silver or Gold Leaf

Vark, pronounced varak, is made from a nugget of either pure gold or silver which is hammered between leather pads until it is thinner than paper. Once beaten, each sheet measures about 7.5 x 13 cm (3 x 5 inches). It is available in packets of six sheets, each of which is sandwiched between newspaper or tissue paper. It is placed on top of dishes such as biriani or sweets as an interesting edible garnish. It is completely vegan, has no flavour, and is a great talking point.

To use edible silver or gold leaf do not touch it as it will disintegrate in your fingers. Gently remove the top covering sheet, leaving the leaf resting on an undersheet. Invert it, then dab the undersheet to transfer the leaf on to the food. You may then choose to break it up a little – gentle rubbing with a pastry brush gives the best results.

It was the seventeenth-century Moghul emperors who first used silver and gold leaf in food; they claimed it was an aphrodisiac!

Sapodilla

Native to central America, though now found in Thailand, Indonesia and Malaysia, this small oval fruit grows to around 8 cm (3 inches). Also called the Chico fruit, it has a thin brown skin tinged with green and red, which though edible is best pared. Its flesh is apple-like in texture, though it has a complex taste of honey plum and pear. At its centre are black inedible seeds. Sapodilla contains some minerals and dietary fibre and yields 60 calories per 100 g (3½ oz).

Starfruit

There are two similar starfruits, the cucumber tree fruit, which grows in the Americas, Africa and southern India, and the star apple or carambola from Thailand, Malaysia and Indonesia, and Sri Lanka (where they are also called Chinese gooseberry). The former is green in colour, as illustrated, the latter yellow. In other respects they are similar. They grow to around 8–12 cm (3–5 inches). Unless very ripe, they are best slightly cooked. Cut crossways, the star fruit is very pretty: discard the skin and

enjoy the slightly crunchy flesh. In the subcontinent star fruit is eaten with salt, squeezed for its juice or pickled. The fruit can help reduce blood sugar levels in diabetics, is an excellent source of vitamin C and dietary fibre, and yields 55 calories per 100 g (3½ oz).

Strawberry

Strawberry is another member of the vast rose family. Tiny wild strawberries have been eaten for thousands of years, but cultivation is a relatively recent development, with American varieties being produced by French farmers in the 1700s. Since then many more types have been developed in varying sizes and flavours. Once considered a summer luxury, strawberries are now bred all over the sunny world, with imports available all year round. They are a good source of vitamins C and A and also contain some minerals. Strawberries yield 23 calories per 100 g (3½ oz).

Tamarillo

This attractive fruit is native to Peru and Brazil, and is related to the potato, aubergine, capsicum and tomato. Indeed, one of its alternative names is tree tomato. It is now grown commercially in other continents, and especially in New Zealand. The skin is too bitter to be enjoyable, but the orange flesh and brown seeds may be eaten and taste both sweet and sour. Tamarillo is a good source of vitamins C and A and yields 50 calories per 100 g (3½ oz).

Exotic Fruit Salad

Take a selection of fruit. The more exotic the better. They are readily available in all seasons (the following selection was bought one cold wet March day in southern England). Combine with some canned fruit and its juice and an appropriate liqueur.

apples, cored and sliced

black and white seedless grapes

kiwi fruit, peeled and sliced

kumquats, halved

passion fruit, quartered

peaches, stoned and sliced

phylasis fruit (Chinese lantern)

raspberries, whole

strawberries, quartered

star fruit, sliced

canned orange or satsuma segments, plus their liquid

canned pineapple chunks, plus their liquid

some Cointreau or alternative liqueur

1 Wash and prepare each of the fresh fruits in the most effective way (as suggested above), and place them in a large non-metallic bowl.

2 Add the canned fruits, their liquid and the Cointreau. Cover, chill and serve when ready.

Naadan Paal Payasam
Sago and Lentil (and Rice) Pudding

Payasam's ancestry goes back thousands of years. It is brownish in colour, sweet in taste and semi-fluid in consistency. Variations exist all round India, its ingredients varying depending on location. In this Payasam from south India, the ingredients include rice, dhal and sago. In Kerela it is called prathaman, and bananas and jackfruit are fried in ghee then added.

SERVES 4

400 ml (14 fl oz) coconut milk

200 g (7 oz) jaggery

125 g (4½ oz) cooked gram lentils

50 g (2 oz) cooked green lentils

50 g (2 oz) cooked sago

50 g (2 oz) cooked rice

1 teaspoon cardamom powder

½ teaspoon ginger powder

1 Bring the coconut milk to the simmer. Add the jaggery, and once dissolved, mix in the lentils, sago and rice, cardamom and ginger.

2 Lower the heat and keep stirring so that it thickens but does not burn at the bottom.

3 Simmer until it is semi-thick, then remove from the heat and serve hot.

Kesari Payasam
Vermicelli Pudding with Saffron

This rich payasam is typical to the Tamil Nadu region. Its ingredients include saffron, vermicelli and sago. It is usually served at wedding feasts and special functions. It is brownish in colour, sweet in taste and semi-fluid in consistency. It can optionally be daubed with edible silver leaf (see page 195).

SERVES 4

50 g (2 oz) sago

225 g (8 oz) vermicelli

4 tablespoons butter ghee

1 tablespoon raisins, chopped

2 tablespoons almonds, chopped

1 tablespoon cashew nuts, chopped

20–25 saffron strands

600 ml (1 pint) milk

200 ml (7 fl oz) sweetened condensed milk

1 teaspoon ground green cardamom seeds

GARNISH

some edible silver leaf (optional)

1 Soak the sago in water for 20 minutes, then drain.

2 Roast the vermicelli in a dry pan.

3 Heat the ghee, and stir-fry the raisins and nuts for about 2 minutes.

4 Bring the milk to the simmer in a non-stick saucepan. Add the saffron in milk and the sago and simmer for about 10 minutes.

5 Lower the heat, add the roasted vermicelli, the condensed milk and the cardamom, and stir continuously to achieve a thickish mixture.

6 Serve hot, garnished with edible silver leaf if desired, and sprinkled with the fried nuts and raisins.

Exotic Fruit Salad

Southall

When I was born, in west London's Ealing, the 'Blitz' had just begun. I am thus, what was called at the time, a 'war baby'. My father was serving in the merchant navy on the dreaded Atlantic convoys. My mother had been working as a maternity training sister at the nearby Queen Charlotte's hospital since her arrival from India, until she became assistant matron at a west Ealing nursing home.

Then, in an act of great fortitude, she purchased a huge house – Eaton Rise, Ealing – in an acre of land, now replaced with various building developments. This she converted into her own ten-bed nursing home. I was only two when it opened, but I lived there until 1953, by which time the new National Health Service had drawn expectant parents away to free hospital maternity services. I well remember the joy and happiness in the house in its heyday, and although I wasn't supposed to go into the wards, everyone turned a blind eye when I crept in to say hello to the latest newcomer.

I also remember a doodlebug flying right over the house (a V-1 German unmanned aircraft, for those not familiar with the term). They had a distinctive monotonous drone, and once the engine cut out, it meant they were about to fall on or near you, complete with their bomb load. I remember hiding under my mother's roll-top desk, clinging to one of the resident Irish maids called Lucy, who, now that I am old enough to look back objectively, was scarcely more than a child herself. Fortunately this doodlebug's droning did not stop, and the machine chugged on toward the west where it fell. I also remember an aerial dog-fight taking place one night. It was too dark and too terrifying to go outside and look. The noises were awesome, and bullets were flying about. One came through the stained glass window of our landing and smashed into the mosaic floor. I also remember how at the end of the war a huge flight of Spitfires and Hurricanes flew from RAF Northolt right overhead, towards

the VE day victory fly-past over Buckingham Palace.

At the age of five, I developed a rather strange obsession about London Transport buses, some of which trundled past the house on routes 65 and 97. I soon learned to tell the difference between the AEC and Bristol engines that powered the different types of bus. I had a small bike by the time I was eight, and I would go out and about in Ealing with a friend, whom I think was the original bus freak. As we got older, and our bikes grew bigger, we ventured further afield, and ultimately cycled the entire routes of all the local buses. Route 97's Bristol-engine buses were garaged at Hanwell, and the 607 trolley-buses at Uxbridge. In between was Southall with its huge AEC bus and lorry factory. Now long-gone, this place produced most of London's bus engines and chassis, and was very soon on my frequent-visit list.

The nursing home was a curious place for my school friends to visit, not just because of the all-female staff of nurses, cooks and maids, but because the cooks were generous to us boys. The food at the nursing home was good, wholesome English fare. I remember my mother bottling the copious amounts of fruit grown in the garden each year, and making pies. But she also cooked other, less familiar dishes from time to time: curries. She did this especially when my grandparents (who later came to live with us) or her brothers and sisters visited us.

With the advent of air-freight, and go-ahead shopkeepers like Southall's Sira, the UK is now blessed with a vast array of exotic fruit and vegetables.

We receive daily supplies from the Americas, Kenya and South Africa, Israel, Australasia, the Subcontinent, Thailand, China and Japan.

Such food was regarded by the staff, patients and my friends alike as something to be avoided. For one thing, who in 1940s Britain ate garlic? Indeed just obtaining it was a long, drawn-out process involving special orders at the greengrocer. Spices were quite unknown to the average man on the street, and had to be ordered from and ground by the chemist, who must have been curious when delivering them along with the drugs order for the nursing home. And even the chemist could not locate everything. So, from time to time, a trip was organised into central London to the Bombay Emporium in Grafton Way at the top of Tottenham Court Road, which not long after outgrew its tiny shop there to become the mighty food producer, BE International. At that time, however, it was London's only spice shop. Even Harrods, whose claim then was to be able to supply anything requested, were challenged by my mother's unusual shopping list.

Of course, my mother's family were products of the Raj. They were born into a military family in northern India. My ancestors had been in India since the 1760s. Curry was a way of life for them and its absence, when they first arrived in England, came as a big shock to them. Any curryholic can sympathise with what must have been awful withdrawal symptoms. But the Bombay Emporium (from which I would often buy samosas to nibble on the journey home, having been allocated shopping duty there), and my mother's excellent curry cooking, soon filled the gap.

But to get back to my cycling exploits, it was on one of my bus-route expeditions that I found myself on the railway bridge in Southall looking down at a Great Western steam train, its gleaming green engine and brown and cream coaches thundering off to the west country. As I followed it from one side of the bridge to the other, I suddenly noticed, almost tucked away under the bridge, a gentleman wearing a turban. He was standing outside a shop, in the window of which I was sure I could see things remarkably like my beloved samosas. I sailed down the bridge to get to the shop and sure enough, they were samosas, but not just that – there were pickles and rice, and chutneys and spice, and all things nice. I rushed back home to tell the family. The year was 1953. The shop was Southall's first spice shop, and needless to say, my cycle visits to Southall became more and more frequent after that.

Southall is a few miles west of London, on the road to Uxbridge and the railway to Slough, Reading and the west country. In the 1850s travellers would scarcely notice the tiny village with its eighty-five houses, solitary church and inn, and its large private lunatic asylum. But Southall has been home to Punjabis since the 1930s, with many working at the local AEC factory and living near by. In its post-war boom Britain encouraged Asian immigration and Southall was an ideal area in which new citizens could work in the service industries that so desperately needed them – buses, railways, hospitals, schools and the new Heathrow airport. The community quickly grew and with it came specialist shops and restaurants, cinemas and services, supplying 'the good things from home' which were unavailable in Britain at that time.

Today Southall bus garage has long-gone, as has the AEC factory and the lunatic asylum. That spice shop under the bridge has gone too. But the church remains, along with several others, plus a mosque and more than one Hindu temple. The one inn has now been replaced by numerous pubs, one of which, called the Glassy Junction, is run by Asians, sells Asian food, and has a largely young Asian clientele. Southall

This logistic miracle gets fresh fruit and vegetables picked 24 hours earlier . . .

and some 10,000 miles away, onto our tables . . .

fresh and tasty whenever we wish.

today is no longer a Middlesex village. It is a Greater London suburb with a population approaching 100,000.

Southall is just one of many Asian success stories. It is prosperous, and booming, and ever-expanding. Today a remarkable infrastructure enables Southall's residents to obtain foodstuffs and products superior in many instances to those in the subcontinent. From that tiny one-man spice shop under the bridge, Southall has spawned almost too many to count. Then there are the twenty or more greengrocers selling exotic produce every day of the year. These are backed up by the huge nearby Western International Market, a vegetable wholesaler to which fresh fruit and vegetables are air-freighted on a daily basis from all corners of the earth. There are at least twenty Halal butchers, and over fifty cafés, snack bars, and restaurants, selling all types of Asian food, at all hours and at inexpensive prices.

Ethnic pots and pans and more can be found at Mr Narendra's Bhai Bhai Housewife cash and carry. His business card says it all: 'Importers, exporters, wholesalers, retailers of kitchenware, stainless steel, glassware, clay ovens,

groceries, potatoes, onions and electrical goods.' Such multi-level trading is quite the norm in Southall: Omi's restaurant also organises car hire, while Centrepoint, who specialise mainly in utensils are also suppliers of fireworks all year round. In addition there are jewellers, sari shops, and music shops.

Southall buzzes with activity. Nearly every shop takes advantage of the wide pavements, and you will find as colourful a display of street trading there as anywhere in the world. In front of the butcher's for example, is a pavement trader selling crockery, and in front of that another offers ripe mangoes by the case. Car ownership is above average, as anyone who has ever tried to park or drive there will know. It is one of the few suburbs to have parking meter restrictions on Sundays.

A new generation of restaurants and grocers has begun to expand westwards, among them some specialising in produce and ingredients from Sri Lanka and south India. The remarkable thing about these and indeed most of the shops in Southall is their opening hours: most are open from 9 a.m. until 9 p.m. every day, and some even longer.

Today Britain has many such Asian communities: in London there is Wembley with its largely Gujarati vegetarian community, Brick Lane with its Bengali/ Bangladeshi community, Tooting with south Indian and Sri Lankan residents; Leicester has its Ugandan Asians, again, many with Gujarati roots; in east Birmingham the Pakistani Kashmiri community forms the Balti area; Bradford has a large Pakistani population as does Glasgow; Manchester has its 'golden curry mile' in Rusholme's Wilmslow Road. And all over the UK smaller centres exist too. I am sure that even if you are not lucky enough to have an Asian community nearby, most readers will have visited one. If not, treat yourself to a day out in the community of your choice and enjoy yourself.

As is so often the case, to my mind first is best, and Southall remains the leader. Although I left Ealing twenty years ago, I live close enough to make frequent visits. Every time I do so all the memories come flooding back, and I think how lucky I was to have been in at the birth of Southall as the queen of the spicy suburbs.

Glossary

This glossary is very extensive, and includes some items not specifically mentioned in the recipes. It is intended to be used as a general reference work. If you do not find a particular word here it is worth checking to see whether it is in the index and can be found elsewhere in the book. The 'Indian' words are mostly Hindi or Urdu. The English spelling is 'standard' but can vary as words are translated phonetically.

A

Achar – Pickle

Adrak – Ginger

Ajwain or Ajowain – Lovage seeds

Akhni – Spicy consommé-like stock. Also called yakhni

Aloo – Potato

Am – Mango

Am chur – Mango powder

Anardana – Pomegranate

Aniseed – Saunf

Areca – Betel nut

Asafoetida – Hing. A rather smelly spice

Aserio – Small red-brown seeds with a slight aniseed flavour. Used medicinally

Ata or Atta – Chupatti flour. (Fine wholemeal flour used in most Indian breads. English wholemeal is a suitable alternative.)

B

Badain – Star anise

Badam – Almond

Balti – In Balti dishes cubes of meat or chicken are marinated, then charcoal-grilled, then simmered in a sauce and usually served in a karahi or Balti pan

Bargar – Process of frying whole spices in hot oil

Basil – Used only in religious applications in Indian cooking, but widely used in Thai cooking

Basmati – The best type of long-grain rice

Bay leaf – Tej Pattia. Aromatic spice

Besan – See Gram flour

Bhaji or Bhajee – Dryish mild vegetable curry

Bhajia – Deep-fried fritter, usually onion

Bhare – Stuffed

Bhoona or Bhuna – The process or cooking the spice paste in hot oil. A Bhoona curry is usually dry and cooked in coconut

Bhunana – Roast

Bhindi – Okra or ladies' fingers

Biriani – Traditionally rice baked with meat or vegetable filling with saffron, served with edible silver foil. The restaurant interpretation is a fried rice artificially coloured, with filling added

Black salt – Kala namak. A type of salt, dark grey in colour. Its taste, of sea water, is relished in India but not, I find, in the West

Bombay Potato – Small whole potatoes in curry and tomato sauce

Brinjal – Aubergine

Burfi or Barfi – An Indian fudge-like sweetmeat

C

Cardamom – Elaichi. One of the most aromatic and expensive spices

Cashew nuts – Kaju

Cassia bark – Aromatic spice, related to cinnamon

Cayenne pepper – A blend of chilli powder from Latin America

Ceylon Curry – Usually cooked with coconut, lemon and chilli

Chana – Type of lentil. See Dhal

Charoli – Sweetish pink-coloured, irregularly shaped seeds with no English translation. Ideal in desserts. Sunflower seeds are a good alternative

Chawal – Rice

Chilgoze or Nioze – Small long creamy nuts with brown shells used in cooking or eaten raw

Chilli – Mirch. The hottest spice

Chirongi or Charauli – Cuddapah almond or in Hindi, the chirongi or charauli. They are small, round, pale reddish-brown in colour, resembling Egyptian lentils, however they are quite aromatic, almost minty in flavour. The emperor Barbur described tham as a cross between walnuts and almonds. They are used in puddings, pullaos and paan

Chor magaz – Melon seeds. Used as a thickener

Chupatti – A dry 15 cm (6 inch) disc of unleavened bread. Normally griddle-cooked, it should be served piping hot. Spelling varies: chuppati, chapati, etc.

Chutneys – From the Hindi word chatnee, it can be a fresh or cooked accompaniment. The most common ones are onion, mango and tandoori. See also Sambals

Cinnamon – Dalchini. One of the most aromatic spices

Cloves – Lavang. Expensive and fragrant spice

Coriander – Dhania. One of the most important spices in Indian cookery

Cummin or Cumin – Jeera

Curry – The only word in this glossary to have no direct translation into any of the subcontinent's fifteen or so languages. The word was coined by the British in India centuries ago. Possible contenders for the origin of the word are karahi or karai (Hindi), a wok-like frying pan used all over India to prepare masalas (spice mixtures); kurhi, a soup-like dish made with spices, gram flour dumplings and buttermilk; kari, a spicy Tamil sauce; turkuri, a seasoned sauce or stew; kari phulia, neem or curry leaves; kudhi or hadhi, a yoghurt soup; or koresh, an aromatic Iranian stew

Curry lands – India is the main curry land with 900 million, mainly Hindu, people. Others include Pakistan, Afghanistan, and, to a lesser extent, Iran, to the west, Nepal and Bhutan to the north, Moslem Bangladesh to the east, and Burma and Thailand, to the south-east, and also Malaysia and Singapore. The tiny island of Sri Lanka has a very distinctive curry style

Curry leaves – Neem or kari phulia. Small leaves a bit like bay leaves, used for flavouring

Cus cus – See Poppy seed

D

Dahi – Yoghurt

Dalchini or Darchim – Cinnamon

Degchi, Dekchi or Degh – Brass or metal saucepan without handles also called pateeli or batlio

Dhal – Lentils. There are over 60 types of lentils in the subcontinent, some of which are very obscure. Like peas, they grow into a hard sphere measuring between 1 cm and 3 mm. They are cooked whole or split with the skin, or split with the skin polished off. Lentils are a rich source of protein

Dhania – Coriander

Dhansak – Traditional Parsee dish cooked in a purée of lentils, aubergine, tomato and spinach

Dopiaza – Traditional Moghul dish. Do means two and Piaza means onion. It gets its name because onions appear twice in the cooking process

Doroo – Celery

Dosa or Dosai – A South Indian pancake made from rice and lentil flour. Usually served with a filling

Dum – Steam cooking. Long before the West invented the pressure cooker, India had her own method which lasts to this day. A pot with a close-fitting lid is sealed with a ring of dough. The ingredients are then cooked in their own steam under some pressure

E

Ekuri – Spiced scrambled eggs

Elaichi – Cardamom

F

Fennel – Sunf or soonf. A small green seed which is very aromatic, with aniseed taste

Fenugreek – Methi. This important spice is used as seeds in fresh or dried form

Five-Spice Powder – Combination of five sweet and aromatic spices used in Chinese and Malay cooking. Usually ground. A typical combination would be equal parts of cinnamon, cloves, fennel seeds, star anise and Szechuan pepper

Foogath – Lightly cooked vegetable dish

G

Gajar – Carrot

Galangal or Galingale – A tuber related to ginger but with a more peppery taste. It is used in Thai cooking where it is called kha, and in Indonesian (laos) and Malay (kenkur)

Garam masala – Literally 'hot mixture'

Garlic – Lasan

Ghee – Clarified butter or margarine much used in northern Indian cookery

Ginger – Adrak (fresh), sont (dried), a rhizome which can be used fresh, dried or powdered

Gobi or Phoolgobi – Cauliflower

Goor or Gur – Jaggery (palm sugar) or molasses

Gram flour – Besan. Finely ground flour, pale blond in colour, made from chana

Galub jaman – An Indian dessert with a cake-like texture

H

Halva – Sweets made from syrup and vegetables or fruit

Handi – Earthenware cooking pot

Hindi – the official language of India

Hing – Asafoetida

Hopper – Kind of rice noodle found in Sri Lanka

Huldi – Turmeric

I

Idli – Rice and lentil flour cake served with light curry sauce

Imli – Tamarind

Isgubul – Vegetable seed

J

Jaifal or Taifal – Nutmeg

Jaggery – See Goor

Jal Frezi – Sautéed or stir-fried dish, often with lightly cooked onion, garlic, ginger, green bell pepper and chilli

Jalebi – An Indian dessert made from a flour, milk powder and yoghurt batter, fried and served cold or hot in syrup

Javatri – Mace

Jeera or Zeera – Cummin

K

Kabli chana – Chick peas

Kadhai – Yoghurt soup

Kaju – Cashew nut

Kala jeera – Black cummin seeds

Kala namak – Black salt

Kalonji – See Wild onion seeds

Karahi (Karai, korai etc.) – The Indian equivalent of the wok. A circular two-handled all-purpose cooking pan. Some restaurants cook in small karahis and serve them straight to the table with the food sizzling inside

Karela – Small, dark green vegetable of the gourd family

Kashmir curry – Restaurateurs' creation. A sweetish curry often using lychees or similar ingredient

Katori – Small serving bowls which go on a thali (tray)

Kebab – Skewered food cooked over charcoal

Kecap manis – Indonesian version of soy sauce; the word kecap is pronounced 'kechap' and our word 'ketchup' derived from this. Soy sauce is a good, though more salty, substitute

Keema – Minced meat curry; soya can be used as a vegetarian substitute

Kewra – Screw pine water. An extract of the flower of the tropical screw pine tree – a fragrant clear liquid used to flavour sweets. It is a cheap substitute for rose water

Khir – Technique of making a sort of cream. Milk is cooked with cucumber and puréed

Kish mish – Sultanas

Kofta – Minced meat or vegetable balls in batter, deep-fried, and then cooked in a curry sauce

Kokum or Cocum – A variety of plum, pitted and dried. Prune-like and very sour

Korma – To most restaurants this just means a mild curry. Traditionally it is very rich. Meat, chicken or vegetables are cooked in cream, yoghurt and nuts, and are fragrantly spiced with saffron and aromatic spices

Koya – Milk reduced to a thick sticky solid. Used for sweet making

Kulcha – Small leavened bread

Kulfi – Indian ice cream. Traditionally it comes in vanilla, pistachio or mango flavours

Kus Kus – See Poppy seed

L

Lasan – Garlic

Lassi or Lhassi – A refreshing drink made from yoghurt and crushed ice. The savoury version is lhassi namkeen and the sweet version is lhassi meethi

Lavang – Cloves

Lemon grass – takrai (Thai), serai (Malay). A fragrant-leafed plant which imparts a subtle lemony flavour to cooking. Use ground powder (made from the bulbs) as a substitute

Lentils – See Dhal

Lilva – A small oval-shaped bean which grows in a pod like the European pea

Lime Leaves – Markrut or citrus leaves. Used in Thai cooking, fresh or dried, to give a distinctive aromatic flavour

Loochees – A type of bread made in Bengal using white flour

Lovage – Ajwain or ajowain

M

Mace – Javitri. The outer part of the nutmeg

Madras – Another restaurateurs' invention. But the people of South India do eat hot curries; some original chef must have christened his hot curry `Madras' and the name stuck

Makhani – A traditional dish. Tandoori chicken is cooked in a ghee and tomato sauce

Makke – Cornflour

Makrut or Markut – Thai Citrus or lime leaf

Malai – Cream

Malaya – The curries of Malaya are traditionally cooked with plenty of coconut, chilli and ginger. In the Indian restaurant, however, they are usually mild and contain pineapple and other fruit

Mamra – Puffed basmati rice

Mango Powder – Am chur. A very sour flavouring agent

Masala – A mixture of spices. Any curry powder is therefore a masala. It can be spelt massala, massalla, musala, mosola, massalam, etc.

Massoor – Red lentils

Mattar – Green peas

Meethi – Sweet

Melon seeds – Chor magaz

Methi – Fenugreek

Mirch – Pepper or chilli

Moglai or Moghlai – Cooking in the style of the Moghul emperors

Mollee – Dishes cooked in coconut and chilli

Mooli – Large white radish

Moong – Type of lentil

Mulligatawny – A Tamil sauce (molegoo – pepper, tunny – water) which has become well known as a British soup

Mustard seeds – Rai. Small black seeds which become sweetish when fried

N

Namak – Salt

Naan or Nan – Leavened bread baked in the tandoor

Naan, Peshwari – Naan bread stuffed with almonds and/or cashews and/or raisins and baked in the tandoor

Naryal – Coconut

Neem – Curry leaf

Nigella – A fragrant seed, resembling tiny black nuggets, also called wild onion seeds.

Nimboo – Lime (lemon)

Nutmeg – Jaifal

O

Okra – Bindi, also known as ladies' fingers

P

Pan or Paan – Betel leaf folded around a stuffing – lime paste or various spices (see Supari) – and eaten after a meal as a digestive

Pakoras – To all intents and purposes the same as the bhajia

Palak or Sag – Spinach

Panch Phoran – Mixture of five seeds

Paneer – Cheese made from cows' or buffaloes' milk. Can be fried and curried

Papadom – Thin lentil flour wafers. Spelling variations include popadom, pappadom, and pupodam

Paprika – Mild red ground pepper made from red bell peppers used mainly for its colour

Paratha – A deep-fried bread

Patia – Parsee curry with a thick, dark brown, sweet and sour sauce

Patna – A long-grained rice

Pepper – Mirch. Has for centuries been India's most important spice – can be used whole or ground

Phall or Phal – A very hot curry (the hottest), invented by restaurateurs

Piaz, Peeaz or Pyaz – Onion

Pickles – Pungent, hot pickled vegetables or meats essential to an Indian meal. Most common are lime, mango and chilli

Pine nuts – Chilgoza. Small, flat, cream-coloured oval nut of the neosia pine, which when roasted has a distinctive taste. Used in sweet dishes and paan

Pistachio nut – Pista magaz. A fleshy, tasty nut which can be used fresh (the greener the better) or salted. It is expensive and goes well in savoury or sweet dishes such as biriani or pista kulfi (ice cream)

Poppy seeds – Cus cus or Kus Kus. White seeds used in chicken curries, blue seeds used to decorate bread. (Not to be confused with the Moroccan national dish cous-cous, made from steamed semolina.)

Pullao – Rice and meat or vegetables cooked together in a pan until tender

Pullao rice – The restaurant name for rice fried with spices and coloured yellow

Pulses – Dried peas and beans, including lentils

Puri – A deep-fried unleavened bread

R

Rai – Mustard seeds

Raita – A cooling chutney of yoghurt and vegetable which accompanies the main meal

Rajma – Red kidney beans

Rasgulla – Walnut-sized balls of semolina and cream cheese cooked in syrup (literally meaning 'juicy balls')

Rasmalai – Rasgullas cooked in cream and served cold

Ratin jot – Alkanet root. Used as a deep red dye for make-up, clothing and food

Rhogan Josh Gosht – Literally it means 'red juice meat', or 'lamb in red gravy'. It is a traditional northern Indian dish. There are many spelling variations, including: rogon, roghan, rugon, rugin; jush, joosh, jesh; goosht, goose, gost

Rose water – Ruh gulab. A clear essence extracted from rose petals to give a fragrance to sweets. See Kewra

Roti – Bread

Ruh gulab – Rose water essence

S

Sabzi – A generic term for vegetables

Saffron Kesar or zafron.– The world's most expensive spice, used to give a dish a delicate yellow colouring and aroma

Sag or Saag – Spinach

Salt – Namak

Sambals – A Malayan term describing the side dishes accompanying the meal

Sambar – A south Indian vegetable curry made largely from lentils

Samosa – The celebrated triangular deep-fried meat or vegetable patties served as a starter or snack

Sarson ka sag – Mustard leaves (spinach-like)

Saunf or Souf – Aniseed

Seeng – Drumstick. A bean-like variety of gourd which looks exactly like a drumstick

Sennl – Allspice

Sesame seed – Til. Widely used in Indian cooking

Sonf – Fennel seed

Sont or Sonth – Dry ginger

Subcontinent – Term used to describe India, Pakistan, Bangladesh, Nepal, Burma and Sri Lanka as a group

Supari – Mixture of seeds and sweeteners for chewing after a meal. Usually includes aniseed or fennel, shredded betel nut, sugar balls, marrow seeds, etc.

T

Taipal or Jaiphal – Nutmeg

Tamarind – Imli. A date-like fruit used as chutney, and in cooking as a souring agent

Tandoori – A style of charcoal cooking originating in north-west India (what is now Pakistan and the Punjab) and naan bread. More recently applied to lobster and vegetables

Tarka – Garnishes of spices/onion

Tarka dhal – Lentils garnished with fried spices

Tava or Tawa – A heavy, almost flat, circular wooden-handled griddle pan used to cook Indian breads and to 'roast' spices. Also ideal for many cooking functions from frying eggs and omelettes to making pancakes, etc.

Tej patia – The leaf of the cassia bark tree. Resembles bay leaf which can be used in its place

Thali set – A tray on which is a number of katori (see above) dishes in which different types of curry, rice and chutney, etc. are placed. Breads and papadoms go on the tray itself

Tikka – Literally a skewered small piece, marinated then barbecued or tandoori baked

Til – Sesame seed

Tindla – A vegetable of the cucumber family

Tindaloo – See Vindaloo

Toor or Toovar – A type of lentil

Tukmeria or Tulsi – Black seeds of a basil family plant, used in drinks

Turmeric – Haldi or huldi. A very important Indian spice, used to give the familiar yellow colour to curries. Use sparingly as it can be bitter

U

Udrak – Ginger

Urid – A type of lentil

V

Vark or Varak – Edible silver or gold foil

Vindaloo – A fiery hot dish from Goa. Traditionally it was pork marinated in vinegar with garlic. In the restaurant it has now come to meal just a very hot dish. Also sometimes called bindaloo or tindaloo (even hotter)

W

Wild onion seeds – See Nigella

Z

Zafron – Saffron

Zeera – Cummin

Storing Fresh Vegetables

Fresh produce should be stored in a cool place, although the exact temperature varies from item to item. Remember that all fruits and vegetables contain a lot of water: leaves and soft fruit consist mostly of water, while roots and tubers have less. Thus leaves and soft fruit will keep for the least time; after a day or two they wilt or shrivel and discolour because of a decrease in their water content.

The refrigerator and the commercial chill cabinet are useful for some items, but not others. It is essential that the refrigerator's temperature does not go below 0°C/32°F – freezing point. If it does, the water in the produce will freeze causing it to lose its molecular structure upon thawing. It should not, however, go above 8°C/46°F. The temperature at the top of the fridge is always cooler.

Some items keep better outside the fridge. Tomatoes, courgettes, marrow and gourds require 12–13°C/53–5°F. These vegetables are prone to rapid deterioration if the temperature goes lower than this, but provided it does not, and the humidity is high enough, they can keep well for up to fourteen days.

Capsicum peppers, chillies, beans, peas in pod, and aubergine prefer a slightly cooler temperature of between 6–9°C/43–8°F and will last in the fridge for about ten to fourteen days.

Onions, shallots, ginger, and garlic keep best at 2–5°C/35–41°F, out of the fridge. If they were sound to start with, they can last for months. They should be kept out of direct sunlight (but not in the dark) so that they don't sprout.

Lettuce, leeks, broccoli, cauliflower, cabbage, radish, celery and carrots keep best at around 1°C/34°F in high humidity, in the fridge, when they will last, on average, for up to ten days. However, these vegetables lose vitamin C and sugar (which turns to starch) the longer they are stored, so the fresher the better.

Potatoes, yam, sweet potatoes, horseradish and ginger like 40–50°C/39–41°, and potatoes prefer the dark (to prevent sprouting) where they can last for months.

Vegetables which grow in the high-altitude curry lands (Nepal, Kashmir, northern India northern Pakistan, and in all the hill stations above 7,000 feet in southern India and Sri Lanka), are very similar to those which grow in temperate Britain. The exotic tropical vegetables which grow on the plains (gourds, okra, and aubergine, for example) are becoming increasingly available in the West, and very good they are too, either singly or in combination with other ingredients.

Food Colouring

Authentic tandooris and tikkas in India have always been cooked with natural colours. Red is achieved using paprika or chilli. Oil is coloured deep red using alkanet root (qv). Yellow derives from saffron and turmeric. You can use anatto seed powder for yellow and beetroot powder for red, but though natural, neither is heat stable, so they change colour, becoming browner, when cooked.

The very bright yellow, red, green and orange food that we are accustomed to at the curry house is a restaurateur invention, achieved by using tartrazine food dyes. Made from coal tar, they are said to have side effects, causing allergies, asthma attacks and hyperactivity, particularly in children. These dyes appear, of course, in numerous other factory-produced foods, such as ready meals, confectionery, sauces and bakery goods. The food tastes no different with or without them, but if you wish to have vibrantly coloured tandoori and rice dishes, purchase them in powdered form. Remember they are extremely concentrated, so use just a tiny amount.

The Store Cupboard

Here is a workable list of items you need to make the recipes in this book, and its sister books, the Curry Bible and Balti Bible, subdivided into essential and non-essential. The essential items appear again and again in the recipes; the non-essential appear only in one or two. This list may look a bit formidable but remember, once you have the items in stock they will last for some time. I have listed the minimum quantities you'll need (as supplied by one or more manufacturers) in metric only, as given on most packaging these days.

Essential Whole Spices

Bay leaf	3 g
Cardamom, black or brown	30 g
Cardamom, green or white	30 g
Cassia bark	30 g
Chilli	11 g
Clove	20 g
Coriander seed	60 g
Cummin seed, white	25 g
Curry leaves, dried	2 g
Fennel seed	27 g
Fenugreek leaf, dried	18 g
Mustard seed	65 g
Peppercorn, black	7 g
Sesame seed, white	57 g
Wild onion seed (nigella)	47 g

Non-Essential Whole Spices

Alkanet root	3 g
Allspice	50 g
Aniseed	25 g
Caraway seed	25 g
Celery seed	25 g
Cinnamon quill	6 pieces
Cummin seed, black	25 g
Dill seed	25 g
Fenugreek seed	47 g

Ginger, dried	6 pieces
Lovage (ajwain) seed	27 g
Mace	8 g
Nutmeg, whole	6 nuts
Panch Phoran	30 g
Pomegranate seed	30 g
Poppy seed	52 g
Saffron stamens	0.5 g
Star anise	30g

Essential Ground Spices

Black pepper	100 g
Chilli powder	100 g
Coriander	100 g
Cummin	100 g
Garam Masala	50g
Garlic powder and/or flakes	100 g
Ginger	100 g
Paprika	100 g
Turmeric	100 g

Non-Essential Ground Spices

Asafoetida	50 g
Cardamom, green	25 g
Cassia bark	25 g
Clove	25 g
Galangal	20 g
Lemon grass	20 g
Mango powder	100 g
Salt, black	50g

Essential Dried Foods

Basmati rice	2 kg
Coconut milk powder	100 g
Gram flour	1 kg
Jaggery	100 g

Non-Essential Dried Foods

Food colouring powder, red E129	25g
Ditto, natural (beetroot powder)	25 g
Food colouring powder, yellow E110	25g
Ditto natural (annatto)	25 g

Lentils and Pulses

Black-eyed beans (lobia)	500g
Chana, split	500 g
Chick peas	500g
Massoor (red) lentils	500 g
Moong green, whole	500 g
Red kidney beans	500g
Toor or tovar, split	500 g
Urid, whole black	500 g

Nuts (all shelled)

Almonds, ground	100 g
Almonds, flaked	100 g
Almonds, whole	50 g
Cashews, raw	100 g
Peanuts, raw	100 g
Pistachios, green	100 g

Miscellaneous

Papadoms, spiced and plain (pack)	300 g
Puffed rice (mamra)	100 g
Red kidney beans	500 g
Rice flour	500 g
Rose water, bottle	7 fl oz
Sev (gram flour snack)	200 g
Silver leaf (vark – edible)	6 sheets
Supari mixture	100 g
Tamarind block	300 g

Oils

Mustard blend	250ml
Sesame	250ml
Soya	250ml
Sunflower	250ml
Vegetable ghee	250g

Canned items

Chickpeas	420g
Coconut milk	400g
Lobia beans	420g
Patra	420g
Plum tomatoes	420g
Red kidney beans	420g

The Curry Club

Pat Chapman has always had a deep-rooted interest in spicy food, curry in particular, and over the years he has built up a huge pool of information which he felt could be usefully passed on to others. He conceived the idea of forming an organisation for this purpose.

Since it was founded in January 1982, The Curry Club has built up a membership of several thousand. We have a marchioness, some lords and ladies, knights a-plenty, a captain of industry or two, generals, admirals and air marshals (not to mention a sprinkling of ex-colonels), and we have celebrity names – actresses, politicians, rock stars and sportsmen. We have an airline, a former Royal navy warship, and a hotel chain.

We have 15 members whose name is Curry or Curries, 20 called Rice and several with the name Spice or Spicier, Cook, Fry, Frier or Fryer and one Boiling. We have a Puri (a restaurant owner), a Paratha and a Nan, and a good many Mills and Millers, one Dal and a Lentil, an Oiler, a Gee (but no Ghee), an Onion, a Cummin and a Butter but no Marj (several Marjories though, and a Marjoram and a Minty). We also have several Longs and Shorts, Thins and Broads, one Fatt and one Wide, and a Chilley and a Coole.

We have members on every continent including a good number of Asian members, but by and large the membership is a typical cross-section of the Great British Public, ranging in age from teenage to dotage, and in occupation from refuse collectors to receivers, high street traders to high court judges, tax inspectors to taxi drivers. There are students and pensioners, millionaires and unemployed... thousands of people who have just one thing in common – a love of curry and spicy foods.

Members regularly receive a bright and colourful magazine, which has regular features on curry and the curry lands. It includes news items, recipes, reports on restaurants, picture features, and contributions from members and professionals alike. The information is largely concerned with curry, but by popular demand it now includes regular input on other exotic and spicy cuisines such as those of Thailand, the spicy Americas, the Middle East and China. We produce a wide selection of publications, including the books listed at the front of this book.

Curry diners will be familiar with the Curry Club window sticker and restaurant quality certificate, which adorns the windows and walls of the best thousand curry restaurants. Curry Club members form the national network of reporters, which leads to the selection of these restaurants, in the highly successful *Good Curry Guide*, with its prestigious awards to the top restaurants.

Obtaining some of the ingredients required for curry cooking can be difficult, but The Curry Club makes it easy, with a comprehensive range of products, including spice mixes, chutneys, pickles, papadoms, sauces and curry pastes. These are available from major food stores and specialist delicatessens up and down the country. If they are not stocked near you, there is the Club's associate, well-established and efficient mail-order service. Hundreds of items are in stock, including spices, pickles, pastes, dried foods, canned foods, gift items, publications and specialist kitchen and tableware.

On the social side, the Club holds residential weekend cookery courses and gourmet nights at selected restaurants. Top of the list is our regular Curry Club gourmet trip to India and other spicy countries. We take a small group of curry enthusiasts to the chosen country and tour the incredible sights, in between sampling the delicious food of each region.

If you would like more information about The Curry Club, write (enclosing a stamped, addressed envelope please) to: The Curry Club, PO Box 7, Haslemere, Surrey GU27 1EP.

Index